faith first

Legacy Edition
PARISH

Grade Six

RESOURCES FOR CHRISTIAN LIVING®

www.FaithFirst.com

"The Ad Hoc Committee to Oversee the Use of the Catechism, United States Conference of Catholic Bishops, has found this catechetical series, copyright 2006, to be in conformity with the *Catechism of the Catholic Church*."

NIHIL OBSTAT
Reverend Robert M. Coerver
Censor Librorum

IMPRIMATUR
† Most Rev. Charles V. Grahmann
Bishop of Dallas

September 1, 2004

The Nihil Obstat and Imprimatur are official declarations that the material reviewed is free of doctrinal or moral error. No implication is contained therein that those granting the Nihil Obstat and Imprimatur agree with the contents, opinions, or statements expressed.

Send all inquiries to:
RCL • Resources for Christian Living
200 East Bethany Drive
Allen, Texas 75002-3804

Toll Free   877-275-4725
Fax   800-688-8356

Visit us at www.RCLweb.com
              www.FaithFirst.com

Printed in the United States of America

20476   ISBN 0-7829-1068-8 (Student Book)
20486   ISBN 0-7829-1080-7 (Catechist Guide)

1 2 3 4 5 6 7 8 9 10
05 06 07 08 09 10 11

ACKNOWLEDGMENTS

Scripture excerpts are taken or adapted from the *New American Bible with Revised New Testament and Psalms* Copyright © 1991, 1986, 1970, Confraternity of Christian Doctrine, Washington, DC. Used with permission. All rights reserved. No part of the *New American Bible* may be reproduced by any means without the permission of the copyright owner.

Excerpts are taken or adapted from the English translation of the *Roman Missal* © 1973, International Commission on English in the Liturgy, Inc. (ICEL); the English translation of the Act of Contrition from *Rite of Penance* © 1974, ICEL; the English translation of *A Book of Prayers* © 1982, ICEL; the English translation of *Book of Blessings* © 1988, ICEL. All rights reserved.

Excerpts are taken or adapted from the English translations of *Kyrie Eleison, Nicene Creed, Apostles' Creed, Sanctus and Benedictus, Agnus Dei, Gloria Patri,* and *Te Deum Laudamus* by the International Consultation on English Texts (ICET).

Photography and Illustration Credits appear on page 304.

Faith First Legacy Edition Development Team

Developing a religion program requires the gifts and
talents of many individuals working together as a team.
RCL is proud to acknowledge the contributions
of these dedicated people.

Program Theology Consultants
Reverend Louis J. Cameli, S.T.D.
Reverend Robert D. Duggan, S.T.D.

Advisory Board
Judith Deckers, M.Ed.
Elaine McCarron, SCN, M.Div.
Marina Herrera, Ph.D.
Reverend Frank McNulty, S.T.D.
Reverend Ronald J. Nuzzi, Ph.D.

National Catechetical Advisor
Jacquie Jambor

Catechetical Specialist
Jo Rotunno

Contributing Writers
Student Book and Catechist Guide
Reverend Louis J. Cameli
Christina DeCamp
Judith Deckers
Jack Gargiulo
Mary Beth Jambor
Michele Norfleet

Art & Design Director
Lisa Brent

Electronic Page Makeup
Laura Fremder

Production Director
Jenna Nelson

Designers/Photo Research
Pat Bracken
Kristy O. Howard
Susan Smith

Project Editors
Patricia A. Classick
Steven M. Ellair
Ronald C. Lamping

Web Site Producers
Joseph Crisalli
Demere Henson

General Editor
Ed DeStefano

President/Publisher
Maryann Nead

Contents

We Pray

Dear God,
We are looking forward to an exciting journey in sixth grade. Thank you for calling us to faith and for the opportunity to learn more about you and your love for us this year. With your help, we will grow and accept more responsibility as Christians. Help us to treat all those we meet with justice and care. Amen.

Welcome to Faith First!

My Life

- Where were you baptized?

_____

- Who first taught you about Jesus?

_____

- Where is it easy for you to pray?

_____

- What is a holy place that you would like to visit?

_____

God's Plan of Salvation

Just as the story of your life happens over time, so has the story of God's love for his people unfolded in history. This year you will learn many new things about God and the story of his people. Complete the activities on the next page to see what you already know, and to find out the kinds of things you will learn this year.

We Believe

God revealed his name to Moses in a voice heard from a burning bush. What is the name God revealed, and what does it mean? Look on page 23 to check your answer.

Name _____   Meaning _____

We Worship

Many centuries after the time of Moses, God anointed David, son of Jesse, as king of God's people. David also wrote poems that are part of the Bible. Many of them were used in worship by the Israelites. You will learn what these poems are called on page 123.

_____

We Live

David's poems and songs are part of the wisdom books of the Bible. Another of the wisdom books contains short sayings such as this one:

Better a dry crust with peace,
    than a house full of feasting with strife.

What is the name of this book of the Bible? You can find the answer on page 199.

_____

We Pray

Jesus teaches us that we can call God Father, just as he did. Did you know that there are two versions of the Our Father in the New Testament? Which Gospel has the longer version that we pray today? Look on page 226 to check your answer.

_____

The Lord Is My Shepherd

The leader walks at the head of a procession to the prayer space, holding the Bible high for all to see.

All make the sign of the cross together.

LEADER: Lord, we gather today to honor the gift of your word. We remember your love for us and that you are always with us.

ALL: **The Lord is my shepherd,
I shall not want.**

LEADER: A reading from the Second Book of Samuel. *Proclaim 2 Samuel 7:9–10a, 16.*

ALL: **The Lord is my shepherd,
I shall not want.**

LEADER: Even though I walk in the dark valley
I fear no evil; for you are at my side.

ALL: **The Lord is my shepherd,
I shall not want.**

LEADER: Only goodness and kindness follow me
all the days of my life;
And I shall dwell in the house of the LORD
for years to come.

ALL: **The Lord is my shepherd,
I shall not want.**

BASED ON PSALM 23:1, 4, 6

All come forward and reverence the Bible.

What do we profess in the creeds of the Church?

Getting Ready

What I Have Learned

What is something you already know about these faith terms?

The message of the prophets

_____

_____

Jesus Christ, Savior of the world

_____

_____

The kingdom of God

_____

_____

Words to Know

Put an X next to the faith terms you know. Put a ? next to the faith terms you need to know more about.

Faith Vocabulary

_____ faith

_____ creed

_____ Covenant

_____ oral tradition

_____ redemption

_____ Immaculate Conception

_____ revelation

_____ original sin

_____ salvation

_____ Incarnation

Questions I Have

What questions would you like to ask about God's plan of salvation?

_____

_____

_____

_____

A Scripture Story

Saint Paul dictating to a scribe

What do you know about the letters of Saint Paul in the New Testament?

The Gift of Faith

We Pray

Praise the LORD from the earth, . . .
You mountains and all hills.
PSALM 148:7, 9

We thank you, Father, for making yourself known to us through your Son, Jesus. Amen.

Who do you know better today than you did a year ago? How did you get to know this person well?

Getting to know someone well takes time and effort. The more people show and tell us about themselves, the more we can get to know them. Coming to know God is something like that.

What are some of the ways you come to know God?

God's Own Word to Us

Faith Focus

How do we grow in our faith in God?

Faith Vocabulary

faith. A supernatural gift and power from God; the gift of God's invitation to us that enables us to know and believe in him, and the power God gives us to freely respond to his invitation.

creed. A statement of beliefs, a profession of faith, a summary of the principal beliefs of the Church.

Why did God place his word in our hearts?

God's Word Within Us

God places his word in our hearts, plants his love deep in our souls. Jeremiah the Prophet shared this truth about God and ourselves when he wrote:

> [God said:] "I will give them a heart with which to understand that I am the LORD." JEREMIAH 24:7

Whether we are happy or sad, successful or in trouble, God's word is always within us speaking to us. It acts like the sun to light up our days and like the moon to help us see at night. It is our challenge to access and understand the light of God's word. Here are some ways that will help us.

1. Pray to the Holy Spirit. It is the Holy Spirit who lives in our hearts and gives us the power to call God "Abba, Father."

2. Come to know Jesus Christ personally. Everything God wants to say to us can be found in Jesus Christ.

3. Grow in understanding of God's revelation. Prayerfully read and study Sacred Scripture, the inspired word of God.

4. Study Sacred Tradition and the teachings of the Church. Sacred Tradition and Sacred Scripture make up a single source, or deposit, of the word of God. Together they are like a mirror in which the Church looks and contemplates God.

5. Listen to the preaching and teaching of the pope and the bishops. They teach us in the name of Christ and help us understand God's revelation more clearly and live it in practical ways.

Trusting God

God places both his word and a desire for him within us. So what do we do about it? We are free to say, "So what?" and reject God. We might also say, "Okay, God, there is a lot I don't understand; so help me believe in you." In other words, we can try to grow in confidence and understanding of God. We can accept the gift of **faith.**

Faith is a supernatural gift, or a gift from God. It is not something we can earn or deserve. We cannot claim that we have achieved a deep faith through our own efforts. Growing in faith does not work that way. We must pray for the grace to truly know God and trust in his love. This kind of faith is not easy or automatic.

Jesus, the Word of God

Jesus revealed that we should have complete and total faith in God. God knows everything about us and everything we need before we ask him. He wants nothing but the best for us.

The Gospel tells us that Jesus' whole life on earth showed us that God wants our happiness now on earth and with him forever in heaven. When we come to believe this about God, we also grow in our trust and love of him. We put God at the center of our lives. We value our friendship with God as the most important relationship we have. This is what faith in God is all about.

Describe someone who has helped you grow in your faith. What did this person do to help you? How did you respond to this person?

TRUSTING ONE ANOTHER

_____

_____

_____

_____

_____

_____

_____

_____

We Profess Our Faith

From the beginning the Church has proudly proclaimed its faith in God in the **creeds** of the Church. Creeds are a way of expressing the heart of the Church's faith. The Apostles' Creed and the Nicene Creed are the two main creeds of the Church.

The Apostles' Creed. The Apostles' Creed is one of the earliest creeds of the Church. It is a summary of the faith of the Apostles. It is divided into three parts.

- The first part speaks of our faith in God the Father and the creation of the world.
- The second part speaks of Jesus Christ, the Son of God, and our redemption—or the saving activity of God through Christ delivering humanity from sin.
- The third part speaks of God the Holy Spirit and our sanctification. Our sanctification is the gift of sharing in God's life and love and living and growing in friendship with God with the help of the Holy Spirit.

The Nicene Creed. When we proclaim the Nicene Creed at Sunday Mass, the grace of the Holy Spirit helps us give our hearts in faith and trust to God the Holy Trinity. We unite ourselves with believing Christians throughout the world.

In the circles create a symbol for each part of the Apostles' Creed. On the lines write what each symbol means. Share your symbols and what they tell about the Church's faith.

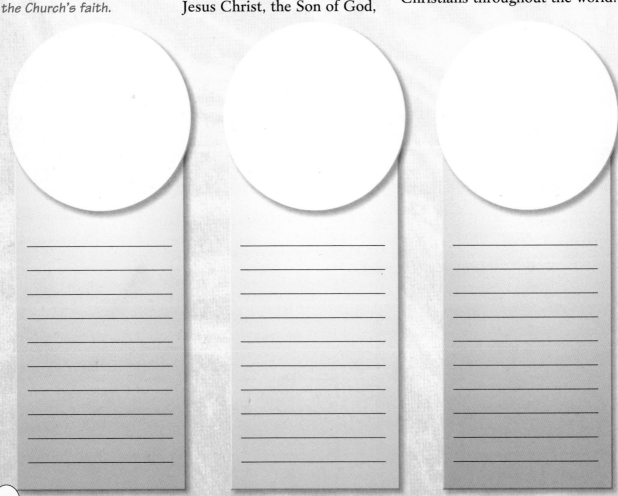

Our Church Makes a Difference

World Youth Day

Every two to three years Catholic youth from all over the world gather together to profess and share their faith in Jesus Christ. They gather at the invitation of the pope to grow in their faith and friendship with Jesus and to live their faith within their communities.

In 2005 Catholic youth from all over the world gathered in Cologne, Germany. This was the ninth World Youth Day. The previous eight World Youth Days were celebrated in 1987 in Buenos Aires, Argentina; in 1989 in Santiago de Compostela, Spain; in 1991 in Czestochowa, Poland; in 1993 in Denver, United States of America; in 1995 in Manila, Philippines; in 1997 in Paris, France; in 2000 in Rome, Italy; and in 2002 in Toronto, Canada.

During World Youth Day celebrations, Catholic youth celebrate their faith. They deepen their understanding of the teachings and practices of the Catholic Church and discuss ways to live their faith. They return to their countries and parishes filled with commitment to live the Gospel with inspired enthusiasm. They return home to build up the kingdom of justice and peace announced by Jesus Christ.

Name some of the ways your parish brings youth together to celebrate, grow in, and live their faith.

Our Catholic Identity

Nicene Creed

The creed we usually profess at Mass on Sundays was written by the Church at the Council of Nicaea in 325 and the Council of Constantinople in 381. This creed clearly states that the Father, Son, and Holy Spirit are one God in three Persons. Jesus Christ is true God and true man and is equally God as the Father.

World Youth Day, Toronto, Canada

What Difference Does Faith Make in My Life?

The Holy Spirit continuously invites you to grow in your faith and friendship with God. The Holy Spirit helps you live the gift of faith with your whole heart.

Write three statements. Write one that expresses your faith in God the Father; a second, your faith in Jesus, God the Son; and a third, your faith in the Holy Spirit. Then describe how that faith helps you make decisions each day.

I Believe in God

1 _____
_____
_____

2 _____
_____
_____

3 _____
_____
_____

My Faith Choice

I profess my faith in God the Holy Trinity each day both by my words and by my actions. This week I will profess my faith in God by

_____

_____ .

We Pray

We Believe in God

At Baptism we first profess our faith in God with the Church.
Pray this profession of faith which is taken from the rite of Baptism.

Leader: Let us profess our faith.
Do you reject sin so as to live in the freedom of God's children?
All: **I do.**

Leader: Do you reject the glamour of evil, and refuse to be mastered by sin?
All: **I do.**

Leader: Do you reject Satan, father of sin and prince of darkness?
All: **I do.**

Leader: Do you believe in God the Father?
All: **I do.**

Leader: Do you believe in Jesus Christ, his only Son, our Lord?
All: **I do.**

Leader: Do you believe in the Holy Spirit?
All: **I do.**

Leader: This is our faith. This is the faith of the Church.
We are proud to profess it, in Christ Jesus our Lord.

FROM THE "PROFESSION OF FAITH," RITE OF BAPTISM

We Remember

Match each term in column A with its meaning in column B.

Column A

____ **1.** faith

____ **2.** Trinity

____ **3.** Nicene Creed

____ **4.** redemption

____ **5.** sanctification

Column B

a. our acceptance of God and our willingness to receive his Revelation

b. the gift of sharing in God's life and love

c. the saving activity of God through Christ delivering humanity from sin

d. a summary of the principal beliefs of the Church

e. the mystery of one God in three divine Persons

To Help You Remember

1. Faith is the supernatural gift from God to believe and trust in him and the grace to freely respond to that gift.

2. Jesus' whole life on earth invited us to faith in God.

3. The creeds of the Church are both a profession and a summary of the Church's faith in God.

1 With My Family

This Week . . .

In chapter 1, "The Gift of Faith," your child learned more about the gift of faith. God reaches out to us and invites us to come to know and believe in him. He invites us to make him the center of our lives and to discover the experience and meaning of true happiness. God created us to know, love, and serve him and to be happy with him now on earth and forever in heaven. The whole life of Jesus Christ on earth most clearly and fully reveals that divine invitation.

For more on the teachings of the Catholic Church on the gift of faith, see *Catechism of the Catholic Church* paragraph numbers 26–38, 50–95, and 144–197.

Sharing God's Word

Read together Jeremiah 24:7. Emphasize that God created us with his word in our hearts and his love deep in our souls.

Praying

In this chapter your child prayed a profession of faith based on the "Profession of Faith" in the rite of Baptism. Read and pray together this prayer on page 19.

Making a Difference

Choose one of the following activities to do as a family or design a similar activity of your own.

• Learn the Apostles' Creed by heart. Make a puzzle to help you. Write the creed on a piece of paper. Then cut the paper into small pieces. Assemble the puzzle to become more familiar with the words of the Apostles' Creed.

• Talk about the things that your family "gives its heart to." Identify which of those things are signs that God is at the center of the life of your family. Discuss how these things are signs to others that you are followers of Christ.

• Read together Exodus 15:1–18. Talk about how much Moses, Miriam, and the Israelites trusted God.

For more ideas on ways your family can live your faith, visit the "Faith First for Families" page at **www.FaithFirst.com**. You will find the "About Your Child" page helpful as your sixth grader begins a new year.

God's Own Word to Us

2

We Pray

Your word is a lamp
 for my feet,
 a light for my path.
PSALM 119:105

Lord God, send the Holy
Spirit to open our minds
and hearts to your holy
word. May we share the
good news of your love
with all we meet.   Amen.

*How do you find the information
that you need?*

Think of a project you have
had to do recently. Maybe you
went to the library and did
research on the Internet, or
interviewed people. There are
many ways to grow in
understanding and living the
gift of faith.

*Why is reading and praying the
Bible vital to your life of faith?*

Faith Focus

In what ways did God reveal himself and his love for all people through the Bible?

Faith Vocabulary

inspiration of the Bible. The Holy Spirit guiding the human writers of Sacred Scripture so that they would faithfully and accurately communicate the word of God, who is the principal Author of the Scriptures.

Covenant. The solemn commitment of fidelity that God and the People of God made with one another, which was renewed in Christ, the new and everlasting Covenant.

God's Inspired Word

The Bible, or Sacred Scripture, is the inspired word of God. This means that God acted through human authors so that they wrote what he wanted. We call this the **inspiration of the Bible.** The various human writers of Sacred Scripture only wrote the truths about God and his saving love for us that God revealed for our salvation.

The Bible contains seventy-three books. These are found in the Old Testament and the New Testament.

Old Testament. The forty-six books of the Old Testament are often grouped this way.

- The Pentateuch, or the first five books of the Bible, tells of God revealing himself and making the **Covenant** with his people.
- The sixteen historical books tell of how God's people sometimes lived the Covenant well and at other times did not.
- The seven wisdom books share advice on how to live the Covenant.
- The eighteen prophetic books remind God's people to be faithful to the Covenant and that God will always be faithful to them.

New Testament. The twenty-seven books of the New Testament are grouped this way.

- The four written accounts of the Gospel are the heart of Sacred Scripture because Jesus Christ is their center.

Antique illustrated Bible on walls of Mexican mission; San Javier, Baja California, Mexico

- The Acts of the Apostles tells the story of the early Church.
- The thirteen epistles, or letters, of Saint Paul help us understand our faith in Jesus and how to live that faith.
- Eight other letters in the New Testament also help us understand and live our faith.
- The Book of Revelation encourages Christians to remain faithful to Jesus when they suffer because of their faith in Jesus Christ.

Open your Bible and briefly page through the Old Testament and New Testament. Locate the Book of Psalms and the four Gospels.

God Reveals His Name

The Pentateuch tells us the story of God revealing his name to Moses and the making of the Covenant between God and the Israelites.

One day while he was tending sheep, Moses saw a bush that was in flames but was not being consumed by the fire. Curious, Moses approached this strange sight and heard a voice coming from the bush, saying:

"Moses! Moses! . . . I am . . . the God of Abraham, the God of Isaac, the God of Jacob. . . . Come, now! I will send you to Pharaoh to lead my people, the Israelites, out of Egypt." EXODUS 3:4, 6, 10

You can just imagine how confused Moses must have been. So he asked:

"[W]hen I go to the Israelites and say to them, 'The God of your fathers has sent me to you,' if they ask me, 'What is his name?' what am I to tell them?" God replied, "I am who am. . . . [T]ell the Israelites: I AM sent me to you." EXODUS 3:13–14

Through this Old Testament story God shares his name with Moses, with the Israelites, and with all people. He says, "I am who am." In Hebrew that name is *YHWH*. By naming himself *YHWH*, God is making it known that he is always with us. Wherever we are, God is always there for us.

Faith-Filled People

People of God

The People of God are the descendants of Abraham to whom God made the promise, "I will make of you a great nation, / and I will bless you. . . . / All the communities of the earth / shall find blessing in you" (Genesis 12:2, 3). The descendants of Abraham are the people whom God chose to be his people and with whom he entered a Covenant. The Bible uses the names *Israelites*, *Hebrews*, and *Jews* for God's people of the Old Covenant.

Reading the Bible

Look up and read Matthew 3:17 in your Bible.
[Matthew = Book of the Bible; 3 = chapter of the book; 17 = verse of the chapter]

Write what the passage reveals about Jesus.

_____

_____

_____

_____

_____

_____

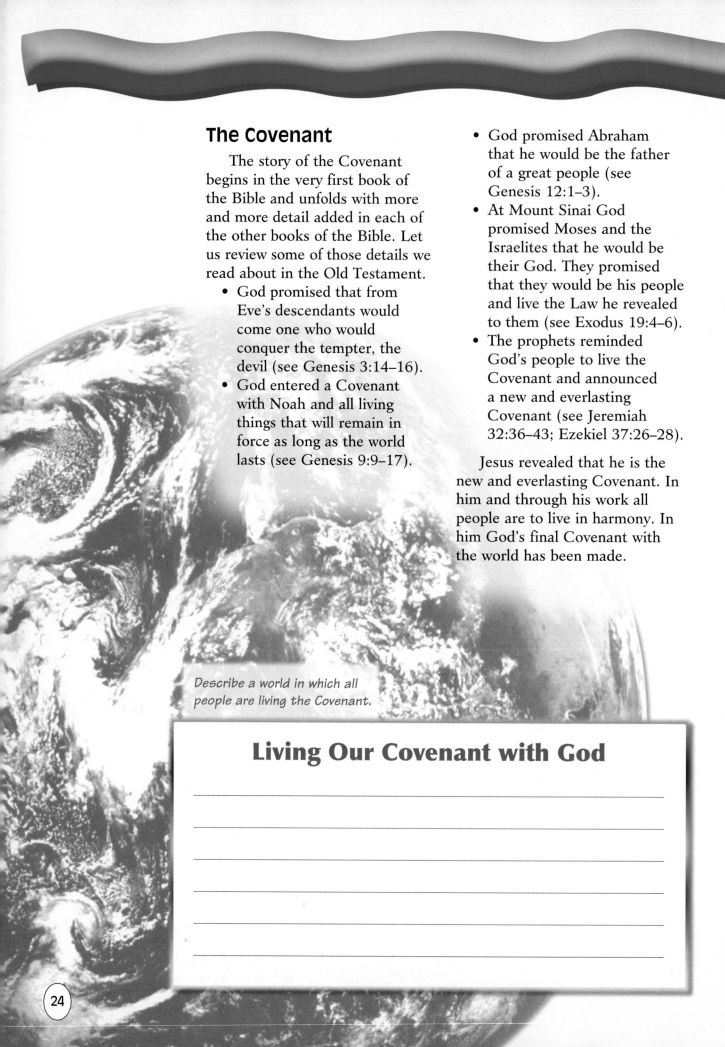

The Covenant

The story of the Covenant begins in the very first book of the Bible and unfolds with more and more detail added in each of the other books of the Bible. Let us review some of those details we read about in the Old Testament.

- God promised that from Eve's descendants would come one who would conquer the tempter, the devil (see Genesis 3:14–16).
- God entered a Covenant with Noah and all living things that will remain in force as long as the world lasts (see Genesis 9:9–17).
- God promised Abraham that he would be the father of a great people (see Genesis 12:1–3).
- At Mount Sinai God promised Moses and the Israelites that he would be their God. They promised that they would be his people and live the Law he revealed to them (see Exodus 19:4–6).
- The prophets reminded God's people to live the Covenant and announced a new and everlasting Covenant (see Jeremiah 32:36–43; Ezekiel 37:26–28).

Jesus revealed that he is the new and everlasting Covenant. In him and through his work all people are to live in harmony. In him God's final Covenant with the world has been made.

Describe a world in which all people are living the Covenant.

Living Our Covenant with God

_____

_____

_____

_____

_____

_____

Our Church Makes a Difference

Services of the Word

Bible reading and faith sharing are vital to the faith life of Catholics. We gain a great deal of inspiration and understanding of our faith by reading Sacred Scripture quietly to ourselves or by prayerfully reading the Scriptures and sharing our faith as a group. Reading the Scriptures makes us aware of God's presence with us. It guides us in living the Covenant God has made with us in Jesus.

The Church encourages us to take part in Scripture services, or services of the word, on the vigils of solemn feasts, such as Pentecost, on Sundays, and on holy days. Taking part in these services on the weekdays of Advent and Lent helps us prepare to celebrate Christmas and Easter.

Taking part in services of the word and prayerfully reading the Scriptures either alone or with other people connects the word of God with our daily lives. The word of God truly becomes "a light for [our] path" (Psalm 119:105). We make living the Commandments and the Beatitudes come alive in the world. We become lights in the world as Jesus commanded us to be.

Make a plan to read the Bible often each week.

What Difference Does Faith Make in My Life?

God is always communicating his word to us. When you prayerfully read the Scriptures alone or with others, God himself speaks to all the People of God, the Church, and to you.

Write three ways your life could be changed by reading, listening to, and studying the Bible.

The Word of the Lord

My Faith Choice

This week I will read and listen to God's word and share my thoughts and feelings with him. I will

_____

_____ .

Your Word Is a Light for My Path

Lectio divina is an important form of prayer of the Church. It is a form of meditation. Follow these steps. Spend quiet time with God, reading and listening to his word.

1. Sit quietly. Be aware that God is present with you. The Holy Spirit dwells within you.

2. Imagine yourself someplace where you can talk and listen to God.

3. Open your Bible to a favorite passage. Sign your forehead, lips, and chest over your heart with a small sign of the cross.

4. Prayerfully and reverently read the passage you selected.

5. Take time to talk and listen to God. Say, "Your word, Lord, is a light for my path" (based on Psalm 119:105).

6. After a few quiet moments, ask the Holy Spirit, "What is your word saying to me?" Write down any key words or phrases that you remember.

7. Make a faith decision and put God's word into action.

We Remember

Write a brief paragraph describing the Church's teaching about Sacred Scripture. Use three or more of these faith terms.

Bible   inspiration of the Bible   prophet

Canon of Scripture   hope

To Help You Remember

1. The Holy Spirit guided, or inspired, the human writers of Sacred Scripture to faithfully and accurately communicate the word of God.

2. Through the Bible God reveals himself and his loving plan of goodness for the world and for all people.

3. The Bible tells the story of the Covenant that God and his people freely entered into.

This Week . . .

In chapter 2, "God's Own Word to Us," your child learned more about the gift of Sacred Scripture, the Bible. Sacred Scripture is the inspired word of God. The heart of Sacred Scripture is the Gospel because Jesus Christ, the Incarnate Word of God, is the heart and fullness of God's Revelation. The Holy Spirit guided, or inspired, the human writers of Sacred Scripture to faithfully and truthfully communicate God's word. The Bible contains the forty-six books of the Old Testament and the twenty-seven books of the New Testament named by the Church to be the inspired word of God. These books are listed in and make up the Canon of Scripture.

For more on the teachings of the Catholic Church on the mystery of God's word to us revealed in Sacred Scripture, see *Catechism of the Catholic Church* paragraph numbers 101–133.

Sharing God's Word

Read together 1 Thessalonians 2:13 and 2 Timothy 3:16–17. Emphasize that the Bible is the inspired word of God.

Praying

In this chapter your child prayed a lectio divina, or a prayer of meditation. Read and pray together this prayer on page 27.

Making a Difference

Choose one of the following activities to do as a family or design a similar activity of your own.

- This week use Bible stories for your family prayer. Invite a different family member to choose the story each day and read it as part of your grace before meals.

- Watch television as a family. Carefully listen to the events that are making the headlines. Now imagine that you are a prophet. Discuss what you would tell the people.

- Create and decorate a special place in your home to display a Bible. Open the Bible each day to a favorite Bible story.

For more ideas on ways your family can live your faith, visit the "Faith First for Families" page at **www.FaithFirst.com**. Click on "Bible Stories" and discuss the Bible story as a family this week.

Living the Covenant
A Scripture Story

We Pray

Happy are those whose hope is in the LORD God.
BASED ON PSALM 146:5

Father, send the Holy Spirit to those you send into the world to announce the Gospel.   Amen.

Who in your school has been chosen to represent the views of the students to the teachers? How do they know what to say?

Ambassadors represent their countries. They speak, not for themselves, but for the governments of the nations they represent. Biblical prophets were chosen by God to speak in his name to the Israelites.

Name some of the prophets in the Bible about whom you have learned.

Byzantine art of six unnamed Old Testament prophets

The Prophets

All the biblical prophets shared a common calling. God chose them and sent them to speak in his name. Their message centered on the two themes of **fidelity** to the Covenant with God and **hope** in his promises for the future.

Fidelity

The prophets often spoke about the fidelity of the Israelites to the Covenant with God. Over and over again they admonished the Israelites when they failed to meet their responsibilities and were unfaithful to the promises they made to God. The prophets addressed the issues of (1) true worship (see Isaiah 1:11), (2) the relationship of God's people with other nations (see Isaiah 1:9), and (3) doing works of justice for the people, especially the poor and the weak (see Isaiah 1:16–17).

Hope

The prophets often invited the Israelites to place their hope in God. While God's people were not always faithful to him, he was always faithful to them. He would be true to his name, YHWH (see Isaiah 53:11). Above all, the poor and humble were signs of this hope. Such holy women as Sarah, Rebecca, Rachel, Miriam, Deborah, Hannah, Judith, and Esther kept this hope of Israel's salvation alive.

Often a prophet simply preached this message. At other times, the message was delivered in a more dramatic way. For example, Jeremiah once wore a yoke that was used to control oxen (see Jeremiah 27:1–2) to get the attention of his listeners.

The messages of the prophets pointed to a new and everlasting Covenant intended for all people, to a new law that would be engraved on people's hearts. All of these promises were fulfilled in Jesus Christ. In him we place our hope.

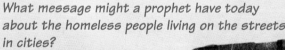

What message might a prophet have today about the homeless people living on the streets in cities?

Reading the Word of God

The Prophet Baruch

There was a time in the history of God's people when they seemed to have very little hope. It was a time of great infidelity of the Israelites to the Covenant. It was a time known as the Exile.

During the Exile God's people were forced to leave their homeland and live in the country of their conquerors, the Assyrians and Babylonians. During this time of suffering, God sent the prophet Baruch and other prophets to speak to his people in Babylonia.

Baruch's message is found in the Book of Baruch. This six-chapter book contains different kinds of writing. This passage is part of a poem, called "Praise of Wisdom in the Law of Moses."

Hear, O Israel, the
   commandments of life:
listen, and know
   prudence! . . .
You have forsaken the
   fountain of wisdom!

Had you walked in the
   way of God,
you would have dwelt in
   enduring peace. . . .
All who cling to [wisdom]
   will live,
but those will die who
   forsake her.
Turn, O Jacob, and
   receive her:
walk by her light toward
   splendor.
   BARUCH 3:9, 12–13; 4:1–2

In this poem Baruch tried to help God's people understand both how their Exile and suffering had happened and how they could find true happiness.

Think about choices people make that result in their being unhappy. Describe one of those choices. What would you do to make a better choice?

Old Testament Prophets

836 B.C.	JOEL
780 B.C.	JONAH
765 B.C.	AMOS
760 B.C.	ISAIAH
755 B.C.	HOSEA
740 B.C.	MICAH
630 B.C.	NAHUM
625 B.C.	ZEPHANIAH
609 B.C.	HABAKKUK
609 B.C.	JEREMIAH
609 B.C.	BARUCH
586 B.C.	EZEKIEL
586 B.C.	DANIEL
586 B.C.	OBADIAH
520 B.C.	HAGGAI
520 B.C.	ZECHARIAH
400 B.C.	MALACHI

Baruch's Challenge

Baruch told the Israelites that they had brought the tragedy of the Exile upon themselves. It was the consequence of their own unwise choices. Baruch's message did not end there. The prophet gave the Israelites hope for the future. He challenged them to learn and act with prudence and wisdom.

Prudence. Prudence is one of the four moral, or cardinal, virtues. It is a blend of good judgment and self-control. It includes the ability to realize that bad judgment can lead to bad consequences. God's people did not act prudently when they turned their backs on God and broke his Law. They thought not keeping God's Law would benefit them. They thought worshiping the false gods of their neighbors would bring them power and wealth. They were wrong. The real consequence of their decision was this: they lost their homeland.

Wisdom. Wisdom is one of the seven gifts of the Holy Spirit. It helps us keep God at the center of our lives. Baruch reminded the Israelites that they needed to turn back to God and be faithful to the Covenant with him. When they did, they would leave their sadness behind. God speaks to us today through the writings of Baruch. We need to listen to and accept his challenge. We are to keep God at the center of our lives. He is the source of true happiness.

Summarize Baruch's message to God's people. Think about decisions you make each day to live as a child of God. Describe what will happen if you follow Baruch's message.

Baruch's Message

What God's People Must Do	What Will Happen
_____	_____
_____	_____
_____	_____
_____	_____
_____	_____
_____	_____
_____	_____

Our Church Makes a Difference

Saint Frances Cabrini (1850–1917), who emigrated from Italy to the United States in 1889 and became a naturalized citizen in 1909

Messengers of Hope

Saint Frances Xavier Cabrini, "Mother Cabrini," was the first citizen of the United States of America to be named a saint. When she was young, geography was her favorite subject in school, and she dreamed of becoming a missionary.

In 1874, at the age of twenty-four, Frances organized the Missionary Sisters of the Sacred Heart at the invitation of her bishop. Later, Pope Leo XIII asked her and the Missionary Sisters to travel to the United States of America to serve Italian immigrants. Frances and the Missionary Sisters arrived in New York City on March 31, 1889. For the next twenty-eight years, they worked together to build hospitals, orphanages, and schools across the United States from New York to Chicago to Seattle.

Today the Missionary Sisters work in Argentina, Brazil, Chile, Panama, Spain, France, and Italy, as well as the United States. They are often joined by the Cabrini Mission Corps to continue the work begun by Mother Cabrini. The Cabrini Mission Corps is a group of laypeople, both single and married. They volunteer for a minimum of one year in the United States and a minimum of eighteen months overseas. Together the Missionary Sisters of the Sacred Heart and the Cabrini Mission Corps live as signs of hope among people.

How can you be a messenger of hope to people?

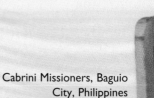

Cabrini Missioners, Baguio City, Philippines

33

What Difference Does Faith Make in My Life?

The Holy Spirit gives you the gift of wisdom. When people see you doing what is good, when you make wise choices, you are showing people that God is at the center of your life. Your choices benefit both yourself and other people too.

Describe a time when you have needed to make an important choice about living your Catholic faith. Tell who helped you and how that person helped you make a wise choice.

Practicing Wisdom

Wise Choice I Made

_____

_____

Who Helped Me

_____

_____

Wisdom Shared with Me

_____

_____

My Faith Choice

This week I will think about what my choices to live the Catholic faith are saying to others. Before I make a decision to say or do something, I will

_____

_____ .

Words of Hope

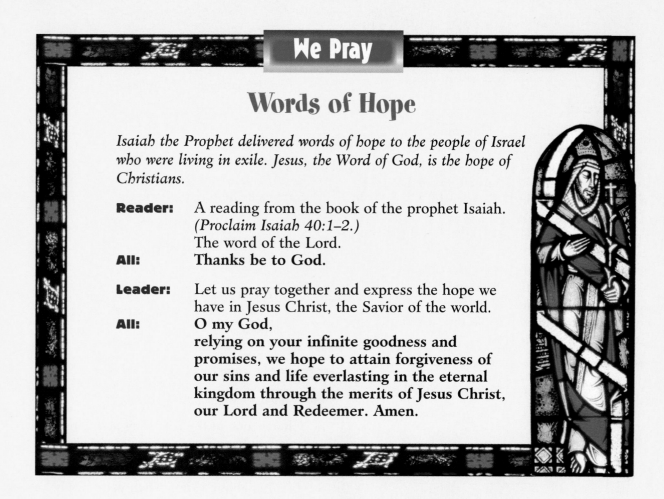

Isaiah the Prophet delivered words of hope to the people of Israel who were living in exile. Jesus, the Word of God, is the hope of Christians.

Reader: A reading from the book of the prophet Isaiah. *(Proclaim Isaiah 40:1–2.)* The word of the Lord.

All: **Thanks be to God.**

Leader: Let us pray together and express the hope we have in Jesus Christ, the Savior of the world.

All: **O my God, relying on your infinite goodness and promises, we hope to attain forgiveness of our sins and life everlasting in the eternal kingdom through the merits of Jesus Christ, our Lord and Redeemer. Amen.**

We Remember

Circle T if the statements are true and F if the statements are false. Make the false statements true.

T   F   1. The promises God made through the prophets of the Old Testament were fulfilled in Jesus Christ.

T   F   2. Baruch the Prophet told the Israelites that they brought the tragedy of the Exile upon themselves.

T   F   3. The consequence of the Israelites' decision to abandon the Covenant was their new wealth and power.

T   F   4. God always remains faithful, even to those who are unfaithful to him.

T   F   5. Wisdom is the cardinal virtue, or habit, of a person blending good judgment and self-control.

To Help You Remember

1. Fidelity to God and hope in his fidelity to his promises were central themes of the prophets.

2. Baruch the Prophet came to God's people during the Exile and promised God would remain faithful to them.

3. Baruch's message focused on living the virtues of wisdom and prudence as the source of happiness and peace.

This Week . . .

In chapter 2, "Living the Covenant: A Scripture Story," your child discovered the important role of the prophets, in particular, the prophet Baruch, in the life of the People of God. The central focus of the prophets' message to God's people was the double-edged message of fidelity and hope. The prophets constantly called people to be faithful to the Covenant as God was always faithful to them. This divine fidelity was always the source of hope, no matter how terrible the suffering God's people experienced.

For more on the teachings of the Catholic Church on the prophets and the virtue of hope, see *Catechism of the Catholic Church* paragraph numbers 64, 201, 214, and 1817–1821.

Sharing God's Word

Read together Baruch 3:9–15, 4:1–4. Emphasize that Baruch tried to help God's people understand that they could find true happiness by remaining faithful to God.

Praying

In this chapter your child prayed an act of hope. Read and pray together this prayer on page 35.

Making a Difference

Choose one of the following activities to do as a family or design a similar activity of your own.

- Think about a time when your family had hope because of your faith in God's love and faithfulness. Describe how that hope helped you at that time.

- Baruch brought a message of hope to the people. Talk about ways that your family can bring hope to each other. How can you bring hope to others?

- Actions speak louder than words. Decide on one way that your family can show others that God is at the center of your lives. Make a conscious effort to implement your decision. Profess your faith in God in both words and actions.

For more ideas on ways your family can live your faith, visit the "Faith First for Families" page at **www.FaithFirst.com**. This week pay special attention to "Questions Kids Ask."

The Mystery of God

4

We Pray

As the heavens tower over
the earth,
so God's love towers
over the faithful.

PSALM 103:11

God and Father of all
gifts, we praise you. You
are the source of all we
have and are.   Amen.

*Why do people enjoy solving
mysteries?*

Mysteries capture our
imagination. Usually, if we
have enough time and insight,
we can solve most mysteries.
God is a mystery unlike every
other mystery. We can never
fully know God, never fully
understand God and his ways.

*What is the most important thing
you have come to believe about
the mystery of God?*

The Revelation of God

The Mystery of Mysteries

Our minds cannot understand the holy mystery of God. God is like and, at the same time, unlike anyone or anything we know. While we can come to know on our own that God exists, we really cannot come to know much about the mystery of who God is without God's revelation of himself. We believe God has done just that. God has revealed that he is:

- Faithful—the One who is always faithful to his people (see Exodus 34:6);
- Truth—all his promises come true (see Deuteronomy 7:9);
- Love—God is love (see 1 John 4:8, 16).

God has revealed these qualities, or attributes, and many others about himself. Each helps us come to know something more about God. But who has God revealed himself to be? That **divine Revelation** has been passed on in Sacred Scripture and the Sacred Tradition of the Church.

The Holy Trinity

God has revealed himself to be the mystery of one God in three divine Persons: Father, Son, and Holy Spirit. This is who God is. We call this revelation of God the mystery of the Holy Trinity. It is at the very center of our faith.

The Holy Trinity, stained glass

Many other mysteries of faith have their beginning in this mystery of mysteries. For example, the story of the human family begins with God creating us out of love. Then, after we had sinned, the Father sent the Son, who became fully human and like us in all ways but sin so that we could become sharers in his divinity. The Father and the Son have sent the Holy Spirit to make us holy, or sanctify us, and to reconcile us with God who created us.

What qualities of a holy person do people see in you?

God the Creator

The very first words of the Bible begin with the story of God's love.

In the beginning, . . .
God created the heavens
and the earth. GENESIS 1:1

If we listen carefully to Genesis, we come to know something about God the Creator. We understand more about the world and ourselves.

- "In the beginning" means that the world had a beginning. The world was not always in existence.
- "God created" means that only God creates. Only he makes everyone and everything out of nothing without any help.
- "Heavens and the earth" is another way of saying "everything, seen and unseen." Angels are part of God's unseen creation. They are spiritual creatures who never stop giving glory to God and who serve his saving plan for all creatures.

God the Father not only created the universe out of love, but also keeps it in existence by his Word, the Son, and by the Holy Spirit, the giver of life.

Images of God

In God's plan of creation, human beings have an extraordinary and unique place. The greatness of every person rests on this revealed truth.

God created man in his image;
in the divine image he
created him;
male and female he
created them.
GENESIS 1:27

Each person is created with a soul that bears the imprint of God's image. Our soul is the innermost spiritual part of us. It is eternal, or lives forever. It gives us the ability to share in his life and love forever. When we choose to live as images of God, we tell others about God's love. We give honor and glory to God.

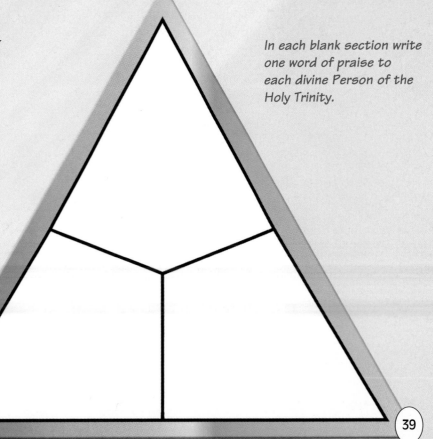

In each blank section write one word of praise to each divine Person of the Holy Trinity.

Sin and Evil

In the beginning God created humanity in a state of original holiness and justice, or friendship with him. Sin and evil, the Bible tells us, made their way into the good world of God's creation through original sin.

Original sin. Original sin is the sin Adam and Eve committed by freely turning away from God's love and friendship. They freely chose to do what they knew God did not want them to do. They sinned and by their sin the original holiness and justice human beings received from God was lost for them and for all humans, except Mary, who came after them.

The biblical story of humanity's fall from grace and original holiness begins with the temptation of Eve by a snake, or serpent. The Bible describes this temptation by putting these words in the mouth of the serpent: "you will be like gods" (Genesis 3:5). Adam and Eve gave in to this temptation and sinned. Their sin, therefore, was a combination of disobedience, pride, ambition, and selfishness.

The loss of original holiness has become part of our fallen human nature. Every human person now shares in the effects of original sin. The world and all of us in the human family are marked by sin. From the very first moment of our existence, or conception, we need to be reconciled with God.

The New Adam

The Son of God, Jesus Christ, became a man, lived on earth, and was raised from the dead to save us and redeem us from sin and death. In Jesus Christ we have been healed, or reconciled, with God, with one another, and with all creation.

Think about the sin of stealing. Describe how stealing separates a person from God and people. Then describe what needs to be done to heal that separation.

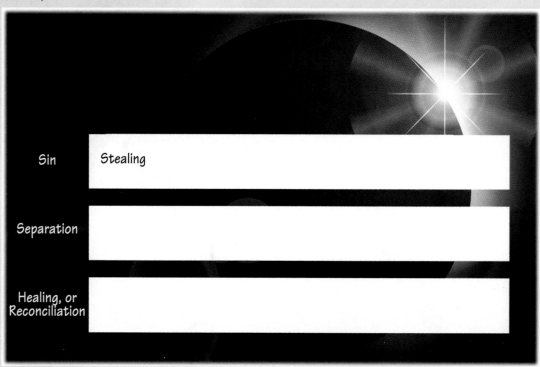

Sin	Stealing
Separation	
Healing, or Reconciliation	

Dove with halo, symbol for Holy Spirit, over Bible open to Gospel of Saint John

Mosaics

Art can help us come to know the mystery of the loving presence of God within us and among us. Long before we had Bibles for everyone to read, Christians used art to help people "hear" the story of creation and redemption.

Mosaics are one of the earliest forms of art used by Christians. The creation of mosaics is an art form consisting of pressing colored pieces of glass called tesserae into soft plaster to form pictures. Mosaics help us enter the mystery of God. They give drama and life to scenes from the Bible that reveal the story of God's love for us. Often decorating the ceilings and walls of churches, they instruct the faithful concerning the majesty and mystery of God, and the lives of Jesus and of Mary and the other saints.

Mosaics and other forms of Christian art, like all the sacramentals of the Church, help us respond in faith to the mystery of the one God, who is Father, Son, and Holy Spirit. They invoke in us a sense of wonder and awe for God. They spark a desire within us to spread the story of God's love by striving to be his living images in the world.

What other art forms inspire and teach us about God? What art in your parish helps you remember God's love for you and for all people?

Our Catholic Identity

Gothic Architecture

Architecture is the art of building. This wonderful art form is used to build churches. Gothic architecture is one form of this art. Gothic churches are tall and have arches that point to heaven. They express the faith of Christians in God and eternal life.

Madonna and Child, Byzantine icon

Detail of *Christ Bearing His Cross* from the Stations of the Cross War Memorial, Dublin, Ireland

What Difference Does Faith Make in My Life?

God always manifests his love. God never stops giving you signs of his love. If you look closely, there are many clues that give you a glimpse into the mystery of God.

Make a collage of words and pictures of people, places, things, and events that have come to be signs of God and his love for you.

Signs of the Mystery of God

My Faith Choice

This week I will try to show that I am made in the image and likeness of God. I will be a sign of God's love by

_____

_____.

Give Thanks to God

The Church prays the Psalms each day. One way we pray the Psalms is by alternately praying the verses aloud. We call this praying the Psalms antiphonally.

All: **Come and see the works of God, awesome in the deeds done for us.**

Group 1: Shout joyfully to God, all you on earth;
Group 2: sing of his glorious name.

All: **Come and see the works of God, awesome in the deeds done for us.**

Group 1: All on earth fall in worship before you;
Group 2: they sing of you, sing of your name!

All: **Come and see the works of God, awesome in the deeds done for us.**

PSALM 66:1, 4, 5

We Remember

Decipher the hidden message. Complete the sentences. Unscramble the highlighted letters to discover the belief about God that is at the center of our faith.

1. God has revealed himself to be the __ __ __ ◯ __ ◯◯ of one God in three divine Persons.

2. Divine __ __ __ __ __ __ __ ◯ __ ◯ is God making himself and his plan of creation and redemption known over time.

3. __ __ __ __ ◯ __ __ __ is God making everyone and everything, seen and unseen, out of nothing and without any help.

4. __ __ __ __ ◯ __ __ __ sin is the name given to the first sin.

The central belief about God is the mystery of the

__ __ __ __ __ __ __ __ __ .

To Help You Remember

1. God is the mystery of mysteries who has revealed himself and his plan of creation and redemption.

2. All creation is destined for the glory of God.

3. Original sin broke the first Covenant uniting creation and God. In Jesus, the final Covenant, God's plan has been restored and creation is reconciled with God.

This Week . . .

In chapter 4, "The Mystery of God," your child learned more about the mystery of God and the divine plan of creation. God is the mystery of mysteries. While we can come to know God exists on our own, we really cannot come to know much about the mystery of who God is and his plan for the world without God's revelation of himself. God has revealed himself to be the Holy Trinity, or one God in three Persons—God the Father, God the Son, and God the Holy Spirit. God created people in his image and likeness to live in happiness and friendship with him. By sinning Adam and Eve broke that original Covenant God made with creation. We call that sin original sin. Jesus Christ, the new Adam, restored us to friendship with God and redeemed us from sin and death.

For more on the teachings of the Catholic Church on the mystery of God and the divine plan of creation, see *Catechism of the Catholic Church* paragraph numbers 51–67, 199–227, 232–260, 279–314, 325–349, 355–379, and 385–412.

Sharing God's Word

Read together Exodus 34:6, Deuteronomy 7:9, and 1 John 4:8, 16. Emphasize that through Sacred Scripture God reveals who he is and his plan of loving goodness for the world.

Praying

In this chapter your child prayed a prayer based on Psalm 66. Read and pray together this prayer on page 43.

Making a Difference

Choose one of the following activities to do as a family or design a similar activity of your own.

- Invite family members to take turns completing the sentence, "God is . . ." Continue until no one is able to complete the sentence. Distribute art materials and create table mats displaying words and phrases your family used to describe God.

- Recall that all people are created in the image and likeness of God. Share ideas about how your family is an image of God.

- Religious art helps us come to know God. This week when you take part in Mass, look at the works of art in your church. Talk about how each work of art helps you come to know God.

For more ideas on ways your family can live your faith, visit the "Faith First for Families" page at **www.FaithFirst.com**. This week take time to read an article from "Just for Parents."

Jesus Christ, the Son of God

We Pray

Hear me, LORD, and
   answer me, . . .
save your servant who
   trusts in you.
                    PSALM 86:1, 2

**Lord God, send your
blessing upon all
who believe in your Son.
May their faith grow
stronger.   Amen.**

*What is one important promise
that you have made? Why was it
easy or difficult to keep?*

Think about the important role
that making and keeping
promises has in our lives.
Making and keeping promises
also plays an important role in
the Bible. We can describe the
Bible as "The Story of the
Promise."

*What is the biggest promise
made in the Bible?*

Cross commemorating site where
Captain Pedro Menendez de
Aviles, Spanish explorer, landed
in 1565 to found Saint Augustine
(Florida), oldest city in America

God Fulfills His Promises

Why is Jesus the fulfillment of all God's promises?

Faith Vocabulary

salvation. The deliverance of humanity from the power of sin and death by God through Jesus Christ who "died for our sins in accordance with the Scriptures."

Incarnation. The term the Church uses to name the faith of the Church that the Son of God became fully human in all things except sin, while remaining fully divine.

Fresco of Jesus on ceiling with smaller portrait of Mary and infant Jesus on nearby alcove, St. Andrew's Church, Chicago, Illinois

God wants everyone to share in his life and love both now and forever. The Church teaches that through the grace of the Holy Spirit, God works quietly and mysteriously to draw all people to himself, even those who have not heard of Jesus. All can be saved who seek to serve and love God with all their heart

Describe things people do that are signs that they are seeking to love God with all their heart.

Jesus, the New Covenant

All of God's promises in the Old Testament and all the events surrounding them point to Jesus Christ. In him all God's promises are fulfilled. Jesus did not abolish the Law and Covenant of Sinai. He fulfilled them and perfected them (see Matthew 5:17–18). Jesus Christ is the new and everlasting Covenant (see 1 Corinthians 11:25). Jesus is the Savior of all people. He is the center of God's plan of **salvation.**

But what about those who have not heard of Jesus? The answer to that question is very important.

Signs of God's Love

1. _____
_____
_____
_____
_____

2. _____
_____
_____
_____
_____

The Church's Faith in Jesus Christ

While Jesus lived on earth and did the work his Father sent him to do, not everyone came to believe he was the Savior and Messiah. Some people were confused and hesitant to believe. Others were hostile. On one occasion when Jesus asked his disciples, "Who do you say that I am?" only Peter spoke out and confessed his faith in Jesus.

> Simon Peter said in reply, "You are the Messiah, the Son of the living God."
> MATTHEW 16:16

The Gospel story of the Apostle Peter's confession of faith in Jesus is the foundation of what the Holy Spirit has led the Church to believe about Jesus. We believe:

- **Jesus is Lord.** Jesus is true God (see 1 Corinthians 12:3).

- **Jesus is the Son of the living God.** Jesus is the second Person of the Holy Trinity and is intimately one with the Father in the Holy Spirit (see John 12:44–45).

- **Jesus is true God and true man.** The Son of God became true man without giving up his divinity. The Son of God became like us in all things but sin. We call this the mystery of the **Incarnation** (see John 1:14).

- **Jesus is the Messiah and Savior.** Jesus is the One whom God promised to send to deliver his people and to lead them to faithfully live the Covenant. Jesus Christ is the one and only Mediator, or "go-between," who links God and the human family. He alone reconciles the human family with God (see 1 Timothy 2:5–6, Hebrews 9:15–28).

Think about some of the choices you recently made that are signs of your faith in Jesus. Share one of those choices with a partner.

Jesus and His Disciples, Ethiopic art

The Paschal Mystery

The center of the work the Father sent Jesus to do on earth is called the Paschal Mystery. The word *paschal* comes from a Hebrew word meaning "the passing over." The Paschal Mystery is Jesus' passing over from life on earth through his Passion, death, Resurrection, and Ascension to a new and glorified life with the Father.

The Crucifixion and Descent of Jesus to the Dead. Jesus sacrificed his life by freely accepting death on the cross and being buried. The dead Christ went down to the dead and opened the gates of heaven for the just who had gone before him and for those who would come after him.

The Resurrection. Three days after he died and was buried, he was raised from the dead with a new and glorified body. All four accounts of the Gospel clearly teach that the Resurrection of Jesus took place. It is at the heart of our faith in Christ (see 1 Corinthians 15:3–5).

The Ascension and Exaltation. Forty days after the Resurrection, the Risen Christ ascended to the Father in heaven, God's domain, where he reigns gloriously at the right hand of the Father (see Luke 24:50–53). From there, Christ, who is hidden from our eyes, will come again in glory at the end of time to judge the living and the dead (see Matthew 25:31–46). Through Christ's Ascension and exaltation in glory, all humanity has been given an unbreakable promise of everlasting life of happiness with the Trinity, with the angels, and with Mary and all the saints (see Revelation 22:4–5).

This great mystery of God's love for us is the center of the Gospel, or Good News. Through the Paschal Mystery all things have been justified, or made right, in Christ with God. Christ is the firstborn from the dead. Through him we are saved and will rise to life everlasting.

The ⊂○ (a fish) is an ancient Christian symbol for Jesus Christ, Son of God, Savior. Reflect on the meaning of the Paschal Mystery. Draw a symbol that expresses your faith in the Paschal Mystery.

Saint Paul of the Cross (1694–1775)

Saint Paul of the Cross

The Passion, death, and Resurrection are the heart of the Gospel. For Paolo (Paul) Francesco Daneo, Saint Paul of the Cross, the Passion and Resurrection of Christ was the greatest work of divine love.

The times during which Paul lived were filled with neglect for the poor, hungry, and sick. Paul believed this was a sign that people had forgotten the suffering and death of Jesus. They were ungrateful for God's love. Paul wrote, "The world lives unmindful of the sufferings of Jesus which are the miracle of miracles of the love of God."

Paul decided to make people more aware of the Passion of Christ and the power of the love of God working in the world. Dressed in a black robe, he traveled up and down Italy and became known as Paul of the Cross. Paul founded the "Barefoot Clerks of the Cross and the Passion," or the Passionists, to help him in his work. Today, there are more than two thousand Passionists who preach the message of the cross to a suffering world in fifty-two nations on all five continents. They see Jesus in people who are suffering. They believe that when they help the suffering, they are helping Jesus who said, "Amen, I say to you, whatever you did for one of these least brothers [or sisters] of mine, you did for me" (Matthew 25:40).

How might Christians today reach out to people who are suffering and share their faith in the Passion, death, and Resurrection of Jesus?

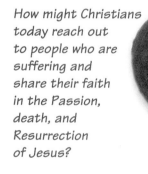

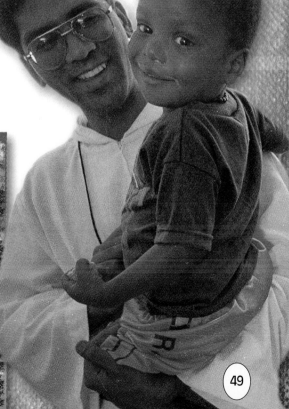

What Difference Does Faith Make in My Life?

Each day you have many opportunities to profess your faith in Jesus Christ either by word or by your actions. Sometimes this is easier to do than at other times. Always the Holy Spirit, the Advocate, is with you to help you.

You will soon be interviewed by a reporter for a Catholic magazine for an article about people living their faith in Jesus. Choose a situation from your life that you will share with the reporter. Write notes for your interview on the pages of this planner.

Living Our Faith in Jesus

My Faith Choice

When I am faced with a difficult decision about living my faith, I will ask myself what Jesus would do. Then I will

_____

_____ .

Scripture-based Stations of the Cross

The Stations of the Cross is a prayer of meditation. This Scripture-based version of the Stations has been given to us by Pope John Paul II. It differs slightly from the traditional Stations, which can be found on page 291. Prayerfully journey the way of the cross with Jesus. Meditate on each of these Stations. Quietly say this prayer after each Station: "We adore you, O Christ, and we bless you. By your holy cross you have saved us and set us free."

1. Jesus is in the Garden of Gethsemane.
2. Jesus, betrayed by Judas, is arrested.
3. Jesus is condemned by the Sanhedrin.
4. Jesus is denied by Peter.
5. Jesus is judged by Pilate.
6. Jesus is scourged and crowned with thorns.
7. Jesus takes up his cross.
8. Jesus is helped by Simon Cyrene to carry his cross.
9. Jesus meets the women of Jerusalem.
10. Jesus is crucified.
11. Jesus promises redemption to the good thief.
12. Jesus is on the cross, with his mother and Saint John at the foot of the cross.
13. Jesus dies on the cross.
14. Jesus is placed in the tomb.

We Remember

Circle the faith words hidden in this heart. Choose two of the faith words you circled and share with a partner a brief description of each.

```
J K L M E R S V      O F R B H S T
Q S A L V A T I O N G H O P D S W X V M F
T P E H B D S V B I N C A R N A T I O N R
M C R U C I F I X I O N C N A T I X L
O P B N R E S U R R E C T I O N W
A B A S C E N S I O N C R T X
N U I O D E S C B M N
K I H Y D
```

To Help You Remember

1. Jesus is the Savior of the world.
2. The Church professes her faith in Jesus Christ, the Son of the living God, who is Lord, Messiah, and the one Mediator between God and humanity.
3. The Paschal Mystery is at the center of the work the Father sent Jesus to do.

This Week . . .

In chapter 5, "Jesus Christ, the Son of God," your child learned more about the mystery of salvation in Jesus Christ. God's plan of salvation began at creation with the promise that a child of Eve would overcome sin and death and reconcile humanity with God. In Jesus Christ, the Son of Mary, the new Eve, that plan was fulfilled. Through the Paschal Mystery—through Christ's passing over from life through his Passion, death, Resurrection, and Ascension to a new and glorified life with his Father—humanity has been saved and redeemed in Christ. Humankind has received the promise of eternal life and happiness.

For more on the teachings of the Catholic Church on the mystery of Jesus Christ and God's plan of salvation, see *Catechism of the Catholic Church* paragraph numbers 410–412, 430–451, 461–469, and 512–679.

Sharing God's Word

Read together Hebrews 9:15–28. Emphasize that Jesus, the Savior of the world, alone reconciles the human family with God.

Praying

In this chapter your child prayed the scriptural Stations of the Cross. Read and pray together the Stations of the Cross on page 51 or the traditional form of the Stations of the Cross on page 291.

Making a Difference

Choose one of the following activities to do as a family or design a similar activity of your own.

- Talk about some of the choices your family has made. How are these choices signs of your faith in Jesus Christ?

- Standing up for our faith can sometimes be difficult. Why? When would you be willing to stand up for your faith?

- When we pray the Sign of the Cross we profess our faith in Jesus who freely died on the cross to save us from sin and death. This week, pray the Sign of the Cross every time you begin to pray.

For more ideas on ways your family can live your faith, visit the "Faith First for Families" page at **www.FaithFirst.com**. This week share some of the ideas on the "Gospel Reflections" page as a family.

God's Plan of Salvation
A Scripture Story

We Pray

Let this be written
   for the next generation,
   for a people not yet born,
   that they may praise
   the LORD.   PSALM 102:19

**Lord our God, may Mary,
the Apostles, and all the
saints help us on our way
of salvation.   Amen.**

*What have you learned from
reading about someone's life?*

Anne Frank wrote an
extraordinary series of letters
that we can read in *The Diary
of Anne Frank*. These letters
pass on for generations to come
the story of the Holocaust. The
letters, or epistles, in the New
Testament pass on to us the
Church's faith in Jesus Christ.

*What is something you know
about Jesus from reading one of
the New Testament letters?*

The Great Theatre in Ephesus,
Turkey. In New Testament
times Ephesus was a chief port
of Asia with a population of
250,000 people.

53

Saint Paul Arriving at Malta, Peter Muller (1637–1701), Dutch painter

The New Testament Letters

The New Testament letters are sometimes called **epistles**. In fact, letters and epistles represent different kinds of writing. When someone had an idea and wanted to explain it in detail, they might call their letter an epistle. Letters, on the other hand, were usually more personal and exchanged between people who knew each other well.

Many letters Saint Paul the Apostle wrote are found in the New Testament. Often these letters were to people who were his converts who came to believe in Jesus Christ through Paul's preaching. He wrote to encourage, support, and instruct his friends. He felt very close to these people. Philippians 1:3–7, for example, is a personal note from Paul.

Paul's writing sometimes addressed a problem that a particular Christian community was facing (see 1 Corinthians 11:17–34). At other times he wrote to remind people of the faith that he preached to them—especially if they were in danger of falling away from the truth (see Galatians 4:1–11).

In addition to the writings of Saint Paul, the New Testament contains other letters. The teachings of all these letters are important for deepening our understanding of and living our faith in Jesus Christ. We will now study part of the Letter to the Ephesians in more detail.

Look up and read Ephesians 4:1–5. What does it tell you about living as a follower of Jesus?

The Letter to the Ephesians

In New Testament times, Ephesus was the capital of the Roman Empire's province of Asia. It was a great commercial center, teeming with merchants, tradespeople, and sailors from all over the world. Paul the Apostle came into this noisy crossroads and stayed for two years before the local silversmiths forced him to flee. They were angry that their trade in shrines to a pagan goddess had suffered due to the growth of the Christian faith.

Read and discover the opening words of the Letter to the Ephesians.

Paul, an apostle of Christ Jesus. . . . Blessed be the God and Father of our Lord Jesus Christ, who has blessed us in Christ with every spiritual blessing in the heavens. . . .

In him we have redemption by his blood, the forgiveness of transgressions, in accord with the riches of his grace that he lavished upon us. . . . In him you also, who have heard the word of truth, the gospel of your salvation, and have believed in him, were sealed with the promised holy Spirit, which is the first installment of our inheritance toward redemption as God's possession, to the praise of his glory.

EPHESIANS 1:1, 3, 7–8, 13–14

This letter was probably written by disciples of Saint Paul. It shares with the Ephesians the heart of the faith in Christ that Saint Paul preached.

What does this passage tell you about the faith of Saint Paul and the early Church in Jesus?

Faith in Christ

_____

_____

_____

_____

_____

_____

_____

You are a youth editor of the advice column, "Let's Live Our Faith," in your diocesan newspaper. How would you respond to these youth?

A Letter for Us Today

The Letter to the Ephesians was written two thousand years ago, but in a very real sense, it is also written to us today. We are chosen by God. We are adopted sons and daughters of God the Father. We are redeemed in Christ. We are temples of the Holy Spirit.

The story of the Ephesians is our story. We believe in Jesus Christ. We have been sacramentally sealed with the promised Holy Spirit who continues to work with us as we proceed along life's bumpy road. In the end, the work of **redemption**, which God the Father has begun in Christ, the Incarnate Son of God, and continues through the Holy Spirit, will be completed.

Let's Live Our Faith

"My best friend has been spreading false rumors about me at school. He is saying that the only reason I make Honor Roll is that I cheat on tests. He doesn't know that I know that he is behind the rumors. It really hurts me. But I am afraid to say anything because I don't want to lose him as a friend."

Jared

"I have a problem that most sixth graders don't have. I want to be a missionary when I grow up. When I told my parents, they said that they didn't think it was a good idea. They wanted me to be a doctor like my grandfather and my mother. 'We have a family tradition of doctors,' they said. 'Look at all the good you could do for people as a doctor.'"

Teri

Dear Jared,

_____

_____

_____

_____

_____

Dear Teri,

_____

_____

_____

_____

_____

Our Church Makes a Difference

Catholic Newspapers

For almost two hundred years the Catholic press has served Catholics in the United States. The *United States Catholic Miscellany* (1822–1861) and the *Truth Teller* (1825–1855) were two of the earliest Catholic newspapers published in the United States. Bishop John England established the *United States Catholic Miscellany,* which today is the *Catholic Miscellany,* to instruct Catholics of the Diocese of Charleston, South Carolina, in the teachings of the Catholic Church. The *Truth Teller* was established in New York to foster religious freedom for Catholics.

The *Pilot,* which is the newspaper published by the Archdiocese of Boston, is the oldest existing Catholic newspaper in the United States. It was established on September 5, 1829, as the *Jesuit,* or *Catholic Sentinel.* The newspaper of the Archdiocese of Cincinnati, the *Catholic Telegraph,* which was established in 1831, is also one of the earliest Catholic newspapers being published today.

Many parishes in the United States provide each family with a copy of its diocesan newspaper. This helps Catholic families grow in their understanding of the teachings of the Catholic Church. It also provides families and Catholic community leaders with the information they need to make informed decisions about living the Catholic faith.

Does your diocese publish a newspaper? If so, what is its name? How does your parish communicate with its members?

Our Catholic Identity

Pastoral Letters

The writing of pastoral letters is one way the bishops of the United States communicate with Catholics and non-Catholics. Through pastoral letters bishops instruct the faithful on Catholic teachings, worship, social concerns, and other topics that are important to the people.

United States Catholic Miscellany photo courtesy of the Diocese of Charleston Archives

The Tidings, published by the Roman Catholic Archdiocese of Los Angeles, California

What Difference Does Faith Make in My Life?

From its beginning the Church has shared her faith through letters. The Holy Spirit invites and helps you to share your faith with others.

Think about several things you can say or do to share your faith in Jesus. Compose an outline of a letter you might write to share your faith.

Sharing Faith in Jesus

_____

_____

_____

_____

_____

_____

_____

_____

_____

My Faith Choice

This week I will try to share my faith in Jesus. I will

_____

_____.

An Act of Faith

Leader: We believe these truths and all that you have revealed, which the Catholic Church faithfully teaches.

Reader 1: God the Father, God the Son, God the Holy Spirit, you are one God in three divine Persons.
All: **We do believe.**

Reader 2: God our Father, you created us because of your love.
All: **We do believe.**

Reader 3: God the Son, Jesus Christ, you became a man and died for our sins and rose from the dead.
All: **We do believe.**

Reader 4: God the Holy Spirit, you are the giver of life, our advocate and teacher.
All: **We do believe.**

We Remember

Define each term by using it in a sentence.

1. epistle _____
   _____

2. letter _____
   _____

3. Ephesians _____
   _____

4. redemption _____
   _____

To Help You Remember

1. The New Testament letters deepen our understanding and love of our faith in Jesus Christ.

2. The Letter to the Ephesians was written to share with us the heart of Saint Paul's preaching about Jesus.

3. The message of Ephesians is as important for us today as it was for the members of the early Church to whom it was addressed.

This Week . . .

In chapter 6, "God's Plan of Salvation: A Scripture Story," your child learned more about Sacred Scripture, especially the literary genre of letter writing in the New Testament. The New Testament Letter to the Ephesians was studied. Your child learned that knowing both the audience and the writing style of a particular book of the Bible helps us better understand its content.

For more on the teachings of the Catholic Church on how to read Sacred Scripture, see *Catechism of the Catholic Church* paragraph numbers 101–133.

Sharing God's Word

Read together Ephesians 1:1–14. Emphasize that this passage is from a letter written to members of the early Church who were living in the city of Ephesus.

Praying

In this chapter your child prayed an act of faith. Read and pray together this prayer on page 59.

Making a Difference

Choose one of the following activities to do as a family or design a similar activity of your own.

- Write letters to family members or friends with whom you have not been in touch for a while. Be sure to include a note of thanks for their friendship.

- Take the time to page through the New Testament and review the names of the New Testament letters. Talk about how the Letter to the Ephesians and the other New Testament letters encourage us to live as followers of Christ.

- Write a letter to each other encouraging one another to live as followers of Christ.

For more ideas on ways your family can live your faith, visit the "Faith First for Families" page at **www.FaithFirst.com**. Click on "Make a Difference" to discuss how your family can live your faith and share it with others.

The Church: The Age of the Spirit

We Pray

[LORD,] teach me to do
 your will,
 for you are my God.
May your kind spirit
 guide me.   PSALM 143:10

God our Father, may your Church always be a sign of your holiness for all the world.   Amen.

What are some of the signs of a school or a team that has spirit?

Spirit days at school are filled with enthusiasm. Excitement and energy fill the school. The Holy Spirit energizes the Church with the gift of enthusiasm. At Baptism you received the gift of the Holy Spirit.

If you were asked to talk to younger students about what it means to belong to a Spirit-filled Church, what would you tell them?

World Youth Day,
Toronto, Canada, 2002

The Holy Spirit

When Christians think of the Holy Spirit, we might think that the Holy Spirit waited until Pentecost to begin his work among us. The truth is that the Holy Spirit has always been at work in the world. We read about the Holy Spirit in the story of creation and the Holy Spirit's work with the Old Testament prophets. We read about the work of the Holy Spirit in the life of Mary in the Gospel story of the Annunciation. When Jesus began his public ministry, he announced in the synagogue in Nazareth, "The Spirit of the Lord is upon me" (Luke 4:18). The work, or mission, of Jesus, the Son of God, and the Holy Spirit always go together and cannot be separated one from the other.

Pentecost

Fifty days after Jesus was raised from the dead, the Holy Spirit came to the disciples as Jesus promised. Filled with enthusiasm, Peter the Apostle and the other disciples went into the streets of Jerusalem. People from many countries listened to Peter. Moved by the Holy Spirit, they were baptized. The **Church** was born.

Pentecost, stained glass

The Church born on Pentecost is a sign and instrument of God's communion with all humanity. It is a sign in the world of the unity of the whole human race. The promise made to Abraham had come true in Christ. The Holy Spirit began the work of gathering people of all races and cultures into the one People of God.

In what ways is the Church a sign of the unity of people of all races and cultures?

The Marks of the Church

At Mass we profess our faith in the "one holy catholic and apostolic Church." These are the four Marks, or the essential features, of the Church that Jesus Christ has given to us.

One. The Church of Jesus Christ is one Church. We profess and celebrate and live our faith in "one Lord, one faith, one baptism; one God and Father of all, who is over all and through all and in all" (Ephesians 4:5–6). What we see in the world today is the one Church founded by Jesus separated into many parts. The whole Church must work to be one, as Jesus and the Father and the Holy Spirit are one.

Holy. The Church is a "holy nation" (1 Peter 2:9). We live in communion with God the Father, God the Son, and God the Holy Spirit.

Catholic. Jesus Christ is the Savior of all people. We invite all people to become disciples of Jesus. All over the world the Church gathers and in many diverse ways celebrates one faith in Christ.

Apostolic. The faith of the Church is rooted in what the Apostles preached and taught in the name of Jesus Christ. There is an unbroken connection, or apostolic succession, between the Apostles and their successors, the pope and the other bishops.

Faith-Filled People

Timothy

Saint Timothy was baptized by Saint Paul the Apostle. Timothy's father was Greek and his mother, Eunice, was Jewish. Timothy traveled with Paul on his missionary journeys and became the first bishop of Ephesus. There are two New Testament letters addressed to Timothy, who was stoned to death in A.D. 97 because he refused to worship the Roman Emperor Dionysius. Saint Timothy's feast day is January 26.

Choose one of the Marks of the Church. Decorate this banner with symbols that tell about that Mark of the Church.

Images for the Church

There are many images in the New Testament for the Church. These images, like the Marks of the Church, help us understand the mystery of the Church. The new People of God, Body of Christ, and Temple of the Holy Spirit are three images for the Church that you have already learned about. Bride of Christ and Mother are two other important images.

Bride of Christ. In the New Testament we read:

Husbands, love your wives, even as Christ loved the church. . . . This is a great mystery, but I speak in reference to Christ and the church.   EPHESIANS 5:25, 32

Christ's love for the Church will never end. Jesus described his love for us this way: "No one has greater love than this, to lay down one's life for one's friends" (John 15:13).

Mother. This image helps us understand that we receive the gift of our life in Christ through the Church. The Church nourishes us as we gather around the table of the Eucharist. The Church teaches us the language of our faith and how we are to live as children of God the Father and followers of Christ.

Picturing the Church

In this space create an image or symbol that you can use to help others understand the Church.

IOANNIS PAULI PP. II
SUMMI PONTIFICIS

LITTERAE ENCYCLICAE

« EVANGELIUM VITAE »

EPISCOPIS
PRESBYTERIS ET DIACONIS
RELIGIOSIS VIRIS ET MULIERIBUS
CHRISTIFIDELIBUS LAICIS
UNIVERSISQUE BONAE VOLUNTATIS HOMINIBUS

DE VITAE HUMANAE INVIOLABILI BONO

LIBRERIA EDITRICE VATICANA
MCMXCV

Our Catholic Identity

Church Documents

The Church issues several types of documents to teach and guide the members of the Church in living the faith of the Church. Among these documents, in order of importance, are apostolic constitutions, issued by the pope or by a council of the Church with the approval of the pope; encyclical letters; apostolic exhortations; apostolic letters; and letters.

Encyclical letter, "Evangelium Vitae," or "The Gospel of Life," of Pope John Paul II, March 3, 1995

Letters from the Church

Beginning with Saint Paul the Apostle and the other writers of the New Testament letters, the Church has a long tradition of letter writing. These letters help the Church and all people understand the meaning of the faith of the Church and the difference living that faith each day will make to bring about peace and unity among all peoples. This tradition continues in the Church today.

Encyclical letters are one of the most important types of letters in the Church. An encyclical letter is a formal letter written by or authorized by the pope. The use of encyclicals as we know them today was begun in 1740 by Pope Benedict XIV.

Encyclicals are official letters of the Church. They spotlight issues on doctrine, morality, or discipline, such as the meaning of the truths of our faith, the Eucharist and the sacraments, war and peace, social and economic justice, moral behavior, and living the Ten Commandments.

In what other ways does the Church teach us?

What Difference Does Faith Make in My Life?

You are a sign, or image, of the Church. The Holy Spirit is always with you, helping you send a clear message to others about the Church.

Use symbols, pictures, and words to create a bulletin board announcement that tells others about the Church.

The People of God

The People of God

My Faith Choice

This week I will try to be a clear image of what the Church is. I will

_____

_____ .

We Pray

"Father, May They All Be One"

At the Last Supper, Jesus prayed for his followers. Let us listen to the prayer of Jesus in John's Gospel and pray to the Father as he did.

Leader: Lord, we gather to listen to your word.
May we always live as the one People of God.

Reader: A reading from the holy gospel according to John.

All: **Glory to you, O Lord.**

Reader: *Proclaim John 17:20–21.*
The gospel of the Lord.

All: **Praise to you, Lord Jesus Christ.**
(Reflect on what it means to be a member of the Church.)

Leader: Lord God, Father of all,
fill us with the love of the Holy Spirit.
Make us one in the fullness of faith and fellowship of love.
We ask this through Jesus Christ, your Son,
who lives and reigns with you and the Holy Spirit,
one God, for ever and ever.

All: **Amen.**

We Remember

Use the clues to describe the identity and mission of the Church.

Across

2. Mark of the Church that tells us Jesus is the Savior of all people
4. Mark of the Church meaning "linked to the Apostles"
5. Image of Church focusing on the Church as the source of our life in Christ

Down

1. Image of Church focusing on the love of Christ for the Church
3. Mark of the Church meaning "living in communion with God"

To Help You Remember

1. The Holy Spirit is at work bringing about the divine plan.

2. The Holy Spirit strengthens the Church to be one, holy, catholic, and apostolic.

3. The Holy Spirit strengthens the Church to be a sign of Christ's love for the Church.

This Week . . .

In chapter 7, "The Church: The Age of the Spirit," your child learned more about the mystery of the Church. In this first of two lessons on the Church, your child learned more about the role of the Holy Spirit in the life of the Church. A closer look was taken at the meaning of the words "We believe in one holy catholic and apostolic church," which we profess in the creed. Finally, the traditional images "Bride of Christ" and "Mother," which are used for the Church, were explored.

For more on the teachings of the Catholic Church on the Holy Spirit and the mystery of the Church, see *Catechism of the Catholic Church* paragraph numbers 687–741, 748–801, and 811–865.

Sharing God's Word

Read together Acts 2:1–13. Emphasize that the Holy Spirit came to the disciples on Pentecost and is at work in the whole Church and in the life of each member of the Church today.

Praying

In this chapter your child prayed a prayer for unity among all the believers in Christ. Read and pray together this prayer on page 67.

Making a Difference

Choose one of the following activities to do as a family or design a similar activity of your own.

- Discuss the four Marks of the Church: one, holy, catholic, and apostolic. Talk about the meaning of each and the ways each of the Marks of the Church is a characteristic of your family.

- One way the pope teaches about the faith is through encyclicals. Discuss other ways that your family can learn more about what the Church teaches.

- Choose one thing your family can do this week to tell others about the work and teachings of the Church.

For more ideas on ways your family can live your faith, visit the "Faith First for Families" page at **www.FaithFirst.com**. Click on "Family Prayer" to find a special prayer to pray together this week.

The People of God

We Pray

LORD, you are the strength
  of your people. . . .
Save your people, bless your
  inheritance;
  feed and sustain them
  forever!   PSALM 28:8, 9

God our Father, may your
Church be a leaven in the
world, transforming us
into your family.   Amen.

*What images do you know that
people use to help us understand
what they are saying?*

When we talk about something
that is difficult to understand,
we sometimes use images and
symbols to help people
understand what we mean.
We use images and symbols to
help us understand the mystery
of the Church.

*What images do you know that
are used to describe the Church?*

The Church

Faith Focus

What images help us understand the mystery of the Church?

Faith Vocabulary

People of God. Biblical image for the Church; the people God has gathered and chosen to be his own; the people through whom God has revealed himself most fully and has invited all nations to live as the one family of God.

Body of Christ. An image for the Church used by Saint Paul the Apostle that teaches that all the members of the Church are one in Christ, the Head of the Church, and all members have a unique and important role in the work of the Church.

Name three people who are members of the Church. Tell what they do to build up the Church.

The New People of God

The **People of God** is one image we use to help us understand what the Church is. The Church is the new People of God, whom God has chosen in Jesus Christ. Like our Old Testament ancestors in faith, who journeyed from slavery in Egypt to freedom, the Church is a people on a journey of faith. Our destination is the kingdom that will be brought to completion by God himself at the end of time when Christ will appear in glory.

After the Risen Jesus returned to his Father, the Holy Spirit helped the early Church understand what Jesus taught and did. This included helping them understand what the Church is. In his writing Saint Paul the Apostle teaches that the Church is a community of saints and the Temple of the Holy Spirit.

The Communion of Saints

The Church, the new People of God, is the Communion of Saints. We are a communion of "holy people" and "holy things."

Holy People. The Communion of Saints includes all the faithful members of the Church on earth and those who have died. It includes both the saints living with God in heaven and those faithful in purgatory who are being prepared to receive the gift of eternal life in heaven.

Holy Things. The Church shares in the one faith revealed in Sacred Scripture and passed on in Sacred Tradition from the times of the Apostles. We share in the sacraments, above all the Eucharist. We share in the charisms, or gifts, of the Holy Spirit. We share with all people the goods, the blessings, that God shares with us.

_____
(Name)

_____

_____
(Name)

_____

_____
(Name)

_____

The Temple of the Holy Spirit

In his First Letter to the Corinthians, Saint Paul the Apostle asks the Christian community in Corinth:

> Do you not know that your body is a temple of the holy Spirit within you, whom you have from God?
>
> 1 Corinthians 6:19

The Church is the Temple of the Holy Spirit. The Holy Spirit dwells within each of the baptized and within the whole Church. The Holy Spirit is the source of the Church's life and of its unity as the one People of God. The Holy Spirit is also the one source of the richness of the Church's many gifts and charisms. Charisms are graces of the Holy Spirit that are given to build up the Church and to help the Church fulfill her work in the world.

The Body of Christ

Saint Paul teaches that the Church is the **Body of Christ**. He wrote:

> Now you are Christ's body, and individually parts of it.
>
> 1 Corinthians 12:27

The Church is both visible and spiritual, human and divine. Christ is the Head of the Body, and we are its members. All the members of the Church—the ordained, members of religious communities, and laypeople—make up the one Body of Christ. Each member of the Church has different gifts and responsibilities to build up the Church.

Jesus gave Saint Peter a unique responsibility in the Church (see Matthew 16:18–19). This unique responsibility is known as the Petrine ministry. It is continued today by the pope, who is the successor of Saint Peter and the bishop of Rome. The pope is the immediate and universal pastor, or shepherd, of the whole Church on earth. His ministry includes the responsibility to:

- keep the Church together as one,
- keep it faithful to the truth of Jesus,
- strengthen and encourage his brothers and sisters.

Describe three ways that the Church shows she is the People of God, a communion of holy people.

The Kingdom of God

All throughout his work on earth Jesus described the kingdom, or reign, of God. At its core, it is a kingdom of truth, mercy, and eternal life, of holiness and grace, of justice, love, and peace triumphing over injustice, hatred, and war.

All the people of the Church join together to continue the work of Christ in our world and to prepare for the coming of the kingdom of God. Here are some of the ways we fulfill that responsibility:

We pray. Each time we pray the Lord's Prayer, we pray, "Thy kingdom come." Every time we celebrate the Eucharist, we pray for the coming of the Lord Jesus to fulfill his work and to bring about the kingdom of God.

We prepare the way. We do not make the kingdom of God happen. It is God's work. We do, however, prepare the way for the coming of the kingdom. We bring the truth of God to those who have not heard it. We are forgiving, just, merciful, and compassionate as Jesus was.

We live the Beatitudes. We seek the kingdom of God first in all we do. Living the Beatitudes (see page 287) will lead us to the happiness God created us to have. We will discover happiness here on earth and eternal life and happiness with God the Holy Trinity.

Describe two things you can do to live these Beatitudes and prepare the way for God's kingdom.

Preparing for the Kingdom

"Blessed are the merciful,
for they will be shown mercy."
MATTHEW 5:7

"Blessed are the peacemakers,
for they will be called children of God."
MATTHEW 5:9

_____   _____

_____   _____

_____   _____

_____   _____

_____   _____

_____   _____

Our Church Makes a Difference

peace and pursue it, to be the first to hold out our hands in friendship and forgiveness [and] to achieve peace in our hearts, in our homes, in our neighborhoods, and in our troubled world."

Who helps you live the Gospel? How do you help others?

Benedictines for Peace

Christians look to one another and need one another to live the Gospel. Saint Benedict of Nursia (480–547) wrote a rule of life that spelled out a clear way to live the Gospel. His rule of life was so helpful that people came from all over to live together to follow it. Saint Scholastica (480–543), Benedict's twin sister, was the first woman to choose to follow his rule of life. Soon other women came to live together to follow the same rule.

The followers of Saint Benedict and Saint Scholastica are consecrated religious and are known as Benedictines. Many Benedictines today have joined together to live the Gospel by giving nonviolent responses to the violence that threatens the world. They are known as Benedictines for Peace and work "to seek

Saints Benedict and Scholastica and their followers, stained glass

73

What Difference Does Faith Make in My Life?

You are a member of the Body of Christ, the People of God, the Church. The Holy Spirit dwells within you, giving you the grace to live the Gospel and continue the work Jesus began while he lived on earth.

Think about all the things your parish does. Name at least three things you can do with other members of your parish to live the Gospel.

Living the Gospel

_____

_____

_____

_____

_____

_____

_____

_____

My Faith Choice

 This week I will use the gifts the Holy Spirit has given me to work with other members of the Church to continue Christ's work in the world. I will

_____

_____.

We Pray

Prayer for Vocations

Every member of the Church, young people and adults, is called to continue the work of Jesus. We all have the vocation to live our life in Christ.

Leader: God calls each member of the Church to share in the work of Christ. All the baptized have the responsibility to prepare the way for the coming of the kingdom of God.

Let us pray that we hear and respond to God's invitation to spread the Gospel.

Reader: *Proclaim Matthew 9:35–38.*

All: Lord God,
we pray that all the members of the Church
may hear your call to serve your people.
We ask this in the name of Christ, our Lord.
Amen.

We Remember

Use the words in the word box to complete each sentence. Not all words will be used.

> **ordained ministers**   **kingdom of God**   **blessings**
>
> **Petrine ministry**   **Charisms**   **Communion of Saints**

1. Bishops, priests, and deacons are
   _____.

2. _____ are graces of the Holy Spirit given to help the Church fulfill her work in the world.

3. The _____ is the special ministry of the pope, the bishop of Rome.

4. The _____ includes all the faithful members of the Church, those on earth and those in heaven and in purgatory.

5. The _____ is all people and creation living in communion with God.

To Help You Remember

1. The Church is the new People of God, the Temple of the Holy Spirit, and the Communion of Saints.

2. Jesus Christ is the Head of the Church, the Body of Christ. The lay faithful, the ordained, and consecrated religious are her members.

3. The kingdom of God begun by the Father and announced in the Gospel is mysteriously present in the Church and will come about in its fullness at the end of time.

This Week . . .

In chapter 8, "The People of God," your child continued to deepen his or her understanding of the mystery of the Church. The Church is the new People of God, the Temple of the Holy Spirit, and the Communion of Saints. Called by the Father, all the baptized are joined to Christ through the power of the Holy Spirit. The whole Church, Christ the Head and all the members (the lay faithful, the ordained, and consecrated religious), is the Body of Christ. Together the entire Body of Christ continues the work of Christ on earth with the help and guidance of the Holy Spirit until the kingdom announced by Christ comes about in its fullness at the end of time.

For more on the teachings of the Catholic Church on the mystery of the Church as the People of God, the Temple of the Holy Spirit, the Body of Christ, and the Communion of Saints, see *Catechism of the Catholic Church* paragraph numbers 770–801, 871–933, 946–959, and 1020–1150.

Sharing God's Word

Read together 1 Corinthians 6:19. Emphasize that the Holy Spirit is the source of the Church's life and its unity as the holy People of God.

Praying

In this chapter your child prayed a prayer for vocations. Read and pray together this prayer on page 75.

Making a Difference

Choose one of the following activities to do as a family or design a similar activity of your own.

- Invite all family members to share three things they are doing to fulfill their responsibilities to live as faithful members of the Church. Discuss ways that you can support one another.

- Talk about the work of the Benedictines of Peace. Share ideas about ways that your family might grow as a family of peace. Create a banner using the words "Peace Be with Us," or similar words. Display it in your home as a reminder that you made the commitment to be a family of peace.

- Talk about the people who help you live the Gospel. Then name ways your family can help others live the Gospel.

For more ideas on ways your family can live your faith, visit the "Faith First for Families" page at **www.FaithFirst.com**. The "Contemporary Issues" page goes particularly well with this chapter.

Mary, Mother of the Church

We Pray

I lift up my soul to my God.
In you I trust.   PSALM 25:1–2

Father, may Mary's prayer
be your people's joy
through all ages.   Amen.

*Why could someone call you a
person of faith?*

People of faith are at the
center of the story of God's
people. Mary's faith in God is
unequaled among all the
People of God. She is a model
of faith for all Christians.

*How did Mary show her faith
in God?*

Mary, the New Eve, Queen of
Heaven and Earth, wood sculpture

Mary, Woman of Faith

Faith Focus

Why does the Church honor and love Mary?

Faith Vocabulary

Immaculate Conception. Mary's freedom from all sin, both original sin and all personal sin, from the first moment of her existence, or conception, and throughout her entire life.

Women of Faith

People of faith are at the center of the story of God's people. Their names fill the pages of the Bible. Many women stand out among these people of faith.

Old Testament Women of Faith. The Bible opens with the story of Eve. At first you might ask, How is Eve a woman of faith? Didn't she disobey God? While that is true, Eve first heard God's promise of a savior. She first heard and trusted in the promise that her descendants would eventually be victorious over the Evil One.

After Eve comes a long line of our ancestors in faith. Among these are Sarah, Hannah, Deborah, Ruth, Judith, and Esther. All these women believed and trusted in God's word and his promises to them.

Looking back over the faith story of the People of God, we come to see that all of these women of faith in the Old Testament prepared the way for Mary. It was through Mary's great act of faith that God's promise to send the Savior would be fulfilled.

Mary's Faith. The Gospel of Luke tells us that the archangel Gabriel spoke in God's name to the Virgin Mary. Gabriel proclaimed:

"The holy Spirit will come upon you, and the power of the Most High will overshadow you. Therefore the child to be born will be called holy, the Son of God." . . . Mary said, "Behold, I am the handmaid of the Lord. May it be done to me according to your word."

LUKE 1:35, 38

Mary is our model of faith. Mary responded to God's invitation saying, "May it be done to me according to your word." Mary did not understand how Gabriel's message to her would come true. Yet she gave herself completely to God. Wherever God would lead her, she would go.

Write and decorate a prayer honoring Mary, our model of faith.

The archangel Gabriel and Mary, woodcarving

Because of this special honor given to Mary, God's grace kept Mary free from sin. Mary was free from original sin from the very first moment of her existence, or conception. We call this the **Immaculate Conception** of Mary. She remained pure of all personal sin her whole life.

When her life on earth ended, the Most Blessed Virgin Mary was taken up, or assumed, body and soul, into the glory of heaven. There she already shares in the glory of her Son's Resurrection. We call this the Assumption of Mary.

Mother of the Church

The Gospel of John tells us that when the crucified Jesus saw his mother and the disciple he loved standing by the cross, he said:

"Woman, behold, your son." Then he said to the disciple, "Behold, your mother."
JOHN 19:26–27

The "beloved disciple" who is at the foot of the cross stands for all of us who are Jesus' disciples. Mary, the Mother of Jesus, is the mother of all who follow her Son, Jesus. Mary is the Mother of Jesus and the Mother of the Church, the Body of Christ.

Faith-Filled People

The Beloved Disciple

The story of the Crucifixion in John's Gospel teaches that the disciple whom Jesus loved stood with Mary near the cross. This disciple has come to be known as "the beloved disciple." The tradition of the Church believes that Saint John, the writer of the Fourth Gospel, was that disciple. After Jesus' death Saint John cared for Mary as a child cares for their mother.

Take a few moments to pray the prayer you wrote on page 78.

Mother of God

God chose the Blessed Virgin Mary to be the Mother of his Son. She is the handmaid of the Lord, who was a virgin her whole life. Jesus, the child whom the Virgin Mary conceived by the power of the Holy Spirit and gave birth to, is the Son of God. Jesus is the second Person of the Trinity, who took on flesh and became human in all things except sin. That is why the Virgin Mary, the Mother of Jesus, is the Mother of God.

Devotion to Mary

Catholics honor Mary and express their devotion to her throughout the year. During Advent we remember Mary as the one who brings Jesus into the world. During Lent and Holy Week, we remember Mary, the Mother of Sorrows. All throughout the year the Church celebrates other feasts of Mary.

We remember Mary's great faith, her hope, her love for God, and her loving faithfulness to her Son.

At Mass we recognize Mary's presence with us and honor her. Mary joins with us and her Son in giving God the Father our praise and thanksgiving through the power of the Holy Spirit. We look forward to joining Mary and the saints in heaven.

In your own words write a short biography of Mary. Use the Gospel stories or the mysteries of the Rosary to develop your biography. Give your biography a title.

Our Church Makes a Difference

Celebrating Mary

The Church around the world remembers and honors Mary, our mother, throughout the year by celebrating feast days in her honor. The Church in the United States joins with the Church in other countries in celebrating these feasts.

- January 1 brings us the Solemnity of Mary, the Mother of God.
- On May 31 we celebrate the feast of the Visitation, or the visit of Mary to Elizabeth.
- August 15 is the feast of Mary's Assumption, when Mary was taken, body and soul, into heaven.
- December 8 is the feast of the Immaculate Conception, which celebrates that Mary was free from original and personal sin throughout her entire life.
- On December 12, the feast of Our Lady of Guadalupe, we celebrate Mary's appearance to Saint Juan Diego in Mexico in 1531.

Throughout the year, we think about Mary's great faith and how her yes to God changed the world. As we celebrate our love for Mary, we ask God for the grace to listen to his word and say yes to his invitation to bring about his plan for all people.

In what ways does your parish honor Mary?

Junior high girl dressed as Mary standing on float during a procession honoring Mary

A shrine to Nuestra Senora de Guadalupe (Our Lady of Guadalupe) outside private home in Mexico City, Mexico

Statue of Mary with flowers for May Crowning during May, the month of Mary

What Difference Does Faith Make in My Life?

Mary was a woman of strong faith. Mary, the Mother of God, is your mother too. Mary cares about you. She wants to be a very important person in your life.

Think about some of the things that are part of your life or the lives of other people that you would like to share with Mary. Take the time to share your thoughts with her.

Mary, My Mother

Queen of All Saints ❋ Mother of Our Savior

Mother of the Church ❋ Queen of Peace

Holy Mary ❋ Holy Mother of God ❋ Mother of Christ

_____

_____

_____

_____

_____

_____

_____

My Faith Choice

This week I will spend time with Mary in prayer.
I will

_____

_____ .

The Canticle of Mary

The Magnificat is Mary's canticle, or song, of praise of God. Divide into two groups and pray it antiphonally.

All: **"My soul proclaims the greatness of the Lord; my spirit rejoices in God my savior."**

LUKE 1:46–49, 54–55

Group 1: "For he has looked upon his handmaid's lowliness;
Group 2: behold, from now on will all ages call me blessed.

Group 1: The Mighty One has done great things for me,
Group 2: and holy is his name. . . .

Group 1: He has helped Israel his servant, remembering his mercy,
Group 2: according to his promise to our fathers, to Abraham and to his descendants forever."

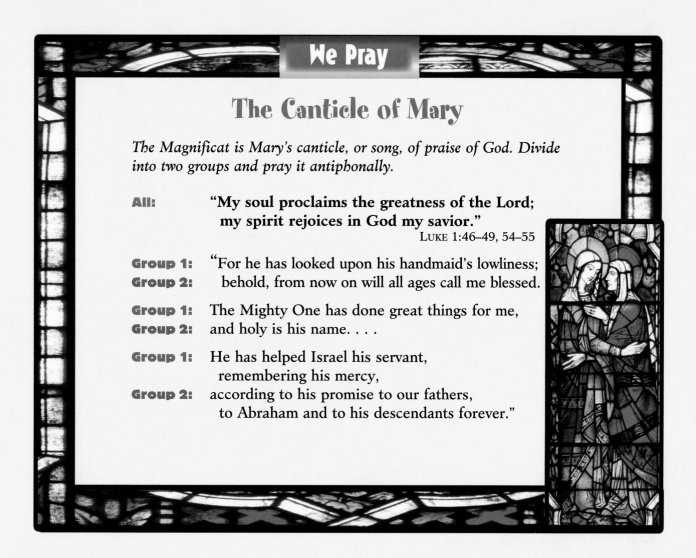

We Remember

Circle the choice in the parentheses that best completes each statement.

1. *(Sarah, Clopas, Mary of Magdala)* was the wife of Abraham and a woman of great faith.

2. The angel *(Michael, Gabriel, Raphael)* announced to the Virgin Mary that she would be the Mother of the Son of God and name him Jesus.

3. The *(Annunciation, Immaculate Conception, Incarnation)* names Mary's unique privilege of being free from sin from the very moment of her existence.

4. The *(Annunciation, Nativity, Assumption)* names Mary being taken to heaven, body and soul.

To Help You Remember

1. Mary is a model of faith for all Christians.

2. The Blessed Virgin Mary is the Mother of God who was free from sin from the first moment of her existence and who was assumed, body and soul, into heaven at the end of her life on earth.

3. Mary is the Mother of the Church, whom we honor throughout the year.

This Week . . .

In chapter 9, "Mary, Mother of the Church," your child learned more about the Church's devotion to Mary. Mary, the Mother of Jesus, is the Mother of God and the Mother of the Church. God's love for Mary is unique. From the first moment of her existence Mary received the unique grace of being free from all sin, both original and personal, and remained free from sin her entire life. At the end of her life on earth, she was assumed, body and soul, into heaven. We look to Mary, as she expects us to, for prayerful guidance.

For more on the teachings of the Catholic Church on Mary, see *Catechism of the Catholic Church* paragraph numbers 484–507 and 963–972.

Sharing God's Word

Read together Luke 1:26–38. Emphasize that Mary, the Mother of Jesus, the Incarnate Son of God, is the Mother of God and the Mother of the Church.

Praying

In this chapter your child prayed part of the Magnificat, Mary's canticle, or song, of praise. Read and pray together this prayer on page 83.

Making a Difference

Choose one of the following activities to do as a family or design a similar activity of your own.

- Use the Canticle of Mary on page 83 as part of your family mealtime prayer this week.

- Take time this week to pray and talk about the meaning of the mysteries of the Rosary. Talk about how Mary is a model of faith for your family. Share ideas on ways Mary inspires you to live as followers of Jesus.

- Talk about how your family honors Mary. Choose to do one thing this week to honor her and to show your love for her.

For more ideas on ways your family can live your faith, visit the "Faith First for Families" page at **www.FaithFirst.com**. Click on "Games" and make learning fun for your child.

"Come, You Who Are Blessed"
A Scripture Story

Jesus the Teacher, stained glass

We Pray

I announced your deed
  to a great assembly. . . .
Your deed I did not hide
  within my heart. . . .
I made no secret of your
  enduring kindness.
PSALM 40:10–11

**God, our loving Father,
prepare us for the day of
the coming of your Son,
Jesus Christ, in glory.**
Amen.

*What good news have you shared
lately?*

We all share good news with
excitement and enthusiasm.
The better the news, the more
excited and enthusiastic we
feel. The Gospel is the best
news the world has ever heard.

*Why should the good news of the
Gospel fill us with excitement
and enthusiasm today?*

Faith Focus

Why is hearing the good news of the Gospel important for all people today and forever?

Faith Vocabulary

Gospels. The first four books of the New Testament, which pass on the faith of the Church in Jesus Christ and in the saving events of his life, Passion, death, Resurrection, and Ascension.

kingdom of God. The fulfillment of God's plan for all creation in Christ at the end of time when Christ will come again in glory.

Sharing the Good News of Jesus

In the New Testament there are four written accounts of the Gospel. The word *gospel* is from the old English word *God-spell*. The **Gospels** according to Matthew, Mark, Luke, and John tell about the life, Passion, death, Resurrection, Ascension, and teachings of Jesus Christ. All of them announce the good news of our salvation in Jesus, who is our Lord and Savior.

The four accounts of the Gospel were formed in three different stages. The *first stage* belongs to the very words and deeds of Jesus. The *second stage* belongs to the time of the Apostles' preaching about Jesus after the Holy Spirit descended on the disciples at Pentecost. The *third stage* belongs to the four Evangelists—Matthew, Mark, Luke, and John. Under the inspiration of the Holy Spirit, they wrote their accounts of the Gospel that the Apostles had passed on about Jesus.

Each of the four accounts of the Gospel tells about Jesus from four individual perspectives.

- Mark emphasizes what it means to be a disciple of Jesus and to walk with him toward the cross.
- Matthew pays special attention to the needs of the Church.
- Luke shows how Jesus' salvation embraces all people.
- John tries to understand the inner meaning of Jesus' words and deeds.

Read Matthew 26:6–13, Mark 14:3–9, Luke 7:36–50, and John 12:1–8. Compare how the same event is reported in different ways.

Matthew

Mark

Luke

John

The Kingdom of God

All four written accounts of the Gospel teach the good news of the **kingdom of God,** or kingdom of heaven. They teach that those who faithfully follow Jesus will be invited to join him in the kingdom that God has prepared since the beginning of creation. Read how Matthew passes on to us that teaching of Jesus.

"When the Son of Man comes in his glory, and all the angels with him, he will sit upon his glorious throne, and all the nations will be assembled before him. And he will separate them one from another, as a shepherd separates the sheep from the goats. He will place the sheep on his right and the goats on his left. Then the king will say to those on his right, 'Come, you who are blessed by my Father. Inherit the kingdom prepared for you from the foundation of the world. For I was hungry and you gave me food, I was thirsty and you gave me drink, a stranger and you welcomed me, naked and you clothed me, ill and you cared for me, in prison and you visited me.' Then the righteous will answer him and say, 'Lord, when did we see you hungry and feed you, or thirsty and give you drink? When did we see you a stranger and welcome you, or naked and clothe you? When did we see you ill or in prison, and visit you?' And the king will say to them in reply, 'Amen, I say to you, whatever you did for one of these least brothers [and sisters] of mine, you did for me.'"

MATTHEW 25:31–40

Jesus clearly teaches us that only those who love one another as he did will enter the kingdom.

Who are the people in need in today's world who Jesus was talking about? How can we reach out to them?

Volunteers gathering food donations outside grocery store on "Make a Difference Day"

Life After Death

The good news proclaimed in this Gospel passage is that God invites all people to live with him forever. When we die, God will judge the way each of us has lived our life. We call this the particular judgment. At our particular judgment we will be assigned to heaven, purgatory, or hell.

Heaven. Those who have been faithful on earth will be invited into the kingdom of heaven. Heaven is everlasting life in communion with God, the Holy Trinity, and with the Virgin Mary, the angels, and all the holy men and women who have lived before us.

Purgatory. Some people who die are not ready to receive the gift of eternal life in heaven. After death, they are purified of their weakness and given the opportunity to grow in their love for God. This opportunity is called purgatory.

Hell. Sadly, some people choose to turn themselves completely away from God's love. They do this by sinning seriously and not asking God for forgiveness. When people do this and die, they choose to stay separated from God forever. We call this eternal separation from God "hell."

On the last day, at the end of time, the lives of everyone will be judged. We call this the Last Judgment. On this day, God will invite all the saints to eternal life in the kingdom. Our bodies will be reunited with our immortal souls. We will rise from the dead just as Christ was raised from the dead and lives forever.

What are some of the ways you can be like the people blessed by God in the story Jesus told?

"Come, You Who Are Blessed"

_____

_____

_____

_____

_____

_____

_____

Our Church Makes a Difference

"Blessed Are the Merciful"

Since the first days of the Church, Christians have continued to help one another as Jesus asked us to do. We reach out to the hungry and thirsty, to those without shelter and in need of clothes, to those who are ill and those in prison.

The people of Saint Elizabeth Parish take this work very seriously. They have named their ministry the "Love Truck." They put into practice exactly what Saint Matthew wrote about. No one in need is left out.

You all know how important it is to be comfortable and nicely dressed for school. When the people of Saint Elizabeth's heard about the children in another parish who needed shoes for the start of school, they saw to it that every child who needed shoes received them. This is certainly the work of the "Blessed" that Saint Matthew wrote about. You might say that they put new shoes on Jesus' feet each and every time a child put on new shoes.

How can you help your parish follow the teaching of Jesus that Saint Matthew shares with us?

Our Catholic Identity

Justice for All

The bishops of the United States have often taught that we need to listen to Jesus and build a world of justice. In the pastoral letter "Economic Justice for All," they clearly taught that the value of a country's economy is measured by how it touches human life and how it protects the dignity of every person. That's what it means to be merciful.

What Difference Does Faith Make in My Life?

Each day the Holy Spirit is helping you see the many opportunities you have to share mercy with others as Jesus did. Every time you help someone, Jesus says that you are helping him.

Describe some of the ways you see others reaching out to people who are poor and vulnerable. Name some of the ways you might do the same.

"Lord, We Saw You Hungry and We . . ."

What I See	What I Can Do

My Faith Choice

ff I know that when I try to help someone in need, I am also treating Christ with kindness. This week I will

_____

_____ .

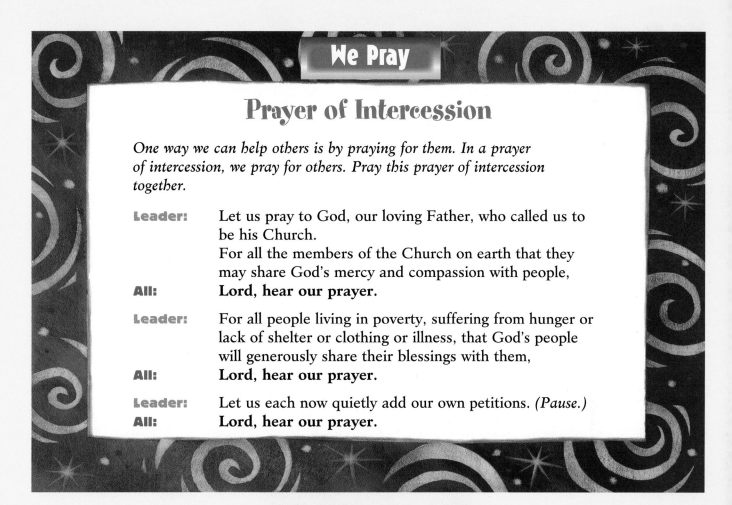

We Pray

Prayer of Intercession

One way we can help others is by praying for them. In a prayer of intercession, we pray for others. Pray this prayer of intercession together.

Leader: Let us pray to God, our loving Father, who called us to be his Church.
For all the members of the Church on earth that they may share God's mercy and compassion with people,

All: **Lord, hear our prayer.**

Leader: For all people living in poverty, suffering from hunger or lack of shelter or clothing or illness, that God's people will generously share their blessings with them,

All: **Lord, hear our prayer.**

Leader: Let us each now quietly add our own petitions. *(Pause.)*

All: **Lord, hear our prayer.**

We Remember

Use the code to discover this important message about the Gospel.

A	B	C	D	E	F	G	H	I	J	K	L	M
1	2	3	4	5	6	7	8	9	10	11	12	13

N	O	P	Q	R	S	T	U	V	W	X	Y	Z
14	15	16	17	18	19	20	21	22	23	24	25	26

4x5 12-4 10÷2   12-5 3x5 24-5 4x4 10÷2 6+6

6-5 2x7 12+2 3x5 22-1 9+5 3+0 10÷2 24-5

4x5 12-4 10÷2   21-10 3x3 28÷2 19-12 2x2 5x3 26÷2

3+12 18-12   13-6 8+7 19-15 .

To Help You Remember

1. The Gospels are the inspired word of God announcing salvation in Jesus Christ.

2. The Gospels teach that we need to live the faith we profess in Jesus.

3. The death of our body is our entrance into life everlasting.

This Week . . .

In chapter 10, "'Come, You Who Are Blessed': A Scripture Story," your child learned that the Gospel is the announcement of the good news of salvation in Jesus Christ. The four Evangelists—Matthew, Mark, Luke, and John—wrote their accounts of the Gospel under the inspiration of the Holy Spirit, who assisted them to write faithfully and without error the saving truth that God revealed in Jesus Christ. Among those truths that Saint Matthew taught is that all those who have faithfully lived as children of God will be invited to enter the kingdom of God, which he has prepared since the beginning of the world.

For more on the teachings of the Catholic Church on the Gospel and life everlasting, see *Catechism of the Catholic Church* paragraph numbers 124–127, 946–959, 1172–1173, and 1402–1405.

Sharing God's Word

Read together Matthew 25:31–40. Emphasize that Jesus clearly teaches us that those who faithfully follow him will be invited to join him in the kingdom of God.

Praying

In this chapter your child prayed a prayer of intercession. Read and pray together this prayer on page 91.

Making a Difference

Choose one of the following activities to do as a family or design a similar activity of your own.

- Jesus taught his disciples to reach out and help people in need. Name the people in need in the world today and talk about what you can do to reach out to them.

- Read and discuss some of the other Bible stories about the kingdom of God. See Matthew 13:24–48, Matthew 20:1–16, Matthew 22:1–14, Luke 13:18–21, and Luke 14:15–24.

- Identify some of the ways that your parish follows what Jesus teaches in Matthew 25:31–40. Decide as a family how your family can join with other members of your parish to follow the teachings of Jesus.

For more ideas on ways your family can live your faith, visit the "Faith First for Families" page at **www.FaithFirst.com**. Click on "Make a Difference" to discover how your family can continue the work of Christ.

Unit 1 Review

A. Best Response

Read each statement and circle the best answer.

1. What is faith?
   - a. a belief of the Church
   - b. a way to pray
   - c. a supernatural gift from God
   - d. a commandment

2. What are summaries of the principal beliefs of the Church?
   - a. Gospels
   - b. proverbs
   - c. psalms
   - d. creeds

3. Where in the Bible do you find stories about the early Church?
   - a. wisdom books
   - b. New Testament
   - c. Old Testament
   - d. historical books

4. The message of the prophets centered on _____.
   - a. wisdom and sacrifice
   - b. fidelity and hope
   - c. faith and love
   - d. understanding and courage

5. We call the mystery of one God in three divine Persons _____.
   - a. divine Revelation
   - b. the Incarnation
   - c. the Holy Trinity
   - d. divine Providence

6. Which of the following is a result of the fall of Adam and Eve?
   - a. original sin
   - b. justice
   - c. happiness
   - d. trust

7. Who is the center of God's plan of salvation?
   - a. Moses
   - b. Abraham
   - c. John the Baptist
   - d. Jesus Christ

8. The events of Jesus' life that make up the Paschal Mystery are his _____.
   - a. public ministry
   - b. arrest, Passion, and Crucifixion
   - c. Passion, death, Resurrection, and glorious Ascension
   - d. baptism

9. Which feast does the Catholic Church not celebrate in honor of Mary?
   - a. Immaculate Conception
   - b. Assumption
   - c. Visitation
   - d. Pentecost

10. Which of the following is not an image of the Church?
    - a. Body of Christ
    - b. Communion of Saints
    - c. Temple of the Holy Spirit
    - d. Breath of God

B. Completing the Paragraph

Use the terms in the word bank to complete the paragraph.

> Covenant   faith   YHWH   revealed
> desire   fidelity   creeds

God has _____ himself in many ways. He places both

his word and a _____ for him within us. God calls us to

respond by accepting his gift of _____. The Pentateuch tells

the story of God revealing his name, _____. The prophets

often spoke about _____ to the promises they made to God.

In the New Testament Jesus reveals that he is the new and everlasting

_____. The Church proclaims her belief in God in the

_____ of the Church.

C. What I Have Learned

Write three things you learned in this unit. Share them with the group.

_____

_____

_____

Look at the list of faith terms in "Words to Know" on page 12.
Circle the terms you know now.

D. From a Scripture Story

In the story of the kingdom of God told by Matthew, Jesus names some
of the ways we are to live as his faithful disciples. In column A list two
ways that his disciples were to live. In column B describe how a faithful
disciple might put those teachings into practice today.

Column A	Column B
_____	_____
_____	_____
_____	_____
_____	_____

Unit 2 • We Worship

What do we celebrate
when we celebrate
the Eucharist?

Getting Ready

What I Have Learned

What is something you already know about these three faith terms?

Sacraments of Christian Initiation

_____

_____

Sacraments at the Service of Communion

_____

_____

Liturgy of the Word

_____

_____

Words to Know

Put an X next to the faith terms you know. Put a ? next to the faith terms you need to know more about.

Faith Vocabulary

_____ liturgy

_____ Passover

_____ Sabbath

_____ Confirmation

_____ Eucharist

_____ parables

_____ Sacraments of Healing

_____ Communion

Questions I Have

What questions would you like to ask about the meaning of the words and actions of the sacraments the Church uses in celebration?

_____

_____

_____

_____

A Scripture Story

Studying the Scriptures

What does Sacred Scripture teach about living a holy life?

Celebrating the Liturgy

We Pray

[L]et us bow down in worship;
let us kneel before the LORD
who made us.   PSALM 95:6

Father, all life,
all holiness comes from
you through your Son,
Jesus Christ our Lord,
by the working
of the Holy Spirit.   Amen.

What rituals are a part of your life?

We all have daily rituals—things we do pretty much the same way each time. We may have the same way of getting ready for school or celebrating a birthday or playing a sport. The Church has rituals too. All over the world, the Church celebrates certain rituals day after day, year after year.

What rituals of the Church do you know?

Blessing of baptismal water
at the Easter Vigil

The Liturgy and the Body of Christ

Faith Focus

Why does the Church celebrate the sacraments?

Faith Vocabulary

liturgy. The Church's work of worshiping God.

sacraments. The seven main liturgical signs of the Church, given to us by Jesus Christ, that make his saving work present to us and make us sharers in the life of God, the Holy Trinity.

The Liturgy

In every celebration of the **liturgy** and **sacraments**, the story of God's loving plan of creation and salvation is proclaimed in our midst. God speaks and we listen attentively. That is why the Liturgy of the Word is always part of our celebration of the sacraments and liturgy. We are made sharers in the Paschal Mystery by the power of the Holy Spirit. The work of the Holy Spirit in the liturgy is to:

- prepare the assembly to meet Christ and
- recall and make Christ known to the assembly.

Every celebration of the liturgy and the sacraments is a celebration of the whole Body of Christ. We join with Christ, the Head of the Church, who himself leads the Church in her celebration. Because Jesus acts in the sacraments, they unfailingly allow us to share in Christ's saving work and make us sharers in the life of God.

What are some of the things that you see and hear during the celebration of the Eucharist and other sacraments? How do these things help you better understand what is really happening?

BAPTISM

CONFIRMATION

EUCHARIST

RECONCILIATION

Sacramental Signs

Each celebration of the sacraments combines words with signs and symbolic actions. Through these sacramental signs and actions, Jesus brings us into the mysteries of his Passion-death-Resurrection-Ascension, his Paschal Mystery. We receive the promise of eternal life.

The Paschal Mystery. Christ died once and was raised once. So how do we share, here and now, in the Paschal Mystery? Through the sacraments, until the end of time when Christ will come again in glory, the Holy Spirit brings Christ's Paschal Mystery to all his believing people.

Promise of Eternal Life. In Jesus, God prepared the way for all to receive the great gift of new and resurrected life (see John 11:25–26). The sacraments both give us a glimpse of and are a pledge of our sharing in that life. On the last day, just as Christ did, we will rise bodily and see God face-to-face!

Look at the stained-glass images of the sacraments on these two pages. Write what each of the images tells about the sacrament it portrays.

Faith-Filled People

Abraham

At Mass the Church proclaims Abraham to be our father in faith. Abraham entered a covenant with God. He believed in God's presence with him and lived a life of hope in the future God promised to him. Abraham was even willing to sacrifice his son Isaac out of love for God. You can find out more about Abraham in Genesis 12:1–7 and 22:2–18.

ANOINTING OF THE SICK

_____

_____

_____

HOLY ORDERS

_____

_____

_____

MATRIMONY

_____

_____

_____

The Liturgical Year

Each year is a time of grace. For Christians it is a yearlong celebration of our life in Christ. The Church's year of celebration, which is made up of seasons and feasts, is called the liturgical year.

Advent. Advent is a time of preparation for Christ's coming among us.

Christmas. The Christmas season celebrates that the Son of God became one of us without giving up his divinity and is the Savior of the world.

Lent. Lent calls us to change our hearts, seek God's forgiveness, prepare candidates for Baptism, and renew our commitment to live our Baptism.

Easter Triduum. The Easter Triduum, or "the three days," is the center of the whole liturgical year. It begins on Holy Thursday evening, continues on Good Friday, and concludes with the celebrations of the Easter Vigil and Easter Sunday.

Easter. The fifty days of the Easter season, which culminates on Pentecost, are a time of proclaiming the mystery of the new life that we have in the Risen Christ.

Ordinary Time. We hear the story of Jesus from one of the four accounts of the Gospel—Matthew, Mark, Luke, or John. We learn what it means to be a disciple of Jesus.

Feasts. The solemnities and feasts of the Lord and of Mary, the Apostles, martyrs, and other holy men and women deepen our sharing in God's work in our world.

Deacon carrying lighted Easter candle, leading procession into church during the Service of Light at the beginning of the Easter Vigil

Illustrate in words or symbols a season or feast of the Church's liturgical year.

One Faith, One Lord

No matter where you go throughout the world, the Catholic Church celebrates the sacraments. The look of the churches may be different. Some churches are massive cathedrals filled with statues and stained-glass windows. Others are simple huts. Some are modern and some are not. But in each church, we gather to proclaim the same Gospel and share the same Eucharist.

The language may be different. The music may be different. The people may even dress differently, but what is essential to our liturgy is always the same: Christ is with us as we celebrate and share in his death and Resurrection.

When the Church gathers to celebrate the sacraments, we proclaim for all to see and hear that Jesus is the Savior of the whole world and of all people. All people are invited to be joined to Christ in Baptism. There is one faith and one Lord, one God who is the Father of all. All people are invited to share in the new life of Christ. All people have the promise of eternal life.

Look at these photos of the celebration of Mass. What do they say to you about the Church and her work in the world?

Our Catholic Identity

The Rites of the Catholic Church

The words and actions used to celebrate the liturgy are called rites. There are different rites in the Catholic Church that are approved by the Church for celebrating the liturgy. The largest number of Catholics celebrate the Roman rite. Other rites include the Byzantine, Alexandrian (or Coptic), Syriac, Armenian, Maronite, Ukranian, Syrian, Romanian, Russian, and Chaldean rites.

Liturgical procession during celebration of the feast of the Virgin of Guadalupe (above)

Nigerian music accompanying celebration of Mass (left)

What Difference Does Faith Make in My Life?

The Holy Spirit prepares you to celebrate the sacraments. Jesus is always there, leading the Church in the celebration.

What are some of the things the Church does at the celebration of the Eucharist? How do these things help you and others take part in the celebration?

Celebrating the Eucharist

What the Church Does	How These Help Me Participate
_____	_____
_____	_____
_____	_____
_____	_____
_____	_____
_____	_____
_____	_____
_____	_____

My Faith Choice

Before Mass this week I will try to spend a few moments remembering that we are joining with Jesus in our celebration. I will

_____

_____.

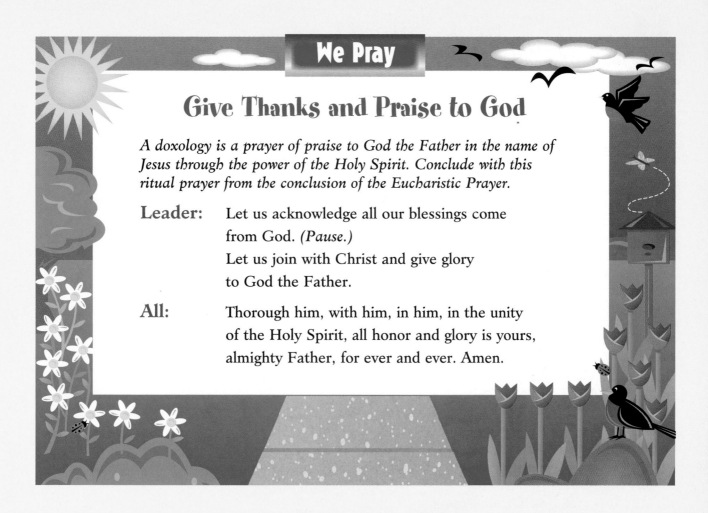

We Pray

Give Thanks and Praise to God

A doxology is a prayer of praise to God the Father in the name of Jesus through the power of the Holy Spirit. Conclude with this ritual prayer from the conclusion of the Eucharistic Prayer.

Leader: Let us acknowledge all our blessings come from God. *(Pause.)*
Let us join with Christ and give glory to God the Father.

All: Thorough him, with him, in him, in the unity of the Holy Spirit, all honor and glory is yours, almighty Father, for ever and ever. Amen.

We Remember

Match the terms in column A with their meanings in column B.

Column A

_____ **1.** liturgy

_____ **2.** Paschal Mystery

_____ **3.** sacraments

_____ **4.** liturgical year

_____ **5.** Easter Triduum

Column B

a. The Church's yearly cycle of seasons and feasts that make up the Church's year of worship

b. Christ's Passion, death, Resurrection, and glorious Ascension

c. The three-day celebration that is at the center of the liturgical year of the Church

d. The seven main celebrations of the Church's liturgy given to us by Christ that make us sharers in the life of God

e. The Church's work of worshiping God

To Help You Remember

1. The celebration of the liturgy and sacraments is the Church's work of worshiping God.

2. The sacraments make us sharers in the life of God through the power of the Holy Spirit.

3. Throughout the year the Church praises God for what he has done and continues to do for us.

This Week . . .

In chapter 11, "Celebrating the Liturgy," your child learned more about the liturgy. The liturgy is the Church's work of worshiping God. The liturgy of the Church centers around the Eucharist and the other sacraments. In the liturgy the members of the Church gather with Christ, the Head of the Church. Through the power of the Holy Spirit, we remember and share in the Paschal Mystery of Christ's saving Passion, death, Resurrection, and glorious Ascension. The whole Church gathers to share in the life of God the Holy Trinity and to bless, praise, and give thanks to the Father with Christ. What Jesus did while he was on earth is made present here and now. We join with Christ all year long and share in his work of salvation. We call the Church's year of worship the liturgical year.

For more on the teachings of the Catholic Church on the liturgy, see *Catechism of the Catholic Church* paragraph numbers 1076–1109, 1136–1186, and 1206.

Sharing God's Word

Read together Psalm 95:1–7. Emphasize that the sacraments are signs and sources of God's grace through which we share the life and work of Jesus Christ, the Good Shepherd.

Praying

In this chapter your child prayed a doxology. Read and pray together this prayer on page 103.

Making a Difference

Choose one of the following activities to do as a family or design a similar activity of your own.

- When you take part in the celebration of Mass this week, notice the liturgical decorations and the priest's vestments. Talk about what they tell you about what liturgical season it is.

- Invite each family member to share their favorite liturgical season. Ask each family member to explain their choice.

- Create a doorknob hanger for the front door of your home. Decorate it so that it is a reminder for the current liturgical season.

For more ideas on ways your family can live your faith, visit the "Faith First for Families" page at **www.FaithFirst.com**. Click on "Family Prayer." This week pray the special prayer as a family.

Passover and the Sabbath
A Scripture Story

We Pray

One thing I ask of the LORD;
 this I seek:
To dwell in the LORD's house
 all the days of my life,
PSALM 27:4

Father, all-powerful
and ever-living God,
we do well always
and everywhere
to give you thanks.   Amen.

What are some customs our nation has for remembering the important events of our history?

Families, communities, and even nations have special customs for celebrating events that are important to them. Many of these customs are passed down from generation to generation. The Church also has customs and rituals for celebrating religious feasts.

What customs do your family and parish use to celebrate the faith of the Church?

People praying at Wailing Wall in Jerusalem during Passover. The West Wall is what is left of the Temple in Jerusalem after its destruction in A.D. 70. This is the holiest shrine of the Jewish people.

105

Bible Background

Faith Focus

What does the Bible tell us about celebrating special days and feasts?

Faith Vocabulary

Sabbath. The seventh day of the week, the Israelites dedicated to God as a holy day and a day of rest.

Passover. The Jewish feast that celebrates the sparing of the Hebrew children from death, and God's saving his people from slavery in Egypt and leading them to freedom in the land he promised them.

The Book of Leviticus

Over the years the people of God have developed rituals. The rituals of the Church are a combination of the words and actions used to celebrate both our faith and hope in God and our love for God. Some of the rituals have developed from the traditions and laws of God's people who lived in Old Testament times. That is why reading the Old Testament can help us learn about the liturgy of the Church.

One of those Old Testament books is Leviticus, the third book of the Pentateuch. Leviticus served as a liturgical handbook for the Levites, or the priests of the Israelites, who were descendants of Levi. Levi is the name of one of the sons of Jacob and Leah. It is also the name of one of the twelve tribes of Israel, which served as a priestly tribe for God's people. The name Levi also appears two times in the genealogy of Jesus in Luke's Gospel (see Luke 3:24, 29).

Leviticus centers on the call of God's people to holiness and the laws and rituals of worship used by the Israelites. Following rituals in the celebration of their liturgy and feasts taught the Israelites the necessity of holiness in every aspect of their lives. It made them aware that observing the laws of the Lord provided a way of life that leads to holiness.

The LORD said to Moses, "Speak to the whole Israelite community and tell them: Be holy, for I, the LORD, your God, am holy." LEVITICUS 19:1–2

Observing Our Laws of Worship

Read this e-mail. How would you respond to it? Share your response with someone in your class.

Jeff from Buffalo writes:
We have a big lacrosse match-up next weekend with St. Bartholomew's—our archrival. Coach Tennyson won't hold practice this Sunday. We need every minute we can get to practice before the game. This "Rest on the Sabbath" is old-fashioned. All the malls are open on Sunday. What's the big deal? It makes no sense!

Holiness Code

The Book of Leviticus contains a section called the Holiness Code. In this section we learn about the rituals and rules for celebrating the **Sabbath** and the Israelite year of worship, including the feasts of **Passover** and Unleavened Bread, Pentecost, New Year's Day, Day of Atonement, and Feast of Booths.

Sabbath

The Holiness Code begins with the Sabbath. We read:

> The LORD said to Moses, . . . "For six days work may be done; but the seventh day is the sabbath rest, a day for sacred assembly, on which you shall do no work. The sabbath shall belong to the LORD wherever you dwell."
>
> LEVITICUS 23:1, 3

Passover

We next read about the feasts of Passover and Unleavened Bread, which are joined as one celebration in Leviticus. We read:

> "The Passover of the LORD falls on the fourteenth day of the first month, at the evening twilight. The fifteenth day of this month is the LORD's feast of Unleavened Bread. For seven days you shall eat unleavened bread. On the first of these days you shall hold a sacred assembly and do no sort of work. On each of the seven days you shall offer an oblation to the LORD. Then on the seventh day you shall again hold a sacred assembly and do no sort of work."
>
> LEVITICUS 23:5–8

Celebrating the Sabbath and Passover rituals helped them share in the love of God. It helped them to remember all God had done for them and to live their covenant with God.

Name your favorite celebration of the Church. How does taking part in that celebration help you lead a life of holiness?

The Liturgy of the Church

The painstaking time devoted to observing the rituals for Passover and the Sabbath was time devoted to God and celebrating his covenant with them. It was time dedicated to helping the Israelites respond to God's invitation to be holy as the Lord God is holy.

Christians remember and celebrate, in faith and gratitude, the mysteries of our faith. Through the power of the Holy Spirit, we hear again and share in the Passover of Christ from his death to his entrance into new life in glory. We journey from slavery to sin to freedom as children of God. We renew the hope that our journey toward God and the promised kingdom will come about as Jesus promised.

Each week Christians keep Sunday as the Lord's Day, a holy day and a day of rest. We remember in faith that Jesus died and was raised for us. He has truly redeemed us from sin and death and given us new life. Out of gratitude, we recognize the wonders of his grace and lift up our hearts and voices and sing out God's praise. We rest from unnecessary work to acknowledge God—Father, Son, and Holy Spirit—to be both the source of our life and the end of our life.

Give Glory to the LORD God

In this space write those things that help you celebrate your life in Christ. Then take a moment to thank God for all his gifts to you.

_____

_____

_____

_____

_____

How great is your goodness, LORD. . . .

Blessed be the LORD,

who has shown me wondrous love.

PSALM 31:20, 22

Our Church Makes a Difference

The Lord's Day

Sunday is the Lord's Day for Christians. It is the day on which Jesus was raised from the dead. It is the day we celebrate the victory of Christ over sin and death.

At one time Christian workers were not always free to join with others in the celebration of the Eucharist on Sundays. Workers were forced to work seven days a week. The Church then made a law forbidding work on Sundays. Today this law is "On Sundays and other holy days of obligation the faithful are bound to participate in Mass; they are also to abstain from those labors and business concerns which impede the worship to be rendered to God, the joy which is proper to the Lord's Day, or the proper relaxation of mind and body" (*Code of Canon Law*, Canon 1247).

The purpose of this law of the Church is to free all workers to have time to celebrate Eucharist and rest on the Lord's Day. The law gives them the freedom to keep the Lord's Day holy and the time to be with their families and to relax. It guides workers from becoming slaves to their work and keeps employers from making workers slaves to their work.

What are some of the ways you see Christians keeping Sunday as the Lord's Day? How does keeping Sunday as the Lord's Day free people to live as children of God?

Our Catholic Identity

Vigils

Some feasts of the Church have a vigil Mass. The celebration of the feast begins on the evening before the feast. This custom comes from the Jewish custom of beginning a day from sundown of one day to sundown of the next day. This is the reason the Catholic Church celebrates the Mass for Sunday on Saturday evening.

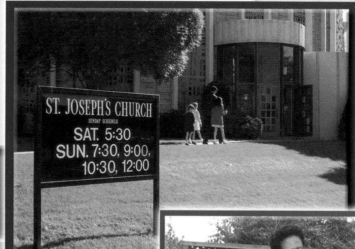

ST. JOSEPH'S CHURCH
SUNDAY SCHEDULE
SAT. 5:30
SUN. 7:30, 9:00,
10:30, 12:00

What Difference Does Faith Make in My Life?

Each week you take part in the celebration of Mass. You give thanks to God and keep him at the center of your life.

It is one of those sunny, warm days at the beach—one of those days when the whole wide world seems to be in one place at one time. Right overhead comes a plane trailing an advertisement. Everyone looks up. Within the banner write an invitation to people that best expresses how we all need to thank and celebrate God.

My Faith Choice

I will try to celebrate Sunday as a holy day. This week I will

_____

_____ .

Bless Us Today

In the Old Testament, kings and priests were anointed with oil. This was a sign that they were chosen by God for a special service to God's people. It was also a sign that God would be with them to help them in their work.

Leader: In Baptism, we were anointed with the oil of chrism as a member of the Body of Christ, the Church. Let us recall our anointing at Baptism.

Lord, you freed us from sin in the water of Baptism. *(Raise a clear bowl of water.)*

All: **Bless us today, Lord.**

Leader: Lord, you anointed us as members of Christ's Body. *(Raise a container of oil.)*

All: **Bless us today, Lord.**

Leader: Lord, you are the Light of the world. *(Lift up a candle.)*

All: **Bless us today, Lord.**

We Remember

Use the letters in the word RITUAL to describe what the Bible tells us about celebrating rituals.

R _____

I _____

T _____

U _____

A _____

L _____

To Help You Remember

1. The Old Testament Book of Leviticus contains the liturgical rituals of the Israelites.

2. The rituals for Passover and the Sabbath and other liturgical rituals helped the Israelites celebrate their faith in God and grow in holiness.

3. Some of the rituals of the Catholic Church have their roots in the rituals of the Israelites, our ancestors in faith.

This Week . . .

In chapter 12, "Passover and the Sabbath: A Scripture Story," your child learned more about the liturgy. They discovered that many of the liturgical rituals of the Church have their roots in the Old Testament. They became familiar with the Old Testament book of Leviticus, which was a liturgical handbook for the Israelites. Leviticus contains many of the liturgical laws and rituals of the Israelites and centers on the call of God's people to be "holy as the LORD God is holy" (Leviticus 19:2).

For more on the teachings of the Catholic Church on the use of rituals in the liturgy of the Church, see *Catechism of the Catholic Church* paragraph numbers 1136–1181.

Sharing God's Word

Read together Leviticus 23:1, 3, 5–8. Emphasize that taking part in the ritual celebrations of their religion helped the Israelites remember and celebrate their faith in God.

Praying

In this chapter your child recalled their Baptism and participated in a prayer asking for God's blessing. Read and pray together this ritual on page 111.

Making a Difference

Choose one of the following activities to do as a family or design a similar activity of your own.

- Talk about the rituals your family has for celebrating Thanksgiving, Christmas, and Easter. Discuss how these rituals began and why they are important to your family.

- Discuss the following questions: What are some of the ways you see people keeping Sunday as the Lord's Day? How does keeping Sunday as the Lord's Day help people live as children of God?

- Choose one thing your family does or will do together to keep Sunday as the Lord's Day.

For more ideas on ways your family can live your faith, visit the "Faith First for Families" page at **www.FaithFirst.com**. This week share some of the ideas on the "Gospel Reflections" page as a family.

Baptism and Confirmation

We Pray

I will live for the LORD.
PSALM 22:31

Lord God,
send your Holy Spirit
to make us witnesses
to Jesus Christ.   Amen.

Describe the way you formally became a member of a group to which you now belong.

Think of a time that you joined with friends to become members of a group. Baptism, Confirmation, and Eucharist initiate us, or bring us, into new life with Jesus Christ and his Body, the Church.

What happens when a person is baptized?

Newly baptized clothed
with white baptismal garments

113

We Belong to Christ

Faith Focus

What happens at the celebration of the sacraments of Baptism and Confirmation?

Faith Vocabulary

Baptism. The Sacrament of Initiation in which we are joined to Jesus Christ, become members of the Church, are reborn as God's adopted children, receive the gift of the Holy Spirit, and original sin and our personal sins are forgiven.

Confirmation. The Sacrament of Initiation that strengthens the grace of Baptism and in which our life in Christ is sealed by the gift of the Holy Spirit.

Baptism

Baptism, Confirmation, and Eucharist are the Sacraments of Christian Initiation. Through the celebration of these three sacraments a person becomes joined to Christ and his Body, the Church. **Baptism** is the first sacrament we receive.

Rite of Baptism. The Church uses water in the celebration of Baptism. In different ways, the sign of water in the Old Testament prepared for its use in the sacrament of Baptism. In the Book of Exodus, for example, we read that God led his people through the water of the Red Sea, saving them from slavery. God saves us from sin in the water of Baptism.

Sacramental Graces, or Effects, of Baptism. What happens to us when we are baptized?

- We are joined to Christ in his dying and rising. We receive new birth in Christ and become adopted daughters and sons of God the Father.

- We receive the gift of the Holy Spirit.
- We become members of the Church, the Body of Christ, and are made sharers in the priesthood of Christ.
- We are freed from all sin—original sin and personal sins.
- We are spiritually marked as belonging to Christ forever. This mark, which no sin can erase, is called a sacramental character. This mark means that Baptism is given once and for all and cannot be repeated.

Since the early days of the Church, both adults and children have been baptized. Baptism is the gateway, or doorway, to new life in the Holy Spirit and to salvation in Christ.

How does the image of water in the Old Testament help us understand Baptism?

114

Confirmation

Most Catholics today are baptized as infants and are confirmed many years later. As we grow older, we confirm our decision.

The Rite of Confirmation. In different ways, the anointing with oil in the Old Testament prepared for its use in the sacrament of **Confirmation**. In the First Book of Samuel, for example, we read about the anointing of Saul (see 1 Samuel 10:1) and David (see 1 Samuel 16:1–13). The anointing was a sign that the Spirit of God lived in the person, helping them to do the work God had chosen them to do.

In Confirmation the bishop or priest-delegate rests his hand on the top of each candidate's head as he anoints each candidate's forehead with chrism, saying:

(Name), be sealed with the gift of the Holy Spirit.

Sacramental Graces, or Effects, of Confirmation. At Confirmation we receive and accept some important responsibilities and the graces to fulfill them.

- We receive the grace of the outpouring of the Holy Spirit in our lives.
- We accept that grace and commit to join Christ in his mission to prepare for the coming of the kingdom of God.
- We cooperate with the grace of the Holy Spirit and bring healing and reconciliation to the world.
- The grace of the Holy Spirit strengthens our bond with the Church and her mission to defend the faith.
- The grace of the Holy Spirit guides us to live as signs of the Covenant as the prophets did.

Confirmation, like Baptism, may be received only once. We receive the grace to remain witnesses for Christ, even in the face of misunderstanding, ridicule, and suffering.

Think of someone you know who is truly living the gifts of Confirmation. Write a description of how that person is a living witness for Christ.

A Living Witness for Christ

_____

_____

_____

_____

_____

Requirements for Confirmation. The Church asks that a person meet certain requirements before they receive the sacrament of Confirmation. They are:

- **Faith.** The person must be baptized. Candidates for Confirmation must profess their faith with the Church.
- **Age.** The grace of Confirmation is a gift of God. Receiving this grace does not depend on how old we are. Today, in some dioceses in the United States, young people who are Roman Catholics are confirmed at various ages. In Eastern Rite Catholic Churches, Confirmation is administered immediately after Baptism and is followed by participation in the Eucharist.
- **Grace.** Candidates must be in the state of grace. Their relationship with God must be close.
- **Will, or choice.** The candidates need to have a clear and deliberate intention to receive the sacrament. They must be open to accept the responsibilities of being a witness for Christ.

Preparation for Confirmation. Confirmation marks our lifelong commitment to be witnesses for Christ. With the help of the Holy Spirit, we prepare ourselves for Confirmation. This preparation includes prayer, service, and reception of the sacrament of Reconciliation. It also includes choosing a sponsor.

A sponsor is someone who gives spiritual help and encouragement to a person who is preparing to receive Confirmation. Because Confirmation continues and deepens the grace of Baptism, it is fitting that our Confirmation sponsor be one of our baptismal godparents.

What qualities would you look for in your sponsor for Confirmation?

_____

_____

_____

_____

_____

_____

_____

Our Church Makes a Difference

Saint of the Holocaust

Maximilian Kolbe was a living witness for Christ. Jesus' greatest sign of his love for God and for all people was his freely giving up his life on the cross. Maximilian Kolbe was a Franciscan priest who lived in Poland. During World War II Father Maximilian and his brother Franciscans gave shelter to more than three thousand people being sought by the Nazis. Because of his work, Father Kolbe was arrested and on May 28, 1941, was sent to Auschwitz and branded prisoner number 16670.

In July 1941 several prisoners tried to escape. As punishment, ten men prisoners were chosen to be put to death. Francis Gajowniczek, a young father, was among the prisoners chosen. Strengthened by the gifts of the Holy Spirit, Father Maximilian stepped forward and volunteered to give up his life in place of the young father. And on August 14, 1941, he was put to death by fatal injection.

Father Maximilian became "a martyr of charity, out of love for Jesus and others" (Pope John Paul II). On October 10, 1982, Pope John Paul II named Father Maximilian a saint of the Church. The pope described him as a "martyr of charity" for us to imitate.

What people do you see living as witnesses for Christ?

Saint Maximilian Kolbe (1894–1941), patron of journalists, families, and the pro-life movement

Our Catholic Identity

Laying On of Hands

The laying on of hands is an important ritual of the Church. This ancient ritual is found in both the Old Testament and the New Testament. Its use signifies a bestowal of an office or a responsibility, of God's blessing, or of God's healing through the invocation of the Holy Spirit. The laying on of hands is an essential part of the rite of Confirmation. Strengthened by the Holy Spirit, we receive the grace to be witnesses for Christ.

Pope John Paul II walking in the Auschwitz concentration camp, after visiting Saint Maximilian Kolbe's cell block 11

What Difference Does Faith Make in My Life?

You are called to be a living witness for Christ. Strengthened with the gift of the Holy Spirit, you continue the work of Christ in the world today.

Look at your life right now. Create a motto or brief statement describing what you can do right now to be a witness for Christ.

Sealed with the Gift of the Holy Spirit

My Faith Choice

This week I will put my witness motto into action.
I will

_____

_____ .

Come, Holy Spirit

We first receive the gift of the Holy Spirit at Baptism and are sealed with the gift of the Holy Spirit at Confirmation.

Leader: On the day of Pentecost tongues of fire parted and came to rest on the disciples. They were all filled with the Holy Spirit.

Reader: *Proclaim Galatians 5:22–26.*

Leader: Remember that the Holy Spirit dwells within us. Let us ask the Holy Spirit to give us the grace to be living witnesses for Christ.

All: **Come, Holy Spirit,**
fill the hearts of your faithful.
And kindle in them the fire of your love.
Send forth your Spirit
and they shall be created.
And you will renew the face of the earth.

We Remember

Compare and contrast the sacraments of Baptism and Confirmation.

Baptism **Confirmation**

Different   **Alike**   **Different**

To Help You Remember

1. A person becomes fully initiated into the Church through the celebration of the three Sacraments of Initiation—Baptism, Confirmation, and Eucharist.

2. Baptism is the first sacrament we receive. It is the doorway to new life in the Holy Spirit and salvation in Christ.

3. Confirmation perfects the grace of Baptism.

This Week . . .

In chapter 13, "Baptism and Confirmation," your child learned more about the sacraments of Baptism and Confirmation. We are joined to Christ and made sharers in the life of the Holy Trinity through the Sacraments of Christian Initiation—Baptism, Confirmation, and Eucharist. Through Baptism we first receive new life and salvation in Christ and become members of the Body of Christ, the Church. By God's gift, through water and the Holy Spirit, original sin and everything that separates us from God is washed away. Confirmation confirms, or seals, Baptism. The Holy Spirit strengthens us to be witnesses for Christ by empowering us to live the Gospel and proclaim Jesus Christ to others.

For more on the teachings of the Catholic Church on the sacraments of Baptism and Confirmation, see *Catechism of the Catholic Church* paragraph numbers 1210–1274 and 1285–1314.

Sharing God's Word

Read together John 3:3–6. Emphasize that through the sacrament of Baptism we are reborn of water and the Holy Spirit.

Praying

In this chapter your child prayed a prayer to the Holy Spirit. Read and pray together this prayer on page 119.

Making a Difference

Choose one of the following activities to do as a family or design a similar activity of your own.

- Water can symbolize many things. Talk about what water symbolizes for you. Share ideas about how water helps you understand what happens in Baptism.

- Place a dish of holy water in a convenient location in your home. Bless each other and yourselves as you come and go during the day and before bedtime. As you bless yourself with the holy water, remember that in Baptism we become members of the Body of Christ.

- Invite family members to name someone they know who is confirmed and is living as a witness for Christ. Describe what this person does to live as a witness for Christ.

For more ideas on ways your family can live your faith, visit the "Faith First for Families" page at **www.FaithFirst.com**. This week click on "Just for Parents."

David, King of Israel
A Scripture Story

We Pray

The LORD swore an oath
  to David,
  a pledge never to be broken:
  "Your own offspring
  I will set upon your
  throne."   PSALM 132:11

**Father, send the Holy Spirit
to guide the ministers
of the Church to carry
out their ministry with
gentleness and concern
for others as Jesus did.**
                    Amen.

*Name some types of writing that
you enjoy reading.*

There are many different types
of literature and other writings.
The writers of the Bible used
many types of writing to
communicate God's word.

*Name some of the types of
writing you know that the writers
of the Bible used.*

David, King of Israel (1040–970 B.C.)
and writer of psalms

Faith Focus

What do the historical books of the Old Testament tell about God and the Covenant?

Faith Vocabulary

consecrate. Set aside and dedicate for a holy purpose.

The Historical Books

The Old Testament contains many different types of writing. Christians divide these writings into four groups: Pentateuch, Historical Writings, Prophets, and Wisdom Writings. In this chapter we will take a look at the historical books. All together, the historical books cover about a thousand years of history. The historical books include:

- Joshua, Judges, and Ruth
- 1 and 2 Samuel
- 1 and 2 Kings
- 1 and 2 Chronicles
- Ezra, Nehemiah
- Tobit, Judith, and Esther
- 1 and 2 Maccabees

The historical books begin with the time Joshua led the Israelites into the land promised them by God and the judges were the leaders of Israel. They next discuss the monarchy, or office of the king, in Israel. This part of the story begins with Saul, David, and Solomon. It continues with the stories of other kings until the destruction of Jerusalem and the exile of God's people in Babylon in the year 587 B.C.

Eventually, the Israelites returned to their homeland and rebuilt their broken lives. The last historical books, 1 and 2 Maccabees, tell of the persecution of the Jewish people and their struggle to keep the faith.

The History of God's People

Look up one of these Scripture passages. Write or illustrate what it says about God's people.

- Joshua 1:1–9
- 2 Samuel 6:11–19
- 1 Kings 8:1–13

Reading the Word of God

The Anointing of David

In the First Book of Samuel we read about Samuel the Prophet anointing David to be king. The Hebrew name *David* means "beloved." Born in Bethlehem, David, the youngest son of Jesse, was chosen by God to be king of God's people.

After the failure of Saul to serve faithfully as king, God rejected Saul and said to Samuel, "I regret having made Saul king, for he has turned from me and has not kept my command" (1 Samuel 15:11). Samuel, who became tremendously upset, went off to tell Saul that God had rejected him. Saul eventually became so angry that he and Samuel never spoke again.

God again came to Samuel and said:

"How long will you grieve for Saul, whom I have rejected as king of Israel? Fill your horn with oil, and be on your way. I am sending you to Jesse of Bethlehem, for I have chosen my king from among his sons." 1 SAMUEL 16:1

Samuel did as God commanded him. He went to Bethlehem where he anointed David to be king of Israel.

David ruled as king for nearly forty years. He drew up the plans to build the Temple in Jerusalem and wrote many of the Psalms. He was an ancestor of Jesus, who would be proclaimed Son of David (see Matthew 21:9–11).

Describe the qualities needed for a leader of God's people.

Time Line of Important Persons and Events in the History of the Israelites

ca. 1900–1700 B.C.
Abraham and Sarah, Isaac and Rebecca, Jacob

ca. 1600–1230 B.C.
Israelites in Egypt

ca. 1230–1200 B.C.
Moses, Exodus, Covenant at Mount Sinai

ca. 1200–1020 B.C.
Joshua and Period of Judges

ca. 1020–800 B.C.
Period of Saul, David, Solomon, and other kings; building of Temple in Jerusalem

ca. 933–587 B.C.
Period of Elijah, Isaiah, Jeremiah, Ezekiel, and other prophets

587–533 B.C.
Exile in Babylon

533–333 B.C.
Return from Exile, rebuilding of Jerusalem

333–167 B.C.
Alexander the Great defeats Persians, rules Israel and other countries in Asia Minor

167–63 B.C.
The Maccabees

Set Aside to Serve God's People

In the Old Testament, kings, priests, and prophets were consecrated for special service among God's people in the ritual of anointing. The word **consecrate** means "to set aside for a holy purpose." From the time of the Apostles the Church has continued this Old Testament practice of consecrating people and things by anointing.

During the rite of Baptism, the newly baptized are anointed with chrism. This shows that the baptized are to serve others as Jesus did.

Confirmation includes the anointing of our forehead with chrism. This is a sign that the person being confirmed is sealed with the gift of the Holy Spirit to serve as a witness for Christ.

In Holy Orders the hands of the newly ordained priests are anointed with chrism. This signifies that they have the ministry to sanctify the people and to offer sacrifices to God.

When we read the historical books, we can see more clearly that God strengthens us for a life of faith, hope, and love in service to God, to the Church, and to all people.

Design a label on this jar that is used to hold chrism. Include on your label the meaning of the use of chrism. Be creative.

Our Church Makes a Difference

United States Conference of Catholic Bishops

The bishops are anointed to serve the People of God, the Church. They are anointed to lead the Church in worshiping God, living the Gospel, and proclaiming the Gospel to all people. In the United States of America the bishops work together to fulfill these responsibilities.

One way they work together is in the United States Conference of Catholic Bishops (USCCB). The USCCB proclaims the teachings of Jesus by writing pastoral letters. These letters often remind Catholics and all Americans of their responsibility to be faithful to the laws of God. They teach about working for justice and peace, for the equal sharing of food and health care by all people, for the protection of all human life and the environment, and other issues that proclaim the dignity of all people.

In a meeting in Rome in 2001, bishops from the United States and other parts of the world discussed this important work. At the end of the meeting, the pope reminded all the bishops that they are "servants of the Gospel for the hope of the world." Just as the anointed leaders in the Old Testament led the people to live the Covenant with God, the bishops of the Church bring hope to the world by courageously leading the Church to live the Gospel.

Christians are an anointed people. How do you see Christians working together to serve others?

Bishops process in the Basilica of the National Shrine of the Immaculate Conception, Washington, D.C., during evening Mass on first day of a general meeting of the United States Conference of Catholic Bishops

125

What Difference Does Faith Make in My Life?

In Baptism the priest or deacon anointed the crown of your head with chrism. He said that God was now anointing you to serve others as Jesus did.

In the circle write one thing you can do to serve others as Jesus did. On the lines coming from the circle, write how that action helps others.

Anointed to Serve

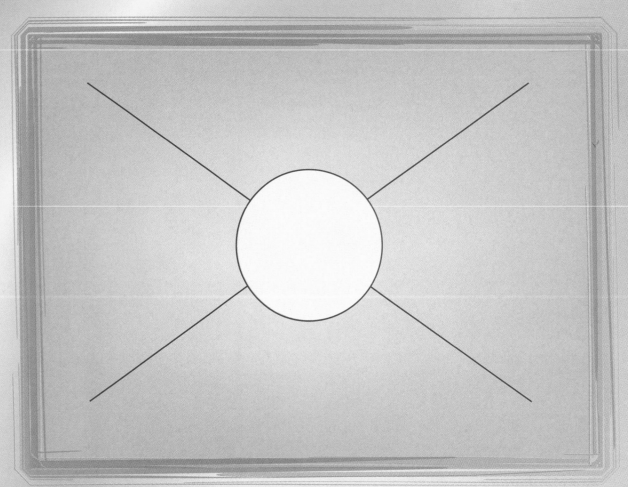

My Faith Choice

This week I will remember that I have been anointed to serve God and others. I will

_____

_____ .

Serve as Jesus Did

We serve as Jesus did when we love God and others as Jesus did. Pray this act of love asking God the Father to help you respond to his call to you to serve others.

Leader: Jesus told us to serve others out of love for God and for them. Close your eyes; imagine you are among the disciples at the Last Supper listening to Jesus.

Reader: *Proclaim Luke 22:24–27.*

All: **Praise to you, Lord Jesus Christ.**

Leader: Think about how you might follow Jesus' example and serve God and one another. *(Pause.)*
Let us join together and pray.

All: **God, Creator and Father,
you created us to know, love, and serve you.
I love you above all things.
I love others as I love myself for love of you.
Send the Holy Spirit to guide me
to love and serve as Jesus did. Amen**

We Remember

Write the letter next to the name of the person in the word box on the line next to the phrase that describes that person.

> **a. Samuel**   **b. Saul**   **c. David**

_____ **1.** Anointed David to be king of Israel

_____ **2.** Wrote some of the Psalms in the Book of Psalms

_____ **3.** Made plans to build the Temple in Jerusalem

_____ **4.** Ancestor of Jesus

_____ **5.** Told by Samuel that he would no longer be king of the Israelites

To Help You Remember

1. The historical books of the Old Testament pass on the story of the Israelites from the time they entered the Promised Land to the persecution of the Jewish people just before the birth of Jesus.

2. The historical books tell us about the anointing of David as king of Israel.

3. The historical books help Christians discover that God is active in the history of the Church.

This Week . . .

In chapter 14, "David, King of Israel: A Scripture Story," your child learned more about the Old Testament and its integral connection with the New Testament. Christians often divide the writings of the Old Testament into the Pentateuch (or Torah), historical writings, the writings of the Prophets, and wisdom writings. In this chapter your child took a deeper look at the historical books. In particular, they learned about David and his anointing as the king of Israel. The historical books of the Old Testament help Christians come to know that God is active and involved in the Church today.

For more on the teachings of the Catholic Church on the unity of Sacred Scriptures, see *Catechism of the Catholic Church* paragraph numbers 54–64, 101–133, and 839.

Sharing God's Word

Read together 1 Samuel 16:1–13. Emphasize that God chose David to serve his people as king.

Praying

In this chapter your child prayed an act of love. Read and pray together this prayer on page 127.

Making a Difference

Choose one of the following activities to do as a family or design a similar activity of your own.

- David was chosen as the leader of God's people. Discuss the following questions: What makes a good leader? In what ways are you a leader? Why do leaders love what they do? How does God help leaders accomplish good things?

- In this chapter is a time line of important events in the history of the Israelites. Make a family time line. Include all the significant dates for your family. Be sure to include the events and people that have had great influence on your family.

- When you take part in Mass this week, find the ambry in your church. The ambry is where the blessed oils are kept. These oils are used in the sacraments. Talk about how you are living out your baptismal anointing.

For more ideas on ways your family can live your faith, visit the "Faith First for Families" page at **www.FaithFirst.com**. Click on "Contemporary Issues" and read about an issue that discusses the connection between faith and life.

The Eucharist

We Pray

They asked and . . .
 with bread from heaven
 [the LORD] filled them.
            PSALM 105:40

**Lord Jesus Christ,
we worship you among us
in the sacrament of your
Body and Blood.   Amen.**

*Name some symbols you
sometimes see or hear and tell
what they point to.*

Symbols point to something
beyond themselves. For
example, when you see smoke
you look for fire. The Church
uses symbols in the celebration
of the sacraments.

*What symbols or symbolic
actions do you see used
at Mass?*

The Bread of Life

Faith Focus

What does the Church celebrate and share in at Mass?

Faith Vocabulary

Eucharist. The sacrament of the Body and Blood of Christ; the Sacrament of Christian Initiation in which we receive the Body and Blood of Christ, who is truly and really present under the appearances of bread and wine, and in which we are most fully joined to Christ and to the Church, the Body of Christ.

Shrub producing manna

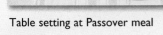

Table setting at Passover meal

The Mass

Many Old Testament events point to, or prefigure, the mystery of the Eucharist, which we celebrate at Mass.

Melchizedek. The story of Melchizedek, king of Salem, also has a deeper meaning for Christians. The three elements in this Old Testament story (see Genesis 14:17–20) prefigure Christ's giving of himself to us in the Eucharist. The elements are bread and wine, the offering of bread and wine as gifts to God, and grateful remembrance of what God has done for his people.

Passover. God commanded his people to celebrate Passover each year with unleavened bread, the Passover lamb, bitter herbs, and wine to remember God's saving them (see Exodus 12:1–20). Jesus gave us a new Passover meal, the Eucharist.

Manna. During the Exodus God gave the Israelites manna to eat (see Exodus 16:1–15). Manna is a breadlike substance produced on a shrub. We say that manna prefigured the Eucharist, the Bread of Life, God gives us.

The Eucharist, prefigured by the manna, the offering of Melchizedek, and the Passover meal, is the great sacrament of God's love. Celebrating the Eucharist recalls and makes present the one sacrifice of Christ, who said:

> "This is my commandment: love one another as I love you. No one has greater love than this, to lay down one's life for one's friends."
> JOHN 15:12–13

Compare Melchizedek, Passover, and manna with what you know about the Mass.

Liturgy of the Word

The proclamation of God's very own word in the Scriptures is the center of the Liturgy of the Word. The word of God

- *feeds* us, nourishing our minds and hearts;
- *reminds* us of God's involvement in our lives;
- *inspires* us to praise and thank God; and
- *shows* us a path for living.

The Scripture Readings. At Mass on Sundays and major feast days, we listen to three readings. The first reading is usually taken from the Old Testament. The second reading is taken from one of the letters of Saint Paul, from one of the other New Testament letters, from the Acts of the Apostles, or from the Book of Revelation.

After the second reading, we stand and sing the Gospel acclamation or another chant. We greet and honor the Lord, who is present with us in the Scriptures. The Gospel is the last of the three readings. The Gospel reading, as well as the other Sunday readings, are on a three-year cycle—Year A (Matthew), Year B (Mark and John), and Year C (Luke). This enables us to hear readings from all four Gospels over a three-year period.

Homily. In the homily the priest or deacon helps us connect the readings to our lives.

Profession of Faith and Prayer of the Faithful. We stand and profess our faith by praying the creed together. We then offer the prayer of the faithful. We pray for the needs of the Church, the world, other people, and ourselves.

Name a favorite Gospel story. What do you think God is saying to you?

Faith-Filled People

Dominic de Guzman

Saint Dominic de Guzman gave his life to preaching the Gospel and explaining the meaning of the word of God. So important was this work for Dominic that many soon joined him. They became the Order of Preachers and today are known as Dominicans. The Church celebrates the feast day of Saint Dominic on August 4.

Speak, Lord. We Are Listening.

_____

_____

_____

_____

_____

_____

_____

_____

Liturgy of the Eucharist

The **Eucharist** is the Church's great prayer of blessing and thanksgiving to God the Father. The work of salvation accomplished by the one sacrifice of Christ is made present, and we are made sharers in it.

Preparation of the Gifts. The Liturgy of the Eucharist begins with the preparation of the gifts. Often there is a procession with the gifts of bread and wine. Bread made from wheat and wine made from grapes are necessary for the celebration of the Eucharist. The priest prays a prayer of blessing that is a form of grace before meals in the Jewish tradition. The preparation of the gifts concludes with the prayer over the offerings.

The Eucharistic Prayer. The priest leads the praying of the preface. He names the reasons we are gathered to give God thanks and praise. We conclude by singing or praying aloud the acclamation, "Holy, holy, holy Lord."

During the Eucharistic Prayer the priest pronounces the words of consecration. Through the words of the priest and the power of the Holy Spirit, the bread and wine are truly changed into the Body and Blood of Christ. Holding the bread, the priest says:

Take this, all of you, and eat it: this is my body which will be given up for you. . . .

Holding the cup of wine, he says:

Take this, all of you, and drink from it: this is the cup of my blood, the blood of the new and everlasting covenant. It will be shed for you and for all so that sins may be forgiven. Do this in memory of me.

The Communion Rite. The consecrated bread is broken for us to share. The faithful in the state of grace are invited to process forward to receive the consecrated bread and wine.

What are some ways that you can participate more actively in the Mass?

Oscar Arnulfo Romero (1917–1980), Archbishop of San Salvador, Martyr of El Salvador

Archbishop Oscar Romero

Christians since the early days of the Church have given their lives out of love for God and others. Oscar Romero, the Archbishop of San Salvador, gave up his life serving Christ and the people of San Salvador. On March 24, 1980, as he began to raise the consecrated bread in his hands, he was shot through his heart and killed. He was assassinated because he truly lived the command we all receive during the concluding rite of the Mass, "Go in peace to love and serve the Lord."

During his homily at that Mass, Archbishop Romero said, "Those who give their lives to the service of the poor through love will live like the grain of wheat that dies. The harvest comes from the grains that die. We know that every effort to improve society, when society is so full of injustice, is an effort that God blesses, God wants, and God demands of us. I am bound by God's command to give my life for all the people of El Salvador, even those who want to kill me."

Archbishop Romero believed that the Gospel demanded that he serve the poor and be their voice. He was truly bread of life for the poor. Like the grain of wheat, he died to bring a harvest of justice to the people of his country.

In what ways do you see people living the Eucharist?

Our Catholic Identity

The Altar

The altar is the table of the Lord. From this table we are fed with the Body and Blood of the Lord Jesus. The altar is also a symbol of Christ. It reminds us that Jesus sacrificed his life for us on the cross. That is why at the beginning of the Mass and at the end of the Mass, the priest venerates, or honors, the altar by kissing and bowing before it.

"Every effort to improve society... is an effort that God blesses."
Archbishop Oscar Romero

Archbishop Romero greeting people after Mass, 1979

What Difference Does Faith Make in My Life?

Each time you participate in Mass you receive the call
and the grace of the Holy Spirit to love and serve the Lord.

*Reflect on Jesus' words, "I am the bread of life" (John 6:35). What do
Jesus' words tell you about being a follower of Christ?*

The Bread of Life

My Faith Choice

This week I will continue to apply Jesus' words "I am
the bread of life" to my life. I will

_____

_____.

We Pray

Bread for the World

The Eucharist strengthens us to live the Gospel. Celebrate this service of the word. Go forth and be bread for the world.

Leader: God, giver of all blessings,
thank you for the gift of Jesus, your Son, the Bread of Life.
Send the Holy Spirit to help us serve others as your Son did.

Reader: *Proclaim John 6:32–35.*
The gospel of the Lord,

All: **Praise to you, Lord Jesus Christ.**

Leader: *Briefly apply the Gospel message to the life of Christians today.*
Let us now pray to God the Father as Jesus taught.

All: **Our Father . . .**

Leader: Let us offer one another a sign of peace. *(Pause.)*
Go in the peace of Christ.

All: **Thanks be to God.**

We Remember

Unscramble the words to complete the sentences.

1. The sacrament of the _____
   shaucerit
   is the sacrament of the Body and Blood of Christ.

2. The _____ meal prefigures
   spaersov
   the Last Supper and the Eucharist.

3. During the Eucharistic Prayer the priest pronounces the

   words of _____. These are the
   crcontionsea
   words Jesus spoke at the Last Supper.

To Help You Remember

1. Many events in the Old Testament prefigure, or point to, the mystery of the Eucharist.

2. The proclamation of the word of God is at the center of the Liturgy of the Word.

3. The Eucharistic Prayer is the heart of the Liturgy of the Eucharist.

This Week . . .

In chapter 15, "The Eucharist," your child learned more about the Mass and the sacrament of the Eucharist. Several events in the Old Testament point to, or prefigure, the Eucharist. Understanding the meaning of the Old Testament stories of the manna, Melchizedek, and the Passover can enrich our understanding of the mystery of the Eucharist. The Eucharist is the sacrament of the Body and Blood of the Lord Jesus, the Bread of Life. At the Eucharist, the bread and wine truly become the Body and Blood of Christ through the power of the Holy Spirit and the words of the priest. When we celebrate the Eucharist, the sacrifice of Jesus is made present.

For more on the teachings of the Catholic Church on the sacrament of the Eucharist, see *Catechism of the Catholic Church* paragraph numbers 1322–1405.

Sharing God's Word

Read together 1 Corinthians 11:17–34. Emphasize that the Eucharist is the sacrament of the Body and Blood of Christ. Sharing in the Eucharist nourishes us and strengthens us to love and serve God and one another.

Praying

In this chapter your child participated in a brief service of the word. Read and take part in this service of the word on page 135 as a family.

Making a Difference

Choose one of the following activities to do as a family or design a similar activity of your own.

- Find a favorite bread recipe and make homemade bread. Gather together and eat the bread for a snack or eat it as part of a special meal. You might even like to make some bread for special neighbors or friends.

- When you take part in Mass this week, think carefully about the readings. After Mass gather together and share your ideas.

- Talk about some ways you can participate in Mass more actively. Invite each family member to choose one thing they will do.

For more ideas on ways your family can live your faith, visit the "Faith First for Families" page at **www.FaithFirst.com**. Check out "Bible Stories." This week read and discuss the Bible story as a family.

The Parable of the Great Feast

A Scripture Story

✛ THE FEAST IS READY ✛

We Pray

Sing joyfully to God our strength;
shout in triumph to the God of Jacob!

PSALM 81:2

Lord God, you feed your people with the Eucharist and strengthen them in holiness.   Amen.

When have you attended a meal that honored someone?

Banquets, or large gatherings of people for special meals, celebrate people and achievements. The writers of the Bible used the image of a banquet to help us understand what it means to belong to the People of God.

What meal stories do you remember from the Bible?

Detail from parable of the Great Feast, stained glass

Bible Background

Faith Focus

How does the biblical image of a great banquet, or feast, help us understand the mystery of the Eucharist?

Faith Vocabulary

parable. A form of story that compares one thing to another to help listeners understand the main point of the story.

Parables

The most famous and important meal in the Gospel is the Last Supper. It is so important that all four evangelists—Matthew, Mark, Luke, and John—wrote about it. Luke includes in his account of the Gospel many other stories that center around meals. There are ten in all, beginning with a banquet at the house of Levi (see Luke 5:27–39) and ending with a meal in Jerusalem just before Jesus' Ascension (see Luke 24:41–42).

Luke and Matthew both include the parable of a great banquet meal that Jesus told. It is called the parable of the Great Feast. In parables Jesus and other storytellers compare two things.

Feast at the House of Levi, Paolo Veronese (1528–1588), Italian painter

A **parable** uses the words *like* and *as* to make its point. In this parable Jesus used his listeners' experiences of meals and banquets to help them understand his message about the kingdom of God.

Look up Matthew 13 to learn about more parables Jesus told. What two things does Jesus compare in each of the parables?

Parables of Jesus

Parable of _____

_____

_____

_____

_____

_____

Parable of _____

_____

_____

_____

_____

_____

The Parable of the Great Feast

Jesus told this parable when he was invited to the home of a leading Pharisee. Some of the Pharisees who were present were criticizing Jesus for sitting down at the same table "with certain people" whose behavior they did not approve. Jesus responded by telling this parable.

"A man gave a great dinner to which he invited many. When the time for the dinner came, he dispatched his servant to say to those invited, 'Come, everything is now ready.' But one by one, they all began to excuse themselves. The first said to him, 'I have purchased a field and must go to examine it; I ask you, consider me excused.' And another said, 'I have purchased five yoke of oxen and am on my way to evaluate them; I ask you, consider me excused.' And another said, 'I have just married a woman, and therefore I cannot come.' The servant went and reported this to his master.

Then the master of the house in a rage commanded his servant, 'Go out quickly into the streets and alleys of the town and bring in here the poor and the crippled, the blind and the lame.' The servant reported, 'Sir, your orders have been carried out and still there is room.' The master then ordered the servant, 'Go out to the highways and hedgerows and make people come in that my home may be filled.' "

LUKE 14:16–23

Jesus invited people who the Pharisees and their guests would have not usually invited. By doing this Jesus was teaching that God invites all people to the kingdom of God and wants them to decide to come.

What does this parable teach about God?

Time Line

ca. 4 B.C.
Birth of Jesus

A.D. 30s
Passion, death, Resurrection, Ascension of Jesus; first Christian Pentecost

A.D. 45–60
Letters of Paul, missionary journey of Paul

A.D. 64
Rome burned, persecution of Nero

ca. A.D. 67
Peter and Paul martyred

A.D. 70
Temple in Jerusalem destroyed

ca. A.D. 70
Gospel of Mark written

ca. A.D. 80
Gospel of Matthew written

ca. A.D. 90–100
Gospel of Luke written, Gospel of John written

The Feast of the Kingdom

Christians have come to understand this parable as a parable about the kingdom of God and the Eucharist. Christ has given the Church the banquet of the Eucharist as both a pledge and an anticipation of the heavenly banquet in the kingdom of God.

We prepare for the coming of the kingdom and sharing in the heavenly banquet by treating all people—without exception—with respect and compassion. We act in such a way that others can see that God invites and desires that everyone share in the banquet in the kingdom of God.

Look at the pictures. Describe what they portray about living for the kingdom of God.

The Kingdom of God

_____
_____
_____
_____
_____
_____
_____
_____
_____
_____
_____
_____
_____

Our Church Makes a Difference

People of God to a new knowledge of today's problems . . . that can lead to some new approaches that promote a greater sense of solidarity."

Every parish in the United States is invited to take part in this work of the Church. One way Catholics do this is by contributing to a special collection at Mass on the Sunday before Thanksgiving. This and the other projects of the Catholic Campaign for Human Development have significantly changed the lives of people living in poverty in our country.

How can you and your friends work with people in your parish to support the Catholic Campaign for Human Development?

Catholic Campaign for Human Development

From its beginning the Church has preached the Gospel message that God desires all people to share in the great banquet in the kingdom of God. The Catholic Campaign for Human Development brings that message to people living in poverty.

Established in 1969, the Catholic Campaign for Human Development shares that Gospel message in practical ways. First, it raises funds to support "organized groups of white and minority poor to develop economic strength and political power." Second, it educates "the

What Difference Does Faith Make in My Life?

You share in the banquet of the Eucharist and look forward to sharing in the great feast in the kingdom of God. The Eucharist strengthens you to live for the kingdom.

Describe how you and your friends might show others that God invites them and all people to share in the great feast in the kingdom of God.

All Are Invited

What We Can Do

_____

_____

_____

_____

What Our Actions Tell Others

_____

_____

_____

_____

My Faith Choice

This week I will remember and live the message of Jesus' parable of the Great Feast. I will

_____

_____.

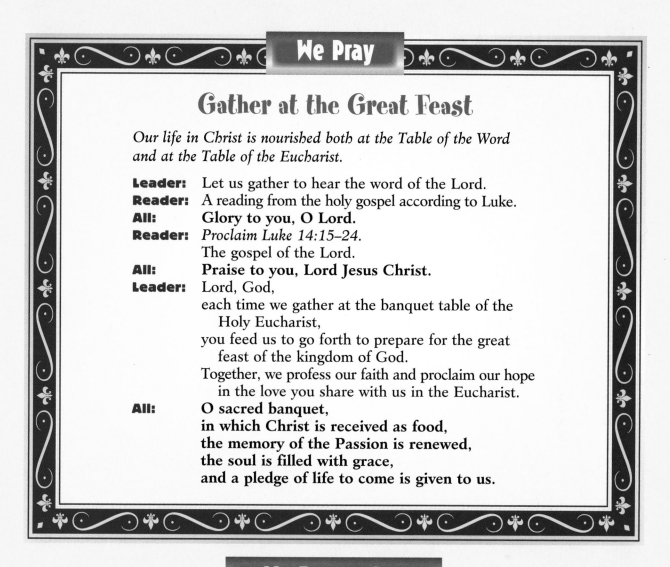

Gather at the Great Feast

Our life in Christ is nourished both at the Table of the Word and at the Table of the Eucharist.

Leader: Let us gather to hear the word of the Lord.
Reader: A reading from the holy gospel according to Luke.
All: **Glory to you, O Lord.**
Reader: *Proclaim Luke 14:15–24.*
The gospel of the Lord.
All: **Praise to you, Lord Jesus Christ.**
Leader: Lord, God,
each time we gather at the banquet table of the
Holy Eucharist,
you feed us to go forth to prepare for the great
feast of the kingdom of God.
Together, we profess our faith and proclaim our hope
in the love you share with us in the Eucharist.
All: **O sacred banquet,**
in which Christ is received as food,
the memory of the Passion is renewed,
the soul is filled with grace,
and a pledge of life to come is given to us.

We Remember

Retell the parable of the Great Feast. Use words or pictures.

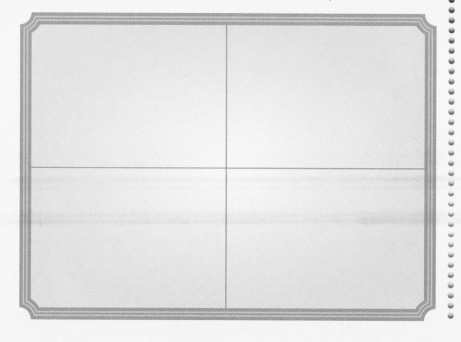

To Help You Remember

1. Jesus used his listeners' experience of meals and banquets in a parable to teach them about the kingdom of God.

2. The parable of the Great Feast teaches that God desires and invites all people to the great feast in the kingdom of God.

3. Sharing in the Eucharist is a pledge of future glory and an anticipation of the great heavenly banquet.

This Week . . .

In chapter 16, "The Parable of the Great Feast: A Scripture Story," your child learned more about the connection between the kingdom of God and the mystery of the Eucharist. Jesus told the parable of the Great Feast to teach about the kingdom of God. This parable helps Christians today deepen their understanding of the mystery of the Eucharist. The Eucharist is a pledge and an anticipation of the great feast of the heavenly kingdom at which all the faithful will be united and will celebrate as the one family of God.

For more on the teachings of the Catholic Church on the Eucharist and the kingdom of God, see *Catechism of the Catholic Church* paragraph numbers 541–554, 1402–1405, and 2816–2821.

Sharing God's Word

Read together Luke 14:7–24. Emphasize that Jesus told this parable to teach what it means to be invited to the kingdom of God.

Praying

In this chapter your child learned and prayed an ancient prayer proclaiming our faith in the Eucharist. Read and pray together this prayer on page 143.

Making a Difference

Choose one of the following activities to do as a family or design a similar activity of your own.

• God invites all people to take their place in his kingdom. His invitation is always being offered to us. Discuss the following questions: Are we reluctant to accept God's invitation? Why or why not?

• One way we show that we are living for the kingdom is by helping people who are in need. Together as a family, choose one thing you can do this week to reach out to others.

• There are many parables in the Bible about the kingdom of God. Read Matthew 13:24–33, 13:44–48; Mark 4:30–34; and Luke 13:18–21 to see what else Jesus teaches us about God's kingdom.

For more ideas on ways your family can live your faith, visit the "Faith First for Families" page at **www.FaithFirst.com**. You will find it helpful to look at "Questions Kids Ask."

Sacraments of Healing

We Pray

LORD, have mercy on me;
   heal me. I have sinned
      against you.   PSALM 41:5

Lord God,
may all who suffer
know and trust that
they are joined to Christ
who suffered for the
salvation of the world.
                    Amen.

When have you or someone you love been in need of healing?

People can get hurt in many ways. Our bodies, our minds, and our feelings can get hurt. We can also get hurt spiritually when we sin. There are many stories in the Gospel that tell about Jesus healing people physically and spiritually.

What stories in the Gospel do you know that tell about Jesus healing people?

Faith Focus

How does Jesus continue his healing ministry in the Church today?

Faith Vocabulary

Reconciliation.
The Sacrament of Healing through which we receive God's forgiveness through the ministry of a priest for sins that we have committed after Baptism.

Anointing of the Sick.
The Sacrament of Healing that strengthens our faith, hope, and love for God when we are seriously ill, weakened by old age, or dying.

The Healing Ministry of Jesus Christ

In the Old Testament Book of Numbers, we read that the people of Israel became ill in the desert during the Exodus (21:4–9). At God's direction Moses lifted up a bronze serpent, and all who looked upon it were healed.

The Church has come to understand that the lifting up of the bronze serpent prefigured the lifting up of Jesus on the cross. Jesus would be the source of healing for the whole human family.

Jesus continues his work today and until the end of time through the Church. He is especially present doing this work through the two Sacraments of Healing, Reconciliation and Anointing of the Sick.

The Ministry of Forgiveness

When we sin, we turn away from the love of God and of other people. We hurt ourselves spiritually and we need healing. We need to heal our relationship with God and with the Church. We need the healing given by God who alone can forgive sins. In his mercy and goodness God shares his power to forgive sins with the Church, the Body of Christ. He shares this forgiveness through the celebration of the sacraments.

Baptism is the first sacrament of forgiveness. In Baptism original sin and all personal sins are forgiven. Jesus also gave the Church the sacrament of **Reconciliation** for the forgiveness of sins committed after Baptism. He said to his disciples,

"Receive the holy Spirit. Whose sins you forgive are forgiven them, and whose sins you retain are retained."
JOHN 20:22–23

This work of forgiveness is continued through the ministry of bishops and priests.

The Eucharist is also a sacrament of forgiveness. Sharing in the Eucharist joins us more closely to Christ and to others. Venial sins are forgiven. Mortal sins, however, must be confessed in the sacrament of Reconciliation. Celebrating Reconciliation and receiving Eucharist regularly helps us deepen our relationship with God and others.

What are some ways we can show that we are truly sorry for our sins?

Freedom from the Punishment of Sin

In Matthew chapter 25, Jesus teaches that there is punishment connected with sin. Punishment for sin is one of the consequences of our sinning. That punishment may be eternal or it may be temporary. Through prayers, good works, and indulgences the faithful can obtain remission, or release, from this temporary punishment. We can do this for ourselves and for the souls in purgatory.

The Graces of Reconciliation

Celebrating Reconciliation heals us spiritually. Some of the effects of this sacrament are:

- Reconciliation restores and strengthens the life of grace with God, which sin caused us to lose or weaken.
- Reconciliation renews our relationship with the Body of Christ, the Church.
- Reconciliation frees us from eternal separation from God. We call that separation from God hell.
- Reconciliation gives us the gifts of peace and forgiveness.
- Reconciliation gives us the grace to faithfully follow Jesus Christ—even in the face of difficulties.

Name several words that describe your feelings when you are forgiven. Use these words in a prayer of thanksgiving to God.

Ministry to the Sick

Jesus healed those who were sick physically and spiritually. He sent his disciples to do the same in his name. Jesus continues his ministry of healing through the sacrament of Anointing of the Sick.

From its very beginning the Church has ministered with the sick in this special way. The New Testament Letter of James states:

Is anyone among you sick? He should summon the presbyters of the church, and they should pray over him and anoint [him] with oil in the name of the Lord, and the prayer of faith will save the sick person, and the Lord will raise him up. If he has committed any sins, he will be forgiven.

JAMES 5:14–15

Anointing of the Sick may be received each time we become seriously ill. We also may receive this sacrament more than once during the same illness if our sickness becomes worse. Elderly people who struggle with the effects of aging and weakness may also receive this sacrament.

In this sacrament we receive many graces. Some of the important graces of this sacrament are:

- We are united to the sufferings of Jesus.
- We receive peace and courage to face our sufferings.
- We can receive the forgiveness of our sins if we are not able to celebrate the sacrament of Reconciliation.
- Our health may be restored.
- We are prepared for our final journey to eternal life when we are very ill and near death.

Through the celebration of Anointing of the Sick, Christ continues his work of healing among us. With faith and trust in God we face our suffering.

Talk with your friends about things you and they can do for people who are sick. Choose one idea and do it together.

Viaticum

The faithful who are terminally ill, or in danger of death, receive the Body and Blood of Christ as viaticum. *Viaticum* is a word which means "food for the journey." Holy Communion received as viaticum is food and strength for a person's journey from life on earth through death to eternal life. If possible, the dying person renews the faith they professed at Baptism during the celebration of viaticum.

End-of-Life Care

Hospice is a ministry of caring for the terminally ill and their families. It is a ministry of the Church throughout the world. "Catholic Hospice" is a ministry of the Archdiocese of Miami and Mercy Hospital. It offers end-of-life care to people of all faiths.

Hospice care is founded on such Gospel virtues and values as compassion, mercy, and respect for the dignity of every person. It gives witness to the faith of the Church that death is the doorway to new and glorified life with God.

Jesus continues his ministry with the dying through hospice care given by the Church. In Catholic Hospice a team of physicians, nurses, social workers, home health aides, chaplains, bereavement and other counselors, and specially trained volunteers care for the dying. The hospice team is available seven days a week, twenty-four hours a day.

What are some of the ways your parish works with people who are sick?

149

What Difference Does Faith Make in My Life?

At times you need to step back from your life and simply look at it. You need to examine your conscience. You need to ask the Holy Spirit to help you take an honest look at the ways you might need healing and that you bring healing to others.

Take a few minutes to think about things you have done and said that brought the gift of healing to people. Create some symbols to recall those moments of healing.

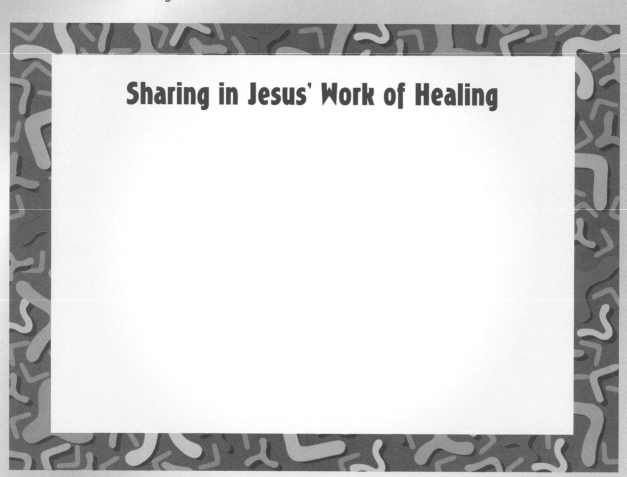

Sharing in Jesus' Work of Healing

My Faith Choice

This week I will be more aware of people and situations that need healing and offer help when I can. I will

_____

_____ .

We Pray

Prayer for the sick

Saint James tells us to pray for the sick. During the care for the sick and dying, the Church prays a brief form of the Litany of the Saints. Think of people you know or have heard about who are sick.

Leader:	**All:**
Holy Mary, Mother of God,	pray for _____.
Saint Joseph,	pray for _____.
Saint Peter,	pray for _____.
Saint James,	pray for _____.
Saint Mary Magdalene,	pray for _____.
Saint Frances Cabrini,	pray for _____.
Saint Paul of the Cross,	pray for _____.
Saint Martin de Porres,	pray for _____.
Saint Terese of the Andes,	pray for _____.

We Remember

The words needed to complete the sentences are hidden in the puzzle. Find and circle the words. Then complete the sentences.

```
K L A X W O G H A K
O T P Q M M F T H O
S S G F O Q I X E D
L C R R R R A N A E
Q B A P T I S M L Y
K S C L A G R E I P
R T E E L I L L N Z
L A E S P A M I G T
```

1. The first sacrament of forgiveness is _____.

2. _____ sins must be confessed in Reconciliation.

3. In Anointing of the Sick we receive the _____ to face our sufferings.

4. In the sacrament of Anointing of the Sick, Christ continues his work of _____ among us.

To Help You Remember

1. Jesus continues this work of healing through the two Sacraments of Healing, Reconciliation and Anointing of the Sick.

2. Reconciliation is the sacrament through which we receive God's forgiveness for the sins we commit after we have been baptized.

3. Anointing of the Sick is the sacrament that strengthens our faith and trust in God when we are seriously ill or dying.

This Week . . .

In chapter 17, "Sacraments of Healing," your child learned more about the two Sacraments of Healing, Reconciliation and Anointing of the Sick. Through Reconciliation we receive forgiveness for sins committed after Baptism. Confession of sins, contrition (or sorrow), penance, and absolution are always a part of the celebration of this sacrament. Throughout his life on earth, Jesus not only healed people physically but also spiritually. Through Anointing of the Sick, Christ continues his healing ministry today with the seriously sick, those weak because of old age, and the dying.

For more on the teachings of the Catholic Church on the Sacraments of Healing, see *Catechism of the Catholic Church* paragraph numbers 1420–1484 and 1499–1525.

Sharing God's Word

Read together John 20:21–23. Emphasize that Jesus gave the Church the power to forgive sins.

Praying

In this chapter your child prayed for the sick, using a form of the Litany of the Saints. Read and pray together this prayer on page 151.

Making a Difference

Choose one of the following activities to do as a family or design a similar activity of your own.

- Talk about the ways your family cares for one another when you are sick. Include the ways you show your care for grandparents, aunts and uncles, and other relatives.

- Find out more about what your parish does to care for the sick and dying. Choose one thing your family can do to reach out to someone who is sick or dying.

- Read Matthew 22:34–40, Matthew 5:1–12, Isaiah 1:10–18, Ephesians 5:1–14. Talk about what the passages teach about forgiveness.

For more ideas on ways your family can live your faith, visit the "Faith First for Families" page at **www.FaithFirst.com**. Click on "Family Prayer" and pray the prayer as a family this week.

Sacraments at the Service of Communion

We Pray

Let your face shine on your
    servant;
    save me in your kindness.
                    PSALM 31:17

God our Father,
may your Church
be for all the world
a sign of your unity
and holiness.   Amen.

*What is one way you see married
couples serving the people of
your parish?*

People very often measure
success by power and wealth.
Being successful in Jesus' eyes
means being a servant just as
he was. The Church celebrates
the sacraments of Holy Orders
and Matrimony to consecrate
some of her members to serve
the Church.

*What is one way you see priests
serving the people of your
parish?*

Called to Serve the Whole Church

Faith Focus

Why do we call Holy Orders and Matrimony Sacraments at the Service of Communion?

Faith Vocabulary

Sacraments at the Service of Communion. The two sacraments of Holy Orders and Matrimony.

communion. A word meaning "sharing with"; the unity in Christ of all the members of the Church, the Body of Christ.

The Service of God and His People

Jesus has set a standard for success that is quite different than the standard the world sets. He says:

"You know that those who are recognized as rulers over the Gentiles lord it over them, and their great ones make their authority over them felt. But it shall not be so among you. Rather, whoever wishes to be great among you will be your servant; whoever wishes to be first among you will be the slave of all. For the Son of Man did not come to be served but to serve and to give his life as a ransom for many."

MARK 10:42–45

To serve God and others as Jesus did means that we must be ready to make sacrifices. To serve as Jesus did means that we strive to serve others by giving ourselves as Jesus did.

The **Sacraments at the Service of Communion,** Matrimony and Holy Orders, consecrate, or set apart, members of the Church to serve the Church, the **communion** of believers in Christ. Married couples give themselves to each other and to the community of faith. Bishops, priests, and deacons dedicate their lives for the benefit of the whole Church. Married and ordained Catholics serve God and the People of God, the Church.

Use the letters of the word, SACRIFICE to describe some of the things you can do to serve others as Jesus did.

S _____
A _____
C _____
R _____
I _____
F _____
I _____
C _____
E _____

Faith-Filled People

The Apostles

The bishops of the Church are the successors of the Apostles. The first Apostles Jesus chose were Peter, John, and his brother James (known as James the Greater), Andrew, Matthew, Philip, Bartholomew, Thomas, James (the son of Alphaeus and also known as James the Less), Thaddeus, Simon, and Judas. After the Resurrection and Ascension of Jesus, Paul and Barnabas were named Apostles.

Holy Orders

Jesus Christ is the one true priest. The baptized can share in the priesthood of Christ in two ways. There is the priesthood of all the faithful and the ordained priesthood. Every Christian is joined to Christ in Baptism and is called to live a life of generous service to God and others as Jesus did.

Holy Orders is the sacrament in which a baptized man shares in the priesthood of Christ in a unique way as a bishop, priest, or deacon.

Bishops continue the ministry of the Apostles. They work in communion with the pope, the successor of Saint Peter the Apostle. Helped by priests, their co-workers, and by deacons, bishops have the duty to authentically teach the faith; celebrate divine worship, above all the Eucharist; and guide their churches as true pastors. Together with the pope, the bishops share in the responsibility for Christ's Church throughout the world.

Describe several ways you see a bishop, priest, or deacon serving the Church. Ask your parish priest how you might help him serve the people of your parish.

155

Matrimony

Matrimony is the sacrament in which a baptized man and a baptized woman join themselves to each other in a lifelong bond of faithful love. They become a sign of Christ's love for the Church. Christian married love, like Christ's love for the Church, is a faithful and lifelong love. It is a sign of the faithful and unbreakable love of God for people.

Christian married couples are to love and serve one another, their children, and others as Christ did. Husbands are to love their wives. Wives are to love their husbands. Parents are to cherish their children and show their children how to live as Christ's followers by the example of their love.

Look at the pictures. Tell how each family is a sign of Christ's love.

1. _____
   _____

2. _____
   _____

3. _____
   _____

Our Church Makes a Difference

The Christian Family, a Domestic Church

When husbands and wives nurture and cherish each other, they become a living sacrament. They become a living sign through which Christ works in the world.

Christian families form a domestic church, the "church of the home." They listen to God's word, pray together, and serve one another with generosity and compassion.

When Christian families serve one another, they are signs of God's loving presence with us. They become living signs that all the baptized are called to serve as Jesus did. They become living signs of God's saving presence among all people and invite everyone to love and serve God and one another as the one family of God.

Describe some of the things the families of your parish are doing that show what it means to be a Christian family.

What Difference Does Faith Make in My Life?

Living your new life in Christ in service to others brings you closer to God and to other people.

Make a check next to those things you can do to be a sign of Christ's love.

I Make a Difference

☐ Read the Bible to a younger brother, sister, or student.

☐ Take part in a neighborhood clean up project.

☐ Criticize my friends for helping out after school.

☐ Ask my parents how I can help them.

Write two more examples of your own.

☐ _____

☐ _____

My Faith Choice

This week I will live my baptismal call to serve others as Jesus did. I will

_____

_____ .

We Pray

A Prayer for Married People

At the sacrament of Matrimony the Church prays for the newly married couple. Our prayers for married couples help them live their vocation to be signs of Christ's love in the world.

Leader: Let us pray for all who have been consecrated in the sacrament of Matrimony to serve the Church.

Reader 1: May the peace of Christ live in their homes.
May they have true friends to help them.
May they be ready to help all who are in need.

All: **Bless them, O Lord.**

Reader 2: May they enjoy their work.
May they solve their daily problems.
May they not care too much about material things.

All: **Bless them, O Lord.**

Leader: May God reward them with a long life and with eternal happiness.

All: **Amen.** ADAPTED FROM THE RITE OF MARRIAGE

We Remember

Fill in the circle next to the word or phrase that completes each sentence correctly.

1. The word _____ is used to point out the sharing of Christians in the life of Christ.

    ○ sacrifice   ○ communion   ○ service   ○ Gentiles

2. The priesthood of all the faithful refers to the sacrament of _____.

    ○ Marriage   ○ Eucharist   ○ Baptism   ○ Holy Orders

3. The ordained priesthood refers to the sacrament of _____.

    ○ Marriage   ○ Eucharist   ○ Baptism   ○ Holy Orders

4. Christian marriage, like _____ love for his Church, is a faithful and lifelong love.

    ○ the pope's   ○ Christ's   ○ the bishop's   ○ the pastor's

To Help You Remember

1. Married and ordained Catholics are living signs that all the baptized are called to serve one another as Christ served his Father and others.

2. Holy Orders consecrates a baptized man to serve the whole Church as a bishop, priest, or deacon.

3. Matrimony unites a baptized man and a baptized woman to be a living sign of Christ's love for the Church.

This Week . . .

In chapter 18, "Sacraments at the Service of Communion," your child learned about the vocation of all the baptized to serve others as Jesus did. While all the baptized are to live this vocation, or calling, God calls some members of the Church to serve the whole community of the Church. Holy Orders and Matrimony are called Sacraments at the Service of Communion. In Holy Orders a baptized man is ordained as a bishop, priest, or deacon to serve the whole Church by continuing the unique work Jesus entrusted to the Apostles. In Matrimony a baptized man and a baptized woman are united in a lifelong bond of faithful love as a sign of Christ's love for the Church.

For more on the teachings of the Catholic Church on the Sacraments at the Service of Communion, see *Catechism of the Catholic Church* paragraph numbers 1533–1589 and 1601–1658.

Sharing God's Word

Read together Mark 10:42–45. Emphasize that each of us receives a special call or vocation from God to serve God and the whole community of the People of God, the Church.

Praying

In this chapter your child prayed a prayer from the rite of Marriage. Read and pray together the prayer on page 159.

Making a Difference

Choose one of the following activities to do as a family or design a similar activity of your own.

• Talk about the ways your family can or already does serve others as Jesus did. Choose one thing you will do together this week.

• Look in your church bulletin to see all the ways your parish serves others. If there are ministries you do not know anything about, take time to find out about them.

• The Christian family is called the church of the home. What are some of the things your family does that the whole Church does? Discuss ways you learn about Jesus, ways you pray, and ways you live the Gospel.

For more ideas on ways your family can live your faith, visit the "Faith First for Families" page at **www.FaithFirst.com**. Click on "Make a Difference" for ideas on how your family can share God's love with others this week.

Name _____

A. The Best Response

Read each question and statement and circle the best answer.

1. What are the seven sacraments?
   - a. Beatitudes
   - b. Corporal Works of Mercy
   - c. main liturgical signs of the Church
   - d. main liturgical seasons of the Church's year

2. Which season of the Church's year celebrates the Resurrection of Jesus?
   - a. Advent
   - b. Christmas
   - c. Lent
   - d. Easter

3. What are rituals?
   - a. codes for happiness
   - b. creeds of the Church
   - c. words and actions used in the celebration of the liturgy
   - d. ways of living the Commandments

4. Which sacrament is a Sacrament of Christian Initiation?
   - a. Confirmation
   - b. Reconciliation
   - c. Matrimony
   - d. Holy Orders

5. Which sacrament uses the rite of anointing?
   - a. Eucharist
   - b. Reconciliation
   - c. Matrimony
   - d. Holy Orders

6. What are the two main parts of the Mass?
   - a. Introductory rites and Liturgy of the Word
   - b. Homily and Prayer of the Faithful
   - c. Eucharistic Prayer and Communion Rite
   - d. Liturgy of the Word and Liturgy of the Eucharist

7. The parable of the Great Feast is about the _____.
   - a. kingdom of God
   - b. Beatitudes
   - c. Ten Commandments
   - d. seven sacraments

8. Which sacrament strengthens our faith and trust in God when we are ill?
   - a. Holy Orders
   - b. Anointing of the Sick
   - c. Reconciliation
   - d. Matrimony

9. What are the Sacraments at the Service of Communion?
   - a. Baptism and Holy Orders
   - b. Confirmation and Holy Orders
   - c. Eucharist and Holy Orders
   - d. Matrimony and Holy Orders

10. Which of these is a Sacrament of Healing?
    - a. Holy Orders
    - b. Reconciliation
    - c. Confirmation
    - d. all of the above

B. Completing the Paragraph

Fill in the blanks in the paragraph by using the terms in the word bank.

> Last Supper   salvation   Holy Communion
>
> Word   sacraments   Paschal Mystery

The story of God's loving plan of creation and _____

in Jesus Christ is proclaimed and celebrated by the Church in the

_____. Through rituals, the Church celebrates the

liturgy, and we are made sharers in the _____ of Jesus

Christ. The sacrament of the Eucharist is celebrated at Mass. During the Liturgy

of the _____, we listen to readings from the Bible. During the

Liturgy of the Eucharist, we do what Jesus did at the _____.

The bread and wine become the Body and Blood of Christ, and we receive the gift

of the Body and Blood of Jesus in _____.

C. What I Have Learned

Write three things you learned in this unit.
Share them with the group.

_____

_____

_____

Look at the faith terms in "Words to Know" on page 96.
Circle the terms you know now.

D. From a Scripture Story

*In the parable of the Great Feast, Jesus teaches what it
means to be invited to the kingdom of God. Describe what
happens in the parable and who is invited.*

What Happens	Who Is Invited
_____	_____
_____	_____
_____	_____

Unit 3 • We Live

How do we show that we share in God's holiness?

163

Getting Ready

What I Have Learned

What is something you already know about these faith terms?

Moral decisions

_____

_____

Virtues

_____

_____

Natural law

_____

_____

Words to Know

Put an X next to the faith terms you know. Put a ? next to the faith terms you need to know more about.

Faith Vocabulary

_____ holiness

_____ theological virtues

_____ morality

_____ capital sins

_____ natural law

_____ justice

_____ moral decisions

_____ venial sins

Questions I Have

What questions would you like to ask about making moral decisions?

_____

_____

_____

_____

A Scripture Story

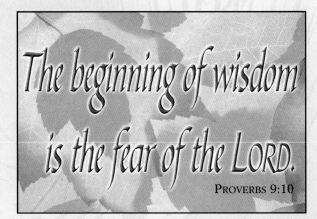

The beginning of wisdom is the fear of the LORD.

PROVERBS 9:10

A proverb from the Book of Proverbs

What does the Book of Proverbs in the Old Testament teach us about living as children of God?

Our Call to Holiness

We Pray

Exalt the LORD, our God; . . .
    holy is the LORD, our God.
                                    PSALM 99:9

God our Father,
you alone are holy.
You sent your Son, Jesus,
to restore us to holiness.
Send the Holy Spirit
to help us become
the holy people
you call us to be.   Amen.

What is something unique about yourself?

Every person is both different from every other person and the same in a unique way. Everyone is created in the image and likeness of God to be holy.

What does it mean to be created in the image and likeness of God?

165

Called to Be Saints

Faith Focus

What does it mean to say that everyone is called to live a holy life?

Faith Vocabulary

holiness. The quality, or condition, of a person who is living in communion and in the right relationship with God, with others, and with all of his creation; being in the state of grace.

theological virtues. The virtues of faith, hope, and love (charity); gifts of God that enable us to live a life of holiness, or a life in communion with the Holy Trinity.

Be Holy

Our life's job description is to share in God's **holiness**. God's command to the Israelites is a command to all his people:

"For I, the LORD, am your God; and you shall make and keep yourselves holy, because I am holy. . . . Since I, the LORD, brought you up from the land of Egypt that I might be your God, you shall be holy, because I am holy." LEVITICUS 11:44–45

God created us to be holy as he is holy. He created us to know him, to love him, to serve him, and to live with him forever in eternal happiness.

The ability and freedom to live a holy life is a gift from God. God not only invites us to live a life in communion with him, but also gives us the powers to live that life. He gives us the **theological virtues**, which help us live as his children.

The theological virtues enable us to grow stronger in the God-life that dwells within us. They are those strengths that begin in God and direct us toward holiness.

There are three theological virtues. They are faith, hope, and love (charity). These three virtues connect us with God—Father, Son, and Holy Spirit—in a very direct way. The more we let these virtues take hold of our lives, the more we grow in holiness.

What can you do to show that the theological virtues are at work in your life? Draw or describe an action for each virtue.

A Life of Faith, Hope, and Love

Faith

Hope

Love

Faith-Filled People

Job

The story of Job is told in the Old Testament. Job was wealthy and faithful to God. He lost all his wealth and became ill with a serious disease. In all of this trouble he did not blame or reject God as his friends tried to convince him to do. Job is a story of grace and freedom and of faith and hope.

Grace and Freedom

Before Christ's life, Passion, death, Resurrection, and glorious Ascension, humanity was under the power of sin and death. With Christ, everything changed. By dying, he destroyed our death and freed us from sin's power. By rising from the dead, he restored our life of holiness.

Grace. At Baptism we are joined to Christ and are made sharers in his work of salvation and redemption. We receive the grace of holiness and are made right with God the Father in Christ. We receive the gift of the Holy Spirit to live holy lives.

God freely gives us the gift of salvation in Christ. It is not something we could ever earn on our own. With the grace of the Holy Spirit, we are made holy again. We call this grace "sanctifying grace."

Freedom of the Children of God. The grace of the Holy Spirit calls us to use the gift of freedom from sin's power responsibly and to grow in holiness. With the grace of the Holy Spirit, we grow in our ability to make the right choices and live as adopted children of God the Father. We turn toward God and away from sin. We accept forgiveness and the gift of having our communion and life with God restored.

Look at the pictures. How are the people in the pictures answering God's call to holiness?

167

_____

_____

_____

_____

_____

_____

_____

_____

_____

Growth in Holiness

God's gift of holiness is not just for us as individuals. It is not something we keep for ourselves. As God shares his life and love with us, we also share our life and love with others. Our growth in holiness involves the way that we live with other people. Holiness is about how we act with others.

Put on then, as God's chosen ones, holy and beloved, heartfelt compassion, kindness, humility, gentleness, and patience, bearing with one another and forgiving one another. . . . And over all these put on love, that is, the bond of perfection.

COLOSSIANS 3:12–14

The Church gives us the Spiritual and Corporal Works of Mercy to guide us in living the life of mercy and compassion that Saint Paul describes. The Church's teaching on social justice, in turn, guides us in living the works of mercy. The works of mercy are concrete, practical things we are to do to live the Gospel. They clearly show that holiness is not just an idea. It is something that we must practice every day. It is a life of true courage, a life that requires God's grace.

Look at the list of Corporal and Spiritual Works of Mercy. Under each picture write the work of mercy it illustrates. In the space on the right draw or write about yourself living one of the works of mercy.

Corporal Works of Mercy

Feed people who are hungry.
Give drink to people who are thirsty.
Clothe people who need clothes.
Visit prisoners.
Shelter people who are homeless.
Visit people who are sick.
Bury people who have died.

Spiritual Works of Mercy

Help people who sin.
Teach people who are ignorant.
Give advice to people who have doubts.
Comfort people who suffer.
Be patient with other people.
Forgive people who hurt you.
Pray for people who are alive and for those who have died.

Our Church Makes a Difference

Volunteers gleaning sweet potatoes, North Carolina Yam Jam

The Gleaning Network

Heroes and saints are not the only ones to take up the challenge to feed the poor and live the works of mercy. People in Catholic parish communities all over the world are working every day to help those in need.

The Gleaning Network is an organization that responds to the needs of many people who are without food. Its thirty-two thousand volunteers provide more than twenty-seven million servings of nourishing food to feed America's hungry each year.

The Gleaners in the Midwest saw that their fertile region produced an abundance of crops, such as tomatoes, oranges, onions, and carrots. Some of this food went to waste. The Gleaners contacted local farmers, who helped them collect the unused crops. The Gleaners grew larger and larger, involved members of other churches, and they purchased their own buildings. They now bring in fresh produce and canned goods from grocery stores and from food drives. They distribute food not just to people in their own community but to the needy throughout the county in which they live.

Remember Ruth in the Old Testament who stood by her mother-in-law, Naomi? The Gleaners chose their name to honor Ruth, who gleaned the fields for crops that were not harvested to support herself and Naomi.

Who do you see living the works of mercy? Tell what they do.

What Difference Does Faith Make in My Life?

God created you to be holy. Living the works of mercy is one way you can strive to live a holy life.

Develop a list of three activities that you could do with others that would help you live a holy life. Choose one and draw up a plan to put it into action.

Signs of a Holy Life

1. _____

_____

2. _____

_____

3. _____

_____

Our Plan

_____

_____

_____

_____

My Faith Choice

This week I will show that I believe I am called to live a life of holiness. I will

_____

_____.

The Road Ahead

The road to living a holy life is not always an easy road to travel. But God always leads us along that road. Quiet yourself. Place your trust in God and quietly pray this prayer.

My Lord,
I have no idea of where I am going.
I do not see the road ahead of me.
I cannot know for certain where it will end.
I hope that I have the desire to please you
in all that I am doing.
And I know that if I do this,
you will lead me by the right road.
Therefore I will trust you.
I will not fear, for you are ever with me,
and you will never leave me.

Adapted from "The Road Ahead"
by Thomas Merton

We Remember

Match each faith term with its description.

Faith Terms

_____ **1.** holiness

_____ **2.** virtues

_____ **3.** faith

_____ **4.** hope

_____ **5.** love

Descriptions

a. the virtue by which we love God above all else and love our neighbor as ourselves

b. good habits that enable us to grow stronger in the God-life that dwells within us

c. the virtue by which we believe in God

d. God's presence in us and our fidelity to God

e. the virtue by which we trust that God is looking after us

To Help You Remember

1. The theological virtues connect us with God and strengthen us to live a life of holiness in communion with God.

2. The grace of the Holy Spirit helps us grow in our ability to freely make choices to grow in holiness.

3. Living the works of mercy is a sign we are trying to live holy lives.

This Week . . .

In chapter 19, "Our Call to Holiness," your child learned more about the call of God to every person to live a holy life. Every person is created in the image and likeness of God. Made sharers in the life of Christ at Baptism, Christians are called to live the way of holiness Jesus lived and taught his disciples to live. Through Baptism we receive the gift of sanctifying grace. We are made sharers in the life and love of God the Father, the Son, and the Holy Spirit. We are joined to Christ and receive the gift of the Holy Spirit and the help to live as adopted sons and daughters of God the Father. God created us with free will and gives us the gift of faith to accept his invitation to live holy lives. Living the Corporal and Spiritual Works of Mercy is one way that we cooperate with the Holy Spirit and strive to live holy lives.

For more on the teachings of the Catholic Church on grace and the universal call to holiness, see *Catechism of the Catholic Church* paragraph numbers 1699–1742, 1803–1832, and 1987–2016.

Sharing God's Word

Read together Leviticus 11:44–45. Emphasize that every person created by God is to live a holy life.

Praying

In this chapter your child quietly prayed a prayer of trust in God. Read and pray together this prayer on page 171.

Making a Difference

Choose one of the following activities to do as a family or design a similar activity of your own.

- Write a family pledge to live holy lives. Be sure that the pledge describes specific behaviors and attitudes that constitute holiness.

- Make a holiness banner. Use the word *holiness*. Decorate the banner and hang it where it can remind all family members of their call to live holy lives.

- Pray the prayer of trust on page 171 as your family prayer this week. This prayer will remind the whole family that God is with you as you journey the road of holiness.

For more ideas on ways your family can live your faith, visit the "Faith First for Families" page at **www.FaithFirst.com**. Click on "Contemporary Issues" to find an article on an especially interesting topic.

Making Moral Choices

20

We Pray

I bless the LORD
who counsels me. . . .
I keep the LORD always
before me.   PSALM 16:7, 8

**God our Father and
Creator, send us your
Holy Spirit to enlighten our
minds and to strengthen
our wills so that we may
walk in the way of Jesus
Christ, your Son.   Amen.**

*What are some skills that you
would like to develop?*

When we need to learn and
develop athletic, dance, or
musical skills, we go to an
instructor and watch performers
who excel at those skills. The
same is true about growing in
the skills that enable us to
make better moral decisions.

*What steps do you follow to learn
how to make good decisions to
live a holy life?*

Morality

Faith Vocabulary

moral decisions. The decisions and choices we make to live as children of God and disciples of Jesus Christ.

morality. A way of judging, or evaluating, whether our choices lead us to God or away from God.

The Sources of Morality

Our moral life is a journey of faith. Where do we go when we need information about making wise **moral decisions**? Moral decisions are decisions we make to live holy lives as disciples of Jesus Christ. Here are some practical starting points we look to:

- the natural law, or the laws inscribed in creation and written in the human heart; for example, "Do good and not evil" and "Treat others as you want them to treat you";
- the Bible, especially the Great Commandment and the Ten Commandments;
- the life and teachings of Jesus;
- the teachings of the Church.

Knowing what determines the **morality**, that is, the goodness or evil of human acts, will also help us make wise moral decisions. Three things determine the morality of an act. They are the object of the act, the intention of the act, and the circumstances surrounding the act.

Object. The object of the act is what we do. It is the good or the bad we do or say. Some things are good in themselves, such as praying. Other things, such as abusing drugs, are evil in themselves.

Intention. The intention of the act is what we want, or our purpose for doing or saying something. A good intention cannot change an evil act into something good. For example, if we steal something to give it to someone as a gift, the act of stealing is still wrong, even though we had a good intention.

Circumstances. The circumstances of the act are those things that surround the decision. Circumstances do not change the goodness or evil of an act, but might make a difference. Circumstances can make something we do or say better or worse. For example, we might tell a lie because we do not want to hurt someone's feelings. The circumstance is kindness. The act of lying is still wrong. The circumstance may make the act of lying less evil. The better choice, of course, is not to lie.

Give examples of circumstances that might make it difficult for people to choose to do something they know is right.

Conscience

Our life is filled with so many things that compete for our attention. Every human being has another voice that constantly calls for our attention. It is our conscience. Our conscience helps us judge what is right and what is wrong. It is important that we train our conscience. We have the responsibility to obey our conscience. The better we train, or form, a good conscience, the better we will be at making decisions that help us live as followers of Jesus Christ.

Not everyone forms a good conscience. People can have a conscience that does not know what is right or wrong. A conscience that is not well formed can lead a person to make wrong moral decisions. A conscience that is not well formed is called an erroneous conscience. When a person deliberately does not work at forming a good conscience, they are forming an erroneous conscience, or a conscience filled with errors and mistakes. Because a person is responsible for their erroneous conscience, they are also responsible for the wrong caused by their actions and for the consequences of their actions.

Solve this dilemma: Your friend approaches you and shows you a pack of firecrackers and a lighter.

What to Do?

1. What is your first reaction?

2. What will you do?

3. Why would you do it?

4. What might be the consequences of your decision?

Sin

The choices we make are not always easy. Sometimes we come close to doing what we know is against God's Law and choose not to do it. At other times we give in to temptation and choose to do something that we know is just plain wrong.

We sin when we deliberately turn away from God and offend him. To help us understand more clearly what sin is all about, the Church speaks about capital sins, mortal sins, and venial sins.

Capital Sins. Capital sins are sins that lead to other sins. There are seven capitals sins. They are pride, covetousness, envy, anger, gluttony, lust, and sloth.

Mortal Sins. Mortal sins are serious offenses against God that break our relationship with him. If we die in this state of separation from God, we remain separated from him forever by our own choice. Being forever separated from God is what we call hell.

Venial Sins. Venial sins are less serious offenses against God. Because all sin turns our heart away from God's love, we should seek forgiveness of all sins, including venial sins.

Jesus died on the cross for our sins. As much as we must be aware of our sins, we must be even more aware of God's mercy and forgiveness.

Write a prayer thanking God for his forgiveness.

Forgiveness   Yurushi   Danh từ

_____

_____

_____

_____

_____

_____

_____

_____

Perdón   Wybaczenie   Perdono

Our Church Makes a Difference

Saint John Bosco

The history of the Church is filled with people like John (Don) Bosco who helped others learn to make good choices. After he was ordained a priest, Don Bosco studied the lives of people living in poverty in large cities. He tried to find out the answer to the question, How does living in poverty in a large city affect the moral decisions people make?

Don Bosco came to realize that many people living in poverty in cities did not have the opportunities for a good education and a good job. Because education is an important part of training ourselves in making moral decisions, Don Bosco decided to create job training programs and professional schools. All the programs in the schools founded by Don Bosco were founded on three values: reason, religion, and kindness.

Many religious priests, brothers, and sisters as well as lay volunteers carry on the work of Saint John Bosco today in more than two hundred schools around the world.

Who helps you learn to make good moral choices?

Saint John Bosco (1815–1888) teaching, stained glass

What Difference Does Faith Make in My Life?

Many of the moral decisions you make are not always easy ones. The Holy Spirit is always with you to teach you and to guide you to make good decisions. God has also created you and every person with a conscience. Your conscience helps you judge what is good and what is evil.

Look over this list of conscience builders. Mark a ✔ next to the actions you use to help build, or form, a good conscience.

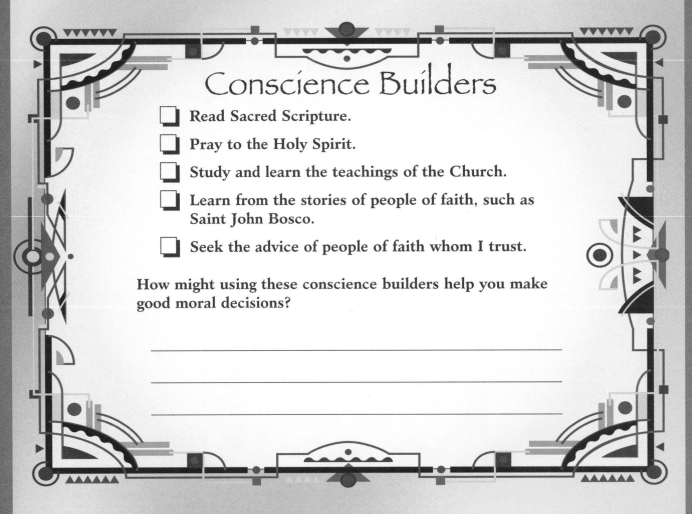

Conscience Builders

- [ ] Read Sacred Scripture.
- [ ] Pray to the Holy Spirit.
- [ ] Study and learn the teachings of the Church.
- [ ] Learn from the stories of people of faith, such as Saint John Bosco.
- [ ] Seek the advice of people of faith whom I trust.

How might using these conscience builders help you make good moral decisions?

_____

_____

_____

My Faith Choice

This week I will try to make moral decisions thoughtfully and responsibly. I will

_____

_____.

An Examination of Conscience

It is important to think about and evaluate our moral decisions.
One way we do this is by examining our conscience.

Leader: Let us look into our hearts and think about the way we have loved or failed to love God and our neighbors as Jesus taught.

All: **Lord, I keep you always before me;**
You will show me the path to life. BASED ON PSALM 116:8, 9

Leader: Reflect in silence after each question.

Reader: How have I kept God first in my life?
(Pause.)

Reader: How have I shown respect to my parents and teachers?
(Pause.)

Reader: How have I been kind and helpful to other people?
(Pause.)

Reader: How have my words and actions shown respect for my body and the bodies of others?
(Pause.)

All: **Lord, I keep you always before me;**
You will show me the path to life. BASED ON PSALM 116:8, 9

We Remember

Read this situation. Name the object, intention, and circumstances of the act. Then discuss the morality of the act.

Sarah and her teammates were playing in the championship game. In the final minutes of the game, Sarah swept by the defender. As she kicked the ball trying to break the 0–0 score, she slipped on the wet grass, and the ball struck the goalkeeper in the face. Stunned from the fall, she looked toward the goal and saw the goalkeeper running toward her.

Object _____

_____

Intention _____

_____

Circumstances _____

_____

To Help You Remember

1. The sources of the morality of our actions are the object of the act, the intention of the act, and the circumstances surrounding the act.

2. Our conscience helps us judge whether an act is good or evil.

3. Sin is turning away from God, freely choosing to do or say what we know is against God's Law.

This Week . . .

In chapter 20, "Making Moral Choices," your child learned about the importance of making moral decisions. We journey through life as a member of the Church, which guides us in making wise decisions to live as faithful followers of Jesus Christ. The things that determine the morality of our acts are the good or evil deed we choose; the intention, or purpose, of doing the act; and the circumstances surrounding the act. A good conscience helps us judge whether an act is good or evil. When we freely and knowingly choose an act that we know is evil, we sin. We turn away from God and offend God.

For more on the teachings of the Catholic Church on conscience, sin, and making moral decisions, see *Catechism of the Catholic Church* paragraph numbers 1749–1794 and 1846–1869.

Sharing God's Word

Read together Psalm 119:1–8. Emphasize that living the Ten Commandments guides us in loving God and our neighbors.

Praying

In this chapter your child used an examination of conscience. Read and use the examination of conscience on page 179 or another form of an examination of conscience.

Making a Difference

Choose one of the following activities to do as a family or design a similar activity of your own.

- Read the statement, "Right is right even if everyone is against it; and wrong is wrong even if everyone is for it." Discuss how the statement applies to making moral decisions.

- Discuss the following questions: What circumstances might make it difficult for people to choose to do what they know is right? What can we do to help us choose to do what we know is right?

For more ideas on ways your family can live your faith, visit the "Faith First for Families" page at **www.FaithFirst.com**. Click on "Family Prayer." Plan to pray this prayer together this week.

Loving God

21

We Pray

The precepts of the LORD
   are right,
   rejoicing the heart.
                    PSALM 19:9

My God,
I love you above all else
because you are all good
and worthy of my love.
                    Amen.

What signs let you know what is important to people?

Think about the people you see every day. From what you see people doing or hear them saying, what seems to be most important to them? Is it God, or is it someone or something other than God?

How can you tell that a person places God first?

Faithfully Living as Children of God

Faith Focus

How do the first three Commandments guide us to love God above all else?

Faith Vocabulary

precepts. Rules or laws that detail responsibilities and impose standards of conduct.

worship. Honor and respect we give to God above all else; faith in, hope in, and love for God above all else.

The Natural Law

We have been created in the image and likeness of God. In God's fatherly love for us, he has etched into our hearts and minds a law, a pattern or design, that helps us live as images of God.

This law helps us discover the way to the true happiness that God has promised us, and to recognize the evil that leads us away from that happiness and away from God. There is something about the way God has created us that moves us naturally, or by nature, to choose what is good for us and others. The Church calls it the natural law.

What are some of the principles, or **precepts**, of this natural law? Here are three.
- Do good and avoid evil.
- Tell the truth to each other.
- Be respectful toward one another.

What others can you think of?

The Ten Commandments

When God entered into the Covenant with Moses and the Israelites, he gave Moses the Ten Commandments. The Commandments reminded the people of the laws he had written on their hearts. They named the ways God wanted his people to live.

Jesus told his disciples they were to live the Commandments. He said that he came to fulfill the Commandments and not to do away with them. Jesus told us to live the Commandments as he did. We are to love God and one another as he did.

Create a bookmark that shows reverence for the name of God. Share it with a friend or a family member.

182

New citizens taking oath at naturalization ceremony

Faith-Filled People

Moses

Moses believed in God above all else. While Moses was on Mount Sinai, the people persuaded Aaron, the brother of Moses, to gather and melt all the gold earrings the women were wearing and create a golden calf to worship. Aaron and the people worshiped the golden calf as the god who freed them from Egypt. Hearing the people dancing and singing, Moses came down from Sinai. He took the golden calf, threw it into the fire, and turned it into powder. (Read the entire account in Exodus 32.)

The First Commandment

I am the LORD your God; you shall not have strange gods before me.
BASED ON EXODUS 20:2–3

The First, Second, and Third Commandments teach us ways that we are to love God above all else. They teach us to love the Lord our God with our whole heart, soul, and mind (see Matthew 22:37).

This First Commandment teaches that we are to **worship** only God. We are to place our faith and hope in God and love him above all else.

This Commandment also warns us about god "substitutes," such things as drugs, alcohol, material possessions, power, and wealth. We all know how easy it is to worship these things and let them take over our lives.

The Second Commandment

You shall not take the name of the LORD, your God, in vain.   BASED ON EXODUS 20:7

The Second Commandment teaches that we are to use the name of God and the names of Mary, Jesus, and the saints reverently and respectfully. Blasphemy is the use of the names of God, of Jesus Christ, of the Virgin Mary, and of the saints in an offensive way.

This Commandment also teaches that we are to take an oath only when it is necessary, as in a court of law. Whenever we call God as our witness, we must tell the truth. To use the name of God or Jesus when we are angry, to show off, or to casually say "I swear to God," is against the Second Commandment.

Sunday is to be kept as the most important holy day of obligation. Catholics have the obligation to take part in Mass on Sunday and on other holy days of obligation. We rest from all work that is not necessary and that turns our hearts and minds away from God.

Name some of the ways that you can keep the Lord's Day holy. Log them on this daily planner.

The Third Commandment

Remember to keep holy the LORD's Day.
BASED ON EXODUS 20:8

In the Old Testament God rested from the work of creation on the seventh day, or the Sabbath. He commanded his people to do the same. The Sabbath is to be kept holy as the Lord's Day. It is to be set aside from all the other days of the week.

Sunday is the Lord's Day for Christians. It is the day on which the Lord Jesus was raised from the dead. It is the first day of the new creation of the world in Christ. It is the day on which we focus on keeping God first in our lives.

The Lord's Day!

Sunday

9:00 A.M.

12:00 P.M.

3:00 P.M.

6:00 P.M.

9:00 P.M.

Our Church Makes a Difference

The Collection at Mass

When we take part in the celebration of Mass, we show our love both for God and for others. The collection at Mass is one sign of that love. This ancient tradition of the Church is one way we generously show our thanks to God and provide for the material needs of the Church.

In the early Church, wealthy people gave money to the Church. Others brought cheese, handwoven cloth, grain, animals, vegetables, bread, and other goods. After gathering at the entrance of the church, they walked in procession to an area near the altar where they left their gifts. After the celebration of the Mass concluded, these gifts were brought and shared with people in need.

What can you contribute to support your parish and the needs of the poor? What do you do now? What more can you do?

Our Catholic Identity

World Mission Sunday

Each year the Church celebrates World Mission Sunday. On that Sunday a special collection is taken up in Catholic Churches. This collection supports the Society for the Propagation of the Faith. The funds collected help mission bishops build churches and chapels, train and support catechists, build health clinics, house and feed missionaries, and many other works. All these works help the Church fulfill Jesus' command, "Go into the whole world and proclaim the gospel to every creature" (Mark 16:15).

What Difference Does Faith Make in My Life?

The Holy Spirit is always inviting you to place your faith, hope, and love in the Holy Trinity above all else. This may not always be easy to do. Many people and things try to take the place of God in your life. It is important that you recognize who these people and things might be.

On the pedestal, describe something that could make it difficult for you to place your trust in God. Then write how you can overcome that obstacle.

Name That Idol

Keeping God First

_____

_____

_____

_____

_____

_____

_____

_____

_____

My Faith Choice

This week I will make God number one in my life. I will

_____

_____.

We Pray

Shema

The Shema is prayed as a morning and evening prayer by Jewish people today. Praying the Shema is the ancient tradition found in the Old Testament.

Hear, Israel, the Lord is our God, the Lord is One.

Sh'ma Yisrael Adonai Elohaynu Adonai Echad.

Blessed be the Name of His glorious kingdom for ever and ever.

Barukh Shem k'vod malkhuto l'olam va-ed.

We Remember

Write First, Second, or Third beside the phrases that describe the Commandments.

_____ **A.** We call God to be our witness to the truth of what we are saying.

_____ **B.** We worship only God.

_____ **C.** Catholics take part in Mass on Sunday.

_____ **D.** We speak the name of God reverently and respectfully.

_____ **E.** We love God above all else.

To Help You Remember

1. The First Commandment teaches us to worship only God and to believe in, hope in, and love God above all else.

2. The Second Commandment teaches us to use the name of God reverently and respectfully.

3. The Third Commandment teaches us to keep the Lord's Day as a holy day, a day set aside for God. Sunday is the Lord's Day for Christians.

This Week . . .

In chapter 21, "Loving God," your child learned more about the first three Commandments. The First Commandment teaches us that we are to worship only God. We are to believe in, hope in, and love God above all else. God alone is and should always be at the center of our lives. The Second Commandment teaches that we are to honor the name of God. We are to speak the name of God reverently and respectfully. The Third Commandment teaches that we are to set aside one day each week as the Lord's Day. For Christians Sunday is the Lord's Day. It is the most important holy day of obligation. On Sundays Catholics have the obligation to take part in the Mass. We are to avoid all work that prevents us from keeping God at the center of our lives.

For more on the teachings of the Catholic Church on the First, Second, and Third Commandments, see *Catechism of the Catholic Church* paragraph numbers 2084–2132, 2142–2159, and 2168–2188.

Sharing God's Word

Read together Exodus 20:1–17. Emphasize that we give glory to God when we live the Ten Commandments.

Praying

In this chapter your child learned to pray the Shema, an ancient prayer of the Jewish people. Read and pray together this prayer on page 187.

Making a Difference

Choose one of the following activities to do as a family or design a similar activity of your own.

- Talk about how your family can make God number one in your lives. Choose one thing you will do together as a family this week to show that God is number one in your lives.

- When you take part in Mass on Sunday, you keep the Lord's Day holy. After you take part in Mass, do something special to keep Sunday as the Lord's Day.

- Create table placemats proclaiming Sunday as the Lord's Day. Use these placemats at your Saturday evening and Sunday family meals.

For more ideas on ways your family can live your faith, visit the "Faith First for Families" page at **www.FaithFirst.com**. Check out "Bible Stories." Read and discuss the Bible story this week.

Loving One Another

22

We Pray

Trust in the LORD and
do good.   PSALM 37:3

**Make known to me
your ways, LORD,
teach me your paths.**
                    Amen.

*What does it mean to be a
disciple of Christ?*

We sometimes ask "Why?"
when we are told or asked to
do something. But even if we
know "why," we often need to
know "how." At the Last
Supper, Jesus gave the answer
to the "how" behind his
teachings on how he wanted
his disciples to live. He said,
"[L]ove one another as I love
you" (John 15:12).

*What does it mean to love as
Jesus did?*

Loving Others and Ourselves

Faith Focus

What do the last seven Commandments teach us about living the second part of the Great Commandment?

Faith Vocabulary

covet. To unjustly desire what rightfully belongs to someone else.

justice. One of the moral, or cardinal, virtues; the good habit of giving to God and to all people what is rightfully due to them.

The Fourth Commandment

Honor your father and your mother. EXODUS 20:12

The Fourth Commandment commands that all family members are to contribute to the family's well-being. Children, even when they are adults, are to honor their parents. They are to respect and obey their parents and offer appropriate assistance when parents are in need. Parents are to teach that the first calling of a Christian is to follow Jesus Christ. They are to care for the physical and spiritual needs of their children. The Fourth Commandment also teaches, in a general way, about our responsibilities as citizens. As long as the authority follows God's Law, it must be obeyed for the common good of everyone.

The Fifth Commandment

You shall not kill. EXODUS 20:13

The principle underlying the Fifth Commandment is: All life is sacred. This Commandment teaches that we must protect and nurture all human life, from the first moment of its conception. We are to respect and care for our own lives, health, and bodies and those of others. We are to act safely and not put ourselves or others in unnecessary danger. We are to live as peacemakers.

The Fifth Commandment forbids (1) the abuse and misuse of food, alcohol, tobacco, or drugs; (2) the direct and intentional killing, or murder, of another human person, born or unborn; (3) the ending of our own life by suicide; (4) the ending of the lives of handicapped, sick, or dying persons; (5) bullying; (6) acts of terrorism or hostage-taking.

The command "not to kill," however, does not prohibit the defending of human life with appropriate force. All people have the right to live safely and securely. A nation may legitimately and justly defend the lives of its citizens. A person may use the force necessary to stop a person or people from unjustly harming him or her.

Jesus asks us to love our enemies. Read Matthew 5:38–41 and Luke 6:27–36. What does this teaching of Jesus tell us about living the Fifth Commandment?

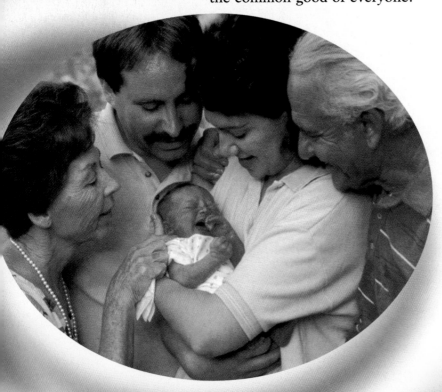

The Sixth Commandment

You shall not commit adultery. Exodus 20:14

The Sixth Commandment commands everyone to live a chaste life. It guides Christians to follow Christ as our model in the way we express our love and friendship with one another. We are always to use our sexuality in appropriate ways.

This Commandment also teaches about marriage. In their marriage commitment, a man and a woman promise to love, honor, and be faithful to each other until death. When a married person has sexual relations with someone other than his or her spouse, that person commits adultery. When adultery occurs, the marriage covenant is broken or seriously weakened. A spouse is treated unjustly, the family is damaged, children are hurt, and society suffers.

Among other sins gravely contrary to the Sixth Commandment are masturbation, fornication, pornography, sterilization and the use of unnatural means to prevent the conception of a child, and homosexual activity. Everyone experiences temptations to misuse their sexuality. To dwell on these thoughts and desires can easily lead us to a misuse of our sexuality. God's grace is always there to help us deal with these temptations.

The Ninth Commandment

You shall not covet your neighbor's wife. Exodus 20:17

The Ninth Commandment commands that everyone respect and honor the promises a man and a woman make to one another in marriage. We are not to do anything, not even desire to do anything, that would break up a marriage.

This Commandment also guides us to train ourselves to be pure in mind and heart, and in our actions. To **covet** something, which is one of the capital sins, is to have an unjust and inordinate desire for something that belongs to someone else.

Name a popular TV show or a popular song that depicts people in a relationship. Are the people in that relationship living according to the Commandments? How might the show or song affect people viewing or listening to it?

Faith-Filled People

Ruth and Boaz

When Ruth's husband died, she took care of her mother-in-law, Naomi. Ruth left her own homeland and took Naomi back to Bethlehem, where Naomi's family came from. Ruth worked in the fields owned by Boaz to feed herself and Naomi. Ruth and Boaz eventually married. Their son Obed was the grandfather of King David, who was an ancestor of Jesus.

The Seventh Commandment

You shall not steal. EXODUS 20:15

The Seventh Commandment commands that we live the virtues of **justice** and charity in our relationships with other people. We are to use the goods of the earth responsibly. How we treat the environment and use water and other natural resources has an impact not only on our own but on future generations.

This Commandment also teaches us about the importance of work. Our work is a participation in the work of God the Creator. Because we are joined to Christ in Baptism, our work is joined to his, and we give honor and glory to God.

This Commandment forbids stealing, cheating, misusing or damaging another's property, paying unjust wages, and treating people as if they were objects to be bought and sold. If we break this Commandment, we have the obligation to repair whatever damage we have caused or to restore what we have unjustly taken.

The Eighth Commandment

You shall not bear false witness against your neighbor. EXODUS 20:16

The Eighth Commandment is about truth. It commands that we live honest and truthful lives. We are to respect the good name of others.

Breaking this Commandment weakens our trust and respect for others. If we break it, we have the obligation to repair the damage that our misuse of the truth has caused. A person's good name is one of their most valued possessions. If we tell lies about a person by spreading false rumors or damaging gossip, we need to get the truth out.

The Tenth Commandment

You shall not covet your neighbor's goods.
BASED ON EXODUS 20:17

The Tenth Commandment commands us to treat others fairly and justly. We are to share the blessings God has given us with others. We are to avoid greed and envy and to be thankful and generous with what we have. Our blessings and the blessings others enjoy are all gifts from God.

What do we mean by the expression "Honesty is the best policy"?

Honesty is the best policy.

Blessed Are the Peacemakers

Living the Ten Commandments prepares the way for the kingdom of God, the kingdom of peace. The Church has the responsibility to help us understand and guide us in living the Ten Commandments as Jesus taught. One way the popes fulfill this responsibility is by writing encyclicals. An encyclical is a teaching letter written to the whole Church.

In 1963 Blessed Pope John XXIII wrote *Pacem in Terris*, or "Peace on Earth." Pope John was very troubled about the many ways human life was being abused. So he wrote this encyclical to remind the world that all human life, the life of every person, without exception, is sacred.

Pope John pointed out clearly that warfare, unjust wages, the misuse of authority, and poverty violate the sacred dignity of people. We must work to correct these injustices and build the kingdom of peace that Jesus announced. We must love one another as Jesus did.

The road to peace is the way of justice. Everyone, people and governments, needs to respect the life and dignity of all people as sacred. We sometimes treat people unjustly because we fear the diversity and differences among people. We need to see that fear as an evil and to embrace diversity and differences as expressions of the infinite beauty of God, who created everyone as a sacred image of himself.

The Holy Spirit teaches us the way of justice. The more we listen, accept his help, and act justly, the more we are building a world of peace as Blessed John XXIII reminded us we are obligated to do.

How do you see people living justly and building a world of peace?

Our Catholic Identity

Fruits of the Holy Spirit

Peace is one of the fruits of the Holy Spirit. The fruits of the Holy Spirit describe what happens when we cooperate with the grace of the Holy Spirit and live as Jesus taught. The fruits of the Holy Spirit are love, joy, peace, patience, kindness, generosity, faithfulness, gentleness, and self-control (see Galatians 5:22–23).

Blessed Pope John XXIII (1881–1963), beatified, or named a Blessed of the Church, by Pope John Paul II on September 3, 2000

What Difference Does Faith Make in My Life?

Each day you cooperate with the Holy Spirit and show respect for yourself and others in many ways. Making such choices builds friendships, families, and safe communities.

Describe several ways you would like others to treat you. Then use them as a guide to the way you treat others.

Living the Golden Rule

My Faith Choice

This week I will look for opportunities to live the Golden Rule. I will

_____

_____.

Prayer for Peace

Peace is one of the fruits of the Holy Spirit. Learn to sign the word peace. *Pray the prayer aloud. Conclude by signing "Peace."*

Lord, make me an instrument of your peace.

Peace

We Remember

Mark the true statements T and the false statements F. Change the false statements into true statements.

F T 1. Adult children who live away from home have less responsibility to honor their parents than do younger children who live at home.

F T 2. All human life is sacred from the first moment a person is conceived in their mother's womb.

F T 3. Everyone is called to live a chaste life.

F T 4. The virtues of justice and generosity help us live the Seventh and Tenth Commandments.

F T 5. The Eighth Commandment is all about living honest and truthful lives.

To Help You Remember

1. The Fourth Commandment teaches that all family members are to contribute to the well-being of their family.

2. The Fifth Commandment teaches that we are to respect all human life and live as peacemakers.

3. The Sixth and Ninth Commandments teach us to live chaste lives in our thoughts and actions.

4. The Seventh and Tenth Commandments command us to treat others justly.

5. The Eighth Commandment is about speaking and living the truth.

This Week . . .

In chapter 22, "Loving One Another," your child learned more about the teachings of the Ten Commandments. The Fourth Commandment teaches that all family members are to contribute to the well-being of the family. Children, young and adult, are to honor and respect their parents. The Fifth Commandment teaches us to respect all human life as sacred and to live as peacemakers. The taking of a human life, even when justified, is a grave evil. The Sixth and Ninth Commandments command all Christians to live a chaste life as Jesus did. The Seventh and Tenth Commandments command that we are to be just and generous. We are to use and care for creation wisely. The Eighth Commandment commands us to live honest and truthful lives.

For more on the teachings of the Catholic Church on the Fourth through Tenth Commandments, see *Catechism of the Catholic Church* paragraph numbers 2196–2550.

Sharing God's Word

Read together John 14:15–21. Emphasize that faithfully living the Ten Commandments is a sign of a faithful disciple of Christ.

Praying

In this chapter your child learned to sign a prayer. Read and sign this prayer on page 195 together.

Making a Difference

Choose one of the following activities to do as a family or design a similar activity of your own.

- Talk about how your family lives as good stewards of creation. Do one thing this week as a family to live as good stewards of creation.

- When we live as peacemakers, we live the Ten Commandments. Talk about how you all live as peacemakers at home, at school or work, and in your community.

- When we show love and respect for others, we live the Ten Commandments. Share stories with each other about times when you were not treated with love or respect. How did being treated this way make you feel?

For more ideas on ways your family can live your faith, visit the "Faith First for Families" page at **www.FaithFirst.com**. Click on "Games" and make learning fun for your child.

The Wisdom Books
A Scripture Story

The Holy Bible, the inspired word of God, stained glass

We Pray

The fear of the LORD is the
beginning of wisdom;
prudent are all who live by it.
PSALM 111:10

Mary,
Mother of God,
Seat of Wisdom,
pray for us.   Amen.

Who do you consider to be a "wise" person?

The good advice of wise people is often passed on from one generation to the next. The wisdom of the Israelites has been gathered and handed on in the wisdom books in the Old Testament.

What words of wisdom from the Old Testament do you know?

Bible Background

How does the gift of wisdom guide us in living as children of God?

Faith Vocabulary

wisdom. One of the seven gifts of the Holy Spirit which helps us to know God's plan of creation and salvation and to make moral decisions according to that divine plan.

oral tradition. The passing on of stories and teachings by word of mouth.

proverb. A short, concise saying stating a well-accepted fact or criterion for making a wise decision.

The Wisdom Books

People living in the Middle East before the time of Christ had an interesting way of gathering, preserving, and expressing common sense. They put their **wisdom** into forms they could learn by heart.

In the Old Testament, wisdom is practical. It is a skill in action. The chief topics of wisdom are the problem of suffering, our origin and destiny, the meaning of happiness, good and evil actions, and death.

The wisdom of the Israelites was collected and passed on in stories, poems, chants, sayings, proverbs, and prayers. These insights were passed from one generation to the next by word of mouth. This word-of-mouth way of doing things is called **oral tradition.**

Eventually, many of the pieces of the oral tradition of the Israelites were collected and written down. There are seven wisdom books in the Old Testament.

The Book of Job is a long poem that is like a play. The wisdom of Job leads us to understand the problem of suffering in our lives.

The Book of Psalms is a collection of prayers in the form of poetry, and the Song of Songs is a poetic hymn portraying the love of God for his people. The wisdom of the Psalms is to refer everything back to God—all our joy, all our sorrow, all our hope.

The Book of Ecclesiastes is a reflection on the emptiness of life. Its wisdom is that our feeling of emptiness can only be filled, in the end, by God.

The Book of Wisdom and the Book of Sirach help people understand the wisdom of staying faithful to God's Law and walking in God's paths.

Give an example of a proverb of your own that you follow to make wise choices.

The Book of Proverbs

The Book of Proverbs is a collection of relatively brief sayings, called **proverbs**, that are meant to guide people through life. These sayings are examples of "skills in action."

This is how the Book of Proverbs describes wisdom:

Wisdom has built her house,
    she has set up her seven
        columns;
She has dressed her meat,
    mixed her wine,
    yes, she has spread her table.
She has sent out her maidens;
    she calls
    from the heights out over
        the city:
"Let whoever is simple turn
    in here;
    to him who lacks
        understanding, I say,
Come, eat of my food,
    and drink of the wine I have
        mixed!

Forsake foolishness that you
    may live;
    advance in the way of
        understanding." . . .

The beginning of wisdom is the
    fear of the LORD,
    and knowledge of the Holy
        One is understanding.

If you are wise, it is to your
    own advantage;
    and if you are arrogant, you
        alone shall bear it.
                    PROVERBS 9:1–6, 10–12

Throughout the Book of Proverbs we are given a series of maxims, or rules of conduct, to make wise decisions. For example:

A mild answer calms wrath,
    but a harsh word stirs up
        anger.   PROVERBS 15:1

You have probably already experienced the wisdom of that proverb.

The beginning of wisdom is the fear of the LORD.

PROVERBS 9:10

199

Understanding the Word of God

Jesus at prayer, stained glass

Jesus, the Wisdom of God

The key to God's wisdom is Jesus Christ himself. He is, according to Paul the Apostle, "[T]he power of God and the wisdom of God" (1 Corinthians 1:24).

Jesus told this proverb to help us understand true wisdom:

"[W]here your treasure is, there also will your heart be."

LUKE 12:34

When we keep our eyes fixed on Jesus, we will live wisely. To grow in wisdom we need to be open to the Holy Spirit, who helps us understand everything Jesus taught. This will make a difference in our lives each and every day.

Describe how what we value influences our decisions.

Value	Influence

Mary, Seat of Wisdom,
artist unknown

Seat of Wisdom

Christians honor and respect Mary for her wisdom. She always kept God at the center of her life. Mary's love for God was the driving force behind all her decisions.

One of the titles Christians honor Mary with is Seat of Wisdom. Mary is called the Seat, or Bearer, of Wisdom because she is the Mother of Jesus, who is "the power and wisdom of God." We honor Mary as the Seat of Wisdom because she lived out her life according to the plan of God.

Mary was eager to hear God's word and to act upon it. Even when she did not understand everything that God asked of her, Mary trusted and believed in God. She believed and trusted in the larger plan of God's wisdom.

We also honor Mary with the title Mother of Good Counsel. We turn to her for advice, or counsel. We ask her to help us make wise decisions.

Take a moment to ask Mary to help you make wise decisions that will help you live as a follower of Christ.

What Difference Does Faith Make in My Life?

There is a difference between acting wisely and acting foolishly. Before you act, ask the Holy Spirit to help you make a wise decision.

Think of someone in a movie or a television program who acts wisely or acts foolishly. Describe how this character's wise or foolish actions affect others.

Actions Have Consequences

My Faith Choice

This week I will begin each day by praying to the Holy Spirit for the gift of wisdom. I will use this gift to help me make decisions about

_____

_____.

Mary, Pray for Us

Leader:	Let us pray to Mary whom Jesus asked to care for us, his disciples.		
Reader:	Holy Trinity, one God	**All:**	**have mercy on us**
	Holy Mary		**pray for us**
	Holy Mother of God		**pray for us**
	Mother most pure		**pray for us**
	Mother of good counsel		**pray for us**
	Virgin most wise		**pray for us**
	Mirror of justice		**pray for us**
	[Seat] of wisdom		**pray for us**
	Cause of our joy		**pray for us**
	Help of Christians		**pray for us**
	Queen of all saints		**pray for us**
	Queen of peace		**pray for us**
Leader:	Pray for us, holy Mother of God		
All:	**That we may become worthy of the promises of Christ.**		

FROM THE LITANY OF THE BLESSED VIRGIN MARY

We Remember

Write a foolish decision and a wise decision for the following situation. Compare the consequences of the decisions.

> The temperature outdoors has just hit 104° F. Two teammates e-mail you to join them to practice your basketball skills on the court outside your school.

Foolish Decision _____

_____

_____

_____

Wise Decision _____

_____

_____

_____

To Help You Remember

1. Wisdom is the gift of the Holy Spirit that helps us know God's plan of creation and salvation, and make decisions according to the plan.

2. The wisdom writings of the Old Testament contain seven books.

3. Jesus is the fullest revelation of the wisdom of God.

This Week . . .

In chapter 23, "The Wisdom Books: A Scripture Story," your child learned more about Sacred Scripture, in particular, the wisdom writings of the Old Testament. This short collection of seven books includes the books of Job, Psalms, Proverbs, Ecclesiastes, Song of Songs, Wisdom, and Sirach. Originally passed on from one generation to the next by word of mouth, this collection of writings contains stories, poems, chants, sayings, proverbs, and prayers. The chief topics of these writings are the problem of suffering, our origin and destiny, the meaning of happiness, the conflict between good and evil, and death.

For more on the teachings of the Catholic Church on Sacred Scripture, see *Catechism of the Catholic Church* paragraph numbers 101–133.

Sharing God's Word

Read together Proverbs 9:10–12. Emphasize that in the Book of Proverbs the sayings are the inspired word of God and guide us through life by helping us make wise choices.

Praying

In this chapter your child prayed a prayer from the Litany of the Blessed Virgin Mary. Read and pray together this prayer on page 203.

Making a Difference

Choose one of the following activities to do as a family or design a similar activity of your own.

- Create a proverb for living as a family. Post it in your home where everyone can see it.

- Brainstorm as many sayings as you can that help us live as children of God. Write one on each month of your family calendar to help you make wise family decisions.

- Watch a movie or television show. List the names of the characters on a sheet of paper. Keep track of the wise and foolish decisions the characters make. Talk about what the characters who made foolish decisions could have done to make wise decisions.

For more ideas on ways your family can live your faith, visit the "Faith First for Families" page at **www.FaithFirst.com**. Check out this week's "Just for Parents" article.

Unit 3 Review

A. Best Response

Read each statement and circle the best answer.

1. Which of these virtues is one of the theological virtues?

   a. wisdom

   b. prudence

   c. faith

   d. courage

2. Which one is not an effect of the grace of the Holy Spirit?

   a. We grow in our ability to make right choices.

   b. We turn toward God and away from sin.

   c. We gain the confidence to grow in holiness.

   d. We reject God's gift of forgiveness.

3. The sources of morality are _____.

   a. object, intention, purpose

   b. intention, reason, effect

   c. object, intention, circumstances

   d. object, circumstances, effect

4. Which one of the following is not the result of an informed conscience?

   a. judging what is right and wrong

   b. making good moral decisions

   c. choosing to do what is against God's Law

   d. living as a follower of Jesus Christ

5. _____ are serious offenses against God.

   a. Venial sins

   b. Mortal virtues

   c. Temptations

   d. Mortal sins

6. Which of the Ten Commandments focus on our relationship with God?

   a. First

   b. First and Second

   c. First, Second, and Third

   d. First, Second, Third, and Fourth

7. Which of the Ten Commandments teaches us not to cheat on a test?

   a. Fifth

   b. Eighth

   c. Seventh

   d. Tenth

8. Which of the Ten Commandments teaches us to live chaste lives?

   a. First

   b. Fifth

   c. Seventh

   d. Ninth

9. Which of the Ten Commandments teaches us to respect all human life as sacred?

   a. First

   b. Fourth

   c. Fifth

   d. Tenth

10. The Book of Proverbs is one of the Old Testament _____.

    a. historical books

    b. books of the prophets

    c. books of wisdom

    d. epistles

B. Completing the Paragraph

Fill in the blanks in the paragraph by using the terms in the word bank.

cardinal	**conscience**
mortal	**venial**
holiness	**moral**

God gives each person the grace to make wise choices and to live a life of

_____. Making choices to live according to God's will is

called living a _____ life. By developing and practicing the four

_____ virtues, we develop good habits and grow in holiness.

Our _____ guides us in judging whether an act is right or

wrong and whether it agrees or does not agree with God's Law. When we

deliberately choose to do or say something that we know is against God's Law, we

sin. _____ sins are grave or serious sins that break our

relationship with God. _____ sins weaken but do not break

our relationship with God.

C. What I Have Learned

Write three things you learned in this unit.
Share them with the group.

_____

_____

_____

Look at the list of faith terms in "Words to Know" on page 164.
Circle the terms you know now.

D. From a Scripture Story

Explain how the following proverb makes a difference
in our daily lives.

> A mild answer calms wrath,
> but a harsh word stirs up anger.
> PROVERBS 15:1

Unit 4 • We Pray

How do we grow as people of prayer?

Getting Ready

What I Have Learned

What is something you already know about these faith terms?

Praying the Psalms

_____

_____

Prayer of adoration

_____

_____

Prayer of contemplation

_____

_____

Words to Know

Put an X next to the faith terms you know. Put a ? next to the faith terms you need to know more about.

Faith Vocabulary

_____ prayer

_____ Book of Psalms

_____ prayer life

_____ vocal prayer

_____ Sermon on the Mount

_____ Lord

Questions I Have

What questions would you like to ask about the Catholic tradition of prayer?

_____

_____

_____

_____

A Scripture Story

Jesus praying in the Garden of Gethsemane

How is Jesus the model of prayer for Christians?

People of Prayer

We Pray

Blessed be God, who did not
    refuse me
  the kindness I sought
    in prayer.   PSALM 66:20

As morning breaks
I look to you, O God,
to be my strength
this day.   Amen.

What do you like to do with friends?

Friends like to spend time with each other. God is the closest Friend we have. He is always with us. He wants us to spend time with him.

What are some of the ways you spend time with God in prayer?

The Prayer of God's People

Faith Focus

What is Christian prayer?

Faith Vocabulary

forms of prayer. The five types of prayers revealed in Sacred Scripture that are the norm for Christian prayer: blessing and adoration, petition, intercession, thanksgiving, and praise.

distractions. Thoughts and ideas that pull us away from prayer.

invocations. Brief prayers we can learn by heart and pray throughout the day.

The Prayer of Christians

Prayer can be defined in many ways. Prayer is an invitation from God to spend time with him. Prayer is "lifting our minds and hearts to God." Another simple and accurate description is "talking with God." We do not need to use fancy words. We just need to speak from our heart. We do not need to impress God. He is always interested in what we have to share with him.

Christian prayer is most often directed to God the Father. Of course, we can and do pray at times directly to Jesus, God the Son, and to God the Holy Spirit. We pray as Jesus did:

At that very moment he rejoiced [in] the holy Spirit and said, "I give you praise, Father, Lord of heaven and earth, for although you have hidden these things from the wise and the learned you have revealed them to the childlike. Yes, Father, such has been your gracious will."

LUKE 10:21

Jesus leads us in prayer. In our prayer Jesus joins us, the Holy Spirit moves in us, and the Father listens with loving attention.

Learn this prayer by heart. Pray it to conclude your prayers.

*Through Christ,
with Christ,
in Christ,
in the unity of the
Holy Spirit,
all honor and glory is yours,
Father,
for ever and ever.*

Abraham, Our Father in Faith

Christians can learn about prayer from the Jewish people, our ancestors in faith. We read about such Old Testament people of prayer as Abraham and Sarah, Jacob and Rebecca, Moses and Miriam, Ruth and Naomi, Judith, David, and Job.

Christians recognize and honor Abraham as our father in faith. With deep faith, Abraham brought his questions and concerns honestly and directly to God. He placed everything in God's hands and placed himself in his care. The Book of Genesis says of Abraham:

[He] put his faith in the LORD, who credited it to him as an act of righteousness.

GENESIS 15:6

The Psalms

King David is another Old Testament model of prayer for Christians. David is considered the author of many of the prayers in the Book of Psalms. Filled with emotion, these prayers are spoken from the heart. In the Psalms we can find five basic **forms of prayer**. They are:

- *Blessing and adoration.* We declare that God is our almighty Creator. Read Psalm 95:1, 6.
- *Petition.* We ask for God's forgiveness and help in all our needs. Read Psalm 38:22–23.

- *Intercession.* We pray that God will help others in their need. Read Psalm 67:2.
- *Thanksgiving.* We express our gratitude to God for all his many blessings. Read Psalm 100:4–5.
- *Praise.* We give glory to God simply because he is God and is deserving of our honor and respect. Read Psalm 29:1–2.

Jesus and Mary and the early Church would have prayed the Psalms. Today, the Church prays the Psalms every day.

Create your own psalm, using one of the five basic prayer forms.

211

Growing as People of Prayer

Christians are people of prayer. It is within our families that we first learn to pray. In and with our families, the Holy Spirit first calls us and teaches us to pray. But how can we continue to grow as people of prayer? There are a number of things we can do.

Be Humble. Sometimes we hesitate to pray because we feel unworthy. We need not worry. Our prayers, like those of the tax collector, are most welcomed by God. (Read Luke 18:9–14.)

Prepare for Prayer. Set aside a special time for prayer. Go to a special place. For example, make a visit to the church or sit before a holy image of Jesus or Mary.

Focus on Praying. Sometimes we are faced with a variety of **distractions** to our prayer. Turn your distracting thoughts and ideas over to the Holy Spirit.

Have Courage and Trust. Sometimes we are not sure if God is listening. We begin to feel discouraged. Even when you are not clear how things will work out, trust God.

The prayer of Christians begins with our loving faith and trust in God the Father. Our prayer is like that of the man in the Gospel who said, "I do believe, help my unbelief!" (Mark 9:24).

Prayer strengthens our faith, hope, and love for God. It also strengthens our communion with God. There is no deep secret to praying. We just need to want to pray and then continue to do so— even when it is difficult.

Describe some of the things that make praying difficult for you. Then choose one of those things and name two ways you can deal with it.

Difficulties	Dealing with Difficulties

Our Church Makes a Difference

The Jesus Prayer

Since the days of the early Church, Christians have prayed in many ways. To help keep in touch with God, Christians have prayed **invocations**. The word *invocation* means "calling on someone." Invocations are brief prayers we can say throughout the day.

One invocation that has been popular for over six hundred years is called the Jesus Prayer. The words of the prayer are simple and often are uttered with a special breathing technique.

The Jesus prayer is a simple prayer to use whenever you want and wherever you are. Memorize the prayer. Pray it often. Teach it to your family and friends. Become a model of prayer for them.

Read the Jesus Prayer on this page. Now try praying the Jesus Prayer yourself, using the breathing actions.

Our Catholic Identity

Prayer Groups

Jesus promised that when his followers come together to pray he would be there with them. Christians often form prayer groups, which the Church calls "schools of prayer." Prayer groups often center their prayer on the Bible. These groups are aware that Jesus, the Word of God, is with them and that it is with and through Jesus that they pray.

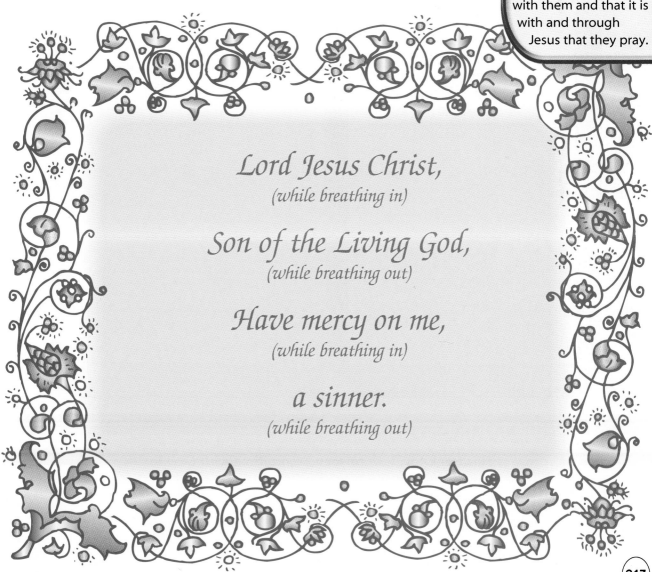

Lord Jesus Christ,
(while breathing in)

Son of the Living God,
(while breathing out)

Have mercy on me,
(while breathing in)

a sinner.
(while breathing out)

What Difference Does Faith Make in My Life?

The Holy Spirit invites you to pray often throughout the day. The Holy Spirit invites you to pray with your family and friends. The Holy Spirit invites you to pray when you are alone.

Take the time to fill out this daily planner. Set aside several different times during the day for praying.

Times for Praying

7:00
7:30
8:00
8:30
9:00
9:30
10:00
10:30
11:00
11:30
12:00
12:30
1:00
1:30
2:00
2:30
3:00
3:30
4:00
4:30
5:00

My Faith Choice

This week I will try to spend more time with God in prayer. I will

_____

_____.

Praise the Lord!

Psalm 150 is the final doxology, or prayer of praise, that concludes the Book of Psalms. This great psalm of praise unites all the prayers of the Book of Psalms into one great prayer.

All: Hallelujah!

Leader: Praise God in his holy sanctuary;
All: give praise in the mighty dome of heaven.

Leader: Give praise for his mighty deeds,
All: praise him for his great majesty.

Leader: Give praise with blasts upon the horn,
All: praise him with harp and lyre.

Leader: Give praise with tambourines and dance,
All: praise him with flutes and strings.

Leader: Give praise with crashing cymbals,
All: praise him with sounding cymbals.
Let everything that has breath
give praise to the LORD!
Hallelujah!   PSALM 150

We Remember

Unscramble the words in the word bank. Use the words to write a brief paragraph about the prayer life of Christians.

> usJes   onraadoti   ylHo   pStiri
>
> aisepr   saPlms   ocatinvions

The Prayer Life of Christians

_____

_____

_____

_____

_____

_____

To Help You Remember

1. The prayer of Christians is most often addressed to God the Father in the name of the Son through the power of the Holy Spirit.

2. Christian prayer finds its roots in the prayer of the Jewish people, our ancestors in faith.

3. Christians grow as people of prayer their whole life long.

This Week . . .

In chapter 24, "People of Prayer," your child learned more about the Church as a people of prayer. They discovered that the tradition of Christian prayer is rooted in the Old Testament. Christians can learn how to pray from Old Testament models of faith such as Abraham and Sarah. Today, Christians express themselves in prayer following the model of praying found in the Old Testament Psalms. We pray prayers of blessing and adoration, petition, intercession, thanksgiving, and praise. Like our ancestors in faith, we need to work at growing as people of prayer.

For more on the teachings of the Catholic Church on prayer, see *Catechism of the Catholic Church* paragraph numbers 2566–2589, 2598–2619, 2623–2643, and 2725–2745.

Sharing God's Word

Read together Luke 10:21. Emphasize that Christians learn to pray from the way Jesus prayed.

Praying

In this chapter your child prayed a prayer of praise. Read and pray together this prayer on page 215.

Making a Difference

Choose one of the following activities to do as a family or design a similar activity of your own.

- Read 1 Samuel 3:1–10. This Bible story is about Samuel listening to God. As you read this story, remember that we all need to spend time in prayer listening to God.

- Saint Ignatius of Loyola is one of the great spiritual guides in the Catholic tradition of prayer. Look on the Internet or at the library to find out more about this great saint.

- When you take part in Mass this week, listen carefully for the doxology, "Through him, with him, in him, in the unity of the Holy Spirit." As you hear and pray these words, recall that the Church prays with and in the name of Jesus to the Father and that it is the Holy Spirit who teaches us how and what to pray.

For more ideas on ways your family can live your faith, visit the "Faith First for Families" page at **www.FaithFirst.com**. Take a look at "Just for Parents" this week.

The Gift of Prayer

25

We Pray

The LORD is my shepherd;
  there is nothing I lack.
                    PSALM 23:1

God our Father,
send the Holy Spirit
to teach and guide us,
to preach the Gospel,
the way of salvation
and love. We ask this
in Jesus' name.   Amen.

What have you practiced and become good at doing?

Champions become champions by taking the time and making the effort to develop their gifts and abilities. God gives everyone the gift of prayer. We need to take the time to develop that gift.

How can you develop the gift of prayer?

Pray Without Ceasing

Faith Focus

What are five practical ways of praying?

Faith Vocabulary

prayer life. The habit of making prayer part of the rhythm of our day.

The Christian Prayer Life

Jesus is our model of prayer. He is the One who best shows us how to develop our **prayer life.** Jesus often spent time in conversation with his Father. He especially did this at important moments in his life. With trust he presented his needs and concerns to the Father. With gratitude he blessed and thanked his Father.

Prayer is important to our life as followers of Christ. Saint Paul reminds us, "Pray without ceasing" (1 Thessalonians 5:17). The Church lives by Paul's advice. We pray as the psalmist prayed, "[a]t dusk, dawn, and noon" (Psalm 55:18).

Morning Prayer

Throughout the world the Church welcomes each new day with prayer. We join Zechariah in thanking God for the dawn of our salvation in Jesus Christ. We pray:

"Blessed be the Lord,
the God of Israel,
for he has visited and
brought redemption
to his people."

LUKE 1:68

Evening Prayer

As the sun sets, the Church throughout the world gathers in prayer. We join Mary in praising God for the wonders of his grace-filled ways.

"My soul proclaims the
greatness of the Lord;
my spirit rejoices in God
my savior."

LUKE 1:46–47

Each time we try to make prayer a regular part of each day, we show that God is at the center of our lives. He is the One in whom we place our faith, hope, and love. We show that we value our friendship with God more than anything else in our lives.

Find the Canticle of Zechariah (Luke 1:68–79) and the Canticle of Mary (Luke 1:46–55) in your Bible. Place a bookmark next to both canticles so that you can join the Church in praying them when you wake up in the morning and when you retire at night.

The Prayer of Adoration

In our prayer of adoration we stand before God as his creatures. We praise God's greatness and acknowledge that he is the Creator. We worship him and admit that we depend on him for everything.

The Church's greatest prayer of adoration is the Eucharist. At Mass we worship God as the community of followers of Jesus. At every Mass, at the end of the preface, we sing or recite the acclamation "Holy, Holy, Holy." We sing or pray aloud:

Holy, holy, holy Lord, God
of power and might,
heaven and earth are full of
your glory.
Hosanna in the highest.
Blessed is he who comes in
the name of the Lord.
Hosanna in the highest.

PREFACE ACCLAMATION,
ROMAN MISSAL

The words of this prayer of adoration are from the Old Testament book of the prophet Isaiah.

We join in this great act of adoration with the Church on earth and all the angels and the saints.

"Holy, holy, holy is the LORD of hosts!" they cried to one another. "All the earth is filled with his glory!"

ISAIAH 6:3

Gestures are a form of prayer. Think about the prayer gestures we use during the celebration of the Eucharist. Describe how each is a prayer of adoration.

Standing _____

_____

_____

Kneeling _____

_____

_____

Bowing _____

_____

_____

Faith-Filled People

Solomon

King Solomon was the son of King David. He changed his name from Jedidiah to Solomon, a name meaning "peace," when he became king. One of Solomon's great achievements was the building of the Temple in Jerusalem to give adoration and glory to God. The innermost part of the Temple, the Holy of Holies, contained the Ark of the Covenant. Two cherubim, fifteen feet high and with fifteen-foot wings, were carved from cedar and stood on either side of the Ark.

Expressions of Prayer

The Holy Spirit teaches us to pray. Christians respond to the Holy Spirit by saying, or expressing, our prayers in three basic ways. They are vocal prayer, meditation, and contemplation. They all share one thing in common—all prayer flows from our heart.

VOCAL PRAYER

We use words all day long. How natural for us to use words when we pray. Vocal prayer is prayer that uses words. Vocal prayers are prayed aloud or silently. They are prayed alone or with others.

The words we speak in our prayers express our thoughts and feelings. They enable us to share with God our joys and sorrows, our achievements and our dreams. They give us the power to share with him everything about ourselves.

But remember, words are not necessary. God knows our innermost thoughts. He knows what we want to say before we put it into words.

MEDITATION

God is a loving Father who every moment is an active part of our life. In a prayer of meditation we connect our lives more closely with God. We use our imagination, mind, and desire to live the new life in Christ that we have received in Baptism. We seek not only to know about Christ but to grow in our love and friendship with him. We spend time with God the Father and give him all our attention. We listen as the Holy Spirit shows us how to live as children of God and disciples of Jesus.

CONTEMPLATION

Saint Teresa of Avila (1535–1582), Doctor of the Church and Spanish mystic, describes the prayer of contemplation as "nothing less than a close sharing between friends; it means taking time frequently to be alone with him who we know loves us." It is communion with God the Father, in Christ, through the power of the Holy Spirit.

Take the time right now. Speak no words. Just be with Jesus, who calls us his friends.

Our Church Makes a Difference

Hildegard of Bingen

The history of the Church is filled with examples of people of prayer. Many have turned and continue to turn to these people. They pray for advice and direction on how to make their lives more prayerful.

Hildegard of Bingen (1098–1179) was blessed with a sense of God's closeness to her and all people. She had a great love of creation as God's great gift to us. At the age of thirty-eight, Hildegard was elected as abbess, or leader, of a group of women who lived together in a religious community. They had joined together to live their lives according to the Rule of Saint Benedict.

Hildegard kept prayer at the heart and center of her life. Through the example of her life she continues to teach people today that through prayer we deepen our friendship with God. Through prayer we speak to God as friend to Friend. The Church honors Hildegard of Bingen as a saint. We celebrate her feast day on September 17.

What can you do to make prayer a regular part of your day?

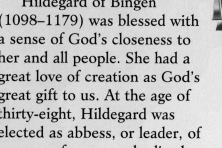

Our Catholic Identity

Spiritual Direction

Everyone needs help to lead a life of prayer. Living a life of prayer is not something we can do on our own. Christians who desire to live a life of prayer seek spiritual direction. They seek the advice of a spiritual director, a person of prayer, who has received the gifts of wisdom, faith, and discernment from the Holy Spirit. The Holy Spirit gives spiritual directors the charism to guide members of the Church in living a life of prayer.

Stained-glass window of Hildegard of Bingen

What Difference Does Faith Make in My Life?

The Holy Spirit teaches you to pray. He is always by your side in everything you do. He is always inviting you to share your life with God.

Prayer can become part of everything you do. Here is a list of things that are part of our lives. Describe how you can make prayer a part of each of them.

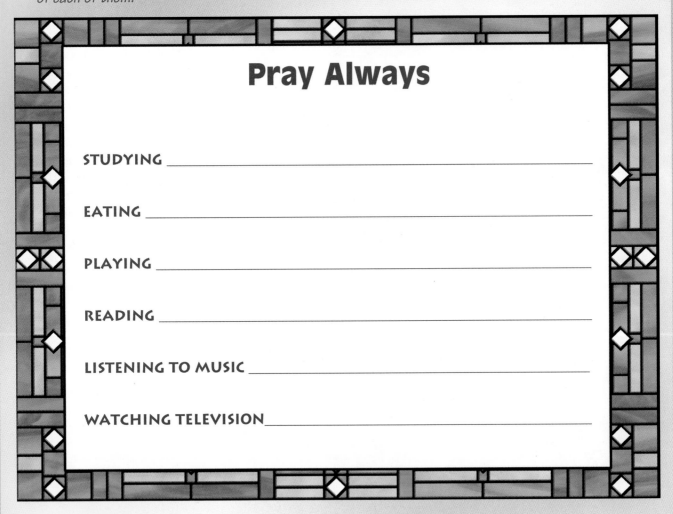

Pray Always

STUDYING _____

EATING _____

PLAYING _____

READING _____

LISTENING TO MUSIC _____

WATCHING TELEVISION _____

My Faith Choice

This week I will try to be more aware that God is always inviting me to spend time with him, friend with Friend. I will

_____

_____.

A Prayer of Meditation

Pray a prayer of meditation following these steps.

1. Remind yourself that you are in the presence of God. Ask the Holy Spirit to teach you to pray.

2. Select and prayerfully read a passage from the Gospel; for example, read Luke 14:7–11, Luke 15:1–10, or John 2:1–11.

3. Imagine yourself in a scene from the Gospel.

4. Reread the passage. Pay careful attention to the conversation between the characters in the Gospel scene. What is Jesus saying to you?

5. Make a decision to put into practice what Jesus is asking of you.

6. Pray a short prayer to the Holy Spirit. Ask the Holy Spirit to help you live as a disciple of Jesus.

We Remember

Match the prayer terms in the word box with their descriptions.

1. vocal prayer   2. meditation   3. contemplation

_____ A prayer that uses words that we say aloud or quietly in our hearts.

_____ A prayer that is a close sharing between friends, and being alone with God who we know loves us.

_____ A prayer that uses our imagination, mind, and desire to live as a faithful disciple of Christ.

To Help You Remember

1. We learn best to pray from Jesus, our model of prayer.

2. In a prayer of adoration we worship God and make him the center of our lives.

3. We often use words to pray. Sometimes we do not use words but just spend time with God.

This Week . . .

In chapter 25, "The Gift of Prayer," your child learned more about the Church as a people of prayer. Jesus is our model of prayer. He is the One who best shows us how to develop our prayer life. Saint Paul the Apostle reminds us that we are to pray without ceasing (see 1 Thessalonians 5:17). The Church follows the advice of Saint Paul and prays throughout the day. Each time we make prayer a regular part of our day, we keep God at the center of our lives. We grow to worship God and value our friendship with him more than all else. We often speak our prayers, either aloud or silently in our heart. As we grow in prayer, we come to realize that prayer is simply spending time with God and words are not always necessary.

For more on the teachings of the Catholic Church on prayer, see *Catechism of the Catholic Church* paragraph numbers 2598–2619 and 2700–2719.

Sharing God's Word

Read together Luke 1:46–47, 68–69. Emphasize that prayer is important to our lives as followers of Christ.

Praying

In this chapter your child prayed a meditation. Read and pray together this prayer on page 223.

Making a Difference

Choose one of the following activities to do as a family or design a similar activity of your own.

- Blessed Mother Teresa of Calcutta used this image to describe prayer. She said, "Prayer enlarges the heart until it is capable of containing God's gift of himself." Ask family members to share how they invite God into their hearts.

- Saint Hildegard of Bingen always felt close to God. Look on the Internet or at the library for more information about this wonderful saint.

- This week when you pray, pray that all your actions will be a reflection of God's love for the world.

For more ideas on ways your family can live your faith, visit the "Faith First for Families" page at **www.FaithFirst.com**. Click on "Family Prayer" and pray the prayer together this week.

The Lord's Prayer
A Scripture Story

26

We Pray

Answer when I call,
   my saving God. . . .
[S]how me favor;
   hear my prayer.   PSALM 4:2

**Our Father,
hallowed be your name.
Your kingdom come.**
                    Amen.

What event have you attended or seen that began with people praying?

Beginning special events and celebrations with prayer is a widespread custom. Many Christians pray the Lord's Prayer, or the Our Father, every day. Christians pray the Our Father all over the world, in all languages.

What do we pray for when we pray the Lord's Prayer?

225

The Prayer of All Christians

The Lord's Prayer is the prayer of all Christians. In the Gospels it has been handed on to the Church in two different forms. A shorter form is found in the Gospel of Luke. A longer form is found in the Gospel of Matthew. It is this form the Church prays today. Both versions address God by name, honor God, and finally ask God to respond to our needs.

Matthew's version of the prayer follows this pattern:

1. God is addressed, or called upon: *Our Father.*
2. Three prayer verses give glory to the Father. We pray that:
   - God's name be made holy;
   - God's kingdom come;
   - God's will be done.
3. Four petitions present our needs to God. We pray that:
   - God will provide for our deepest needs;
   - God will forgive our sins;
   - God will help us overcome temptation;
   - God will help us win the struggle over evil.

The Lord's Prayer is a vast treasure chest of wisdom condensed into a small jewelry box. The ancient Roman writer Tertullian called it a summary of the whole Gospel. Saint Augustine, in one of his letters, described it this way:

Run through all the words of the holy prayers [in Scripture], and I do not think that you will find anything in them that is not contained and included in the Lord's Prayer.

Create a billboard for the Lord's Prayer. Remember, you have to compete with a lot of other messages out there. Grab people's attention with the good news of the Lord's Prayer!

226

Reading the Word of God

The Lord's Prayer

In Matthew's Gospel, the Lord's Prayer is part of the **Sermon on the Mount.** Jesus had just finished warning his disciples about doing good deeds so that everyone could praise them. Then, while teaching his disciples about prayer, he said:

"This is how you are to pray:
Our Father in heaven,
  hallowed be your name,
  your kingdom come,
  your will be done,
    on earth as in heaven.
  Give us today our daily
    bread;
  and forgive us our debts,
  as we forgive our debtors;
  and do not subject us
    to the final test,
  but deliver us from
    the evil one."

MATTHEW 6:9–13

Jesus lived his life as a prayer to the Father. His life gave praise to his Father and he placed total trust in the Father. This trust was especially clear as Jesus approached his death on the cross. Facing his death on the cross, he opened his heart to his Father, saying:

"I am troubled now. Yet what should I say? 'Father, save me from this hour'? But it was for this purpose that I came to this hour. Father, glorify your name."

JOHN 12:27–28

All Jesus did gave glory and honor to the Father.

Look at the words of the Our Father. How might the words "your will be done" help you live as a disciple of Jesus?

The Meaning of the Lord's Prayer

The Lord's Prayer teaches us not only how to pray but also how to live a life of total trust in God as Jesus did.

OUR FATHER. Through our Baptism we are joined to Jesus and become one with him and one another. The Holy Spirit is poured into our hearts, enabling us to call God Abba, or Father, as Jesus did.

WHO ART IN HEAVEN. The word *heaven* points to God's majesty and glory. The Church on earth joins with the angels and saints in heaven in praising God.

HALLOWED BE THY NAME. Glory and praise truly belong to God who creates, redeems, and sanctifies us.

THY KINGDOM COME. We pray that the kingdom announced by Jesus will come to completion when he comes again in glory at the end of time. We promise to prepare a way for the coming of that kingdom.

THY WILL BE DONE ON EARTH AS IT IS IN HEAVEN. God's will is for all people to live in communion with him forever. When we pray "thy will be done," we promise to live according to God's will and plan.

GIVE US THIS DAY OUR DAILY BREAD. Our daily bread is Christ himself, who said, "I am the living bread that came down from heaven" (John 6:51). We ask God to watch over our physical and our spiritual needs.

AND FORGIVE US OUR TRESPASSES AS WE FORGIVE THOSE WHO TRESPASS AGAINST US. Forgiveness is a two-way street. Those who receive God's forgiveness and mercy must be willing to be as forgiving and merciful toward others as God is toward them.

AND LEAD US NOT INTO TEMPTATION. Temptation tries to convince us that there is something better than God's will. We ask God for the courage to face temptation with strong faith, confident hope, and generous love.

BUT DELIVER US FROM EVIL. Satan and forces of evil in the world try to lead us away from God's love. There is no one, no power, stronger than Jesus. We pray that God's victory in Jesus Christ will be our victory as well.

Living the Lord's Prayer

_____

_____

_____

_____

Write two headlines that tell about people living the Lord's Prayer.

Our Church Makes a Difference

Share the Good News

Jesus gave the Church the command to share the good news of God's saving love with the whole world. We are to make disciples of all nations. We are to evangelize the whole world. We are to invite all people to be baptized and join with Jesus in calling God Abba, Father.

This work is called evangelization. It is the most important work of the Church. We carry out this work by preaching the word of God and by living as faithful witnesses for Christ. We celebrate the sacraments and live the Great Commandment. We do all these things and more so that the Good News will enter every heart of every person on earth.

When this happens, the human family will be renewed. Our prayer "Thy Kingdom come" will be fully answered. All people will live as children of God, whom we all honor and love as the one Father of all.

How does each image in the illustration connect to the themes in the Our Father?

Our Catholic Identity

Ecumenism

Jesus prayed that his followers would be one as he and the Father are one. But divisions have arisen in the Church. The followers of Jesus are divided into many churches. Ecumenism is the work of the Church striving to restore unity among all Christians.

What Difference Does Faith Make in My Life?

Jesus gave the Church the Lord's Prayer, or Our Father.
That means he gave it to you. The Holy Spirit gives you
the power to call God Abba, Father. What a wonderful
privilege! Stay in touch with God your Father today.

*You have been given the job of webmaster of a new Web site that tells
the world all about the Lord's Prayer. Design the home page.*

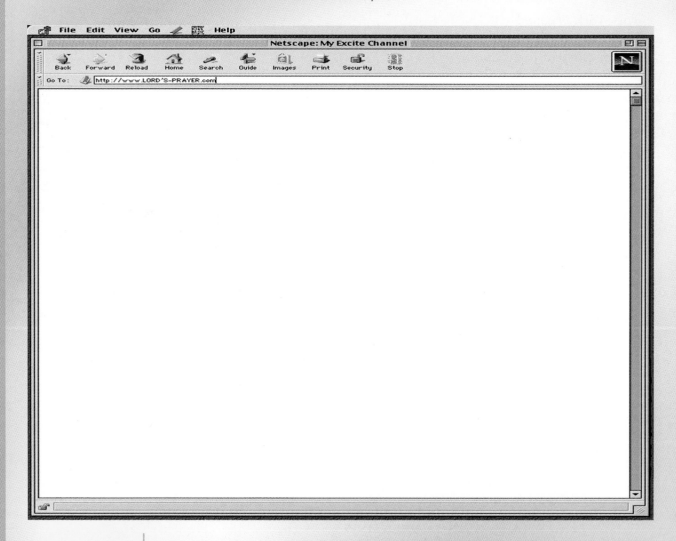

My Faith Choice

Each morning this week I will pray one petition of the
Our Father. I will think about what it means and I will

_____

_____ .

The Lord's Prayer

The Our Father, or Lord's Prayer, is the prayer of all Christians. Take time every day to pray it alone.

Reader: *Our Father, who art in heaven, hallowed be thy name;*

Group 1: *thy kingdom come; thy will be done on earth as it is in heaven.*

Group 2: *Give us this day our daily bread; and forgive us our trespasses*

Group 1: *as we forgive those who trespass against us;*

Group 2: *and lead us not into temptation, but deliver us from evil.*

All: *Amen.*

We Remember

Use the code to discover why the Church says that the Our Father teaches us both how to pray and how to live as children of God.

A ·—	F ··—·	K —·—	P ·——·	U ··—	Z ——··
B —···	G ——·	L ·—··	Q ——·—	V ···—	
C —·—·	H ····	M ——	R ·—·	W ·——	
D —··	I ··	N —·	S ···	X —··—	
E ·	J ·———	O ———	T —	Y —·——	

___ ___ ___ ___ ___ ___ ___
··· ··— —— —— ·— ·—· ·—·—

___ ___ ___ ___ ___
——— —·—· ·—· ·· ·

___ ___ ___ ___ ___ ___ ___
—·— ——— ·· ·—·· · ·—·

To Help You Remember

1. The Lord's Prayer is the prayer of all Christians.

2. The Lord's Prayer teaches us to make our whole life a prayer.

3. The Lord's Prayer shows us how to live as people who place our trust in God above all else.

This Week . . .

In chapter 26, "The Lord's Prayer: A Scripture Story," your child learned more about the Our Father. In Matthew's Gospel, Jesus' teaching of the Our Father, or Lord's Prayer, is part of the Sermon on the Mount. Many biblical scholars think that the version of the Our Father in Matthew is close to the version the early Christians prayed. Saint Thomas Aquinas called the Lord's Prayer the "most perfect of prayers." He said, "This prayer not only teaches us to ask for things, but also in what order we should desire them." When we pray the Our Father, the Holy Spirit teaches us how to pray and to live the Gospel.

For more on the teaching of the Catholic Church on the Our Father, see *Catechism of the Catholic Church* paragraph numbers 2759–2856.

Sharing God's Word

Read together Matthew 6:9–13. Emphasize that Jesus lived his life as a prayer.

Praying

In this chapter your child prayed the Lord's Prayer. Read and pray together the Lord's Prayer on page 231.

Making a Difference

Choose one of the following activities to do as a family or design a similar activity of your own.

- Many of the first Christian communities prayed the Our Father three times a day. This week use the Our Father for family prayer at least once a day.

- Visit the supermarket as a family. Purchase some basic food items and deliver them to a local food bank. Your parish can give you a location.

- Saint Thomas Aquinas wrote that the Our Father "not only teaches us to ask for things, but also in what order we should desire them." Look at the Our Father and discuss what you think Saint Thomas Aquinas meant.

For more ideas on ways your family can live your faith, visit the "Faith First for Families" page at **www.FaithFirst.com**. "Gospel Reflections" will continue to change each week over the summer. Don't forget to check it out.

Unit 4 Review

Name _____

A. The Best Response

Read each statement and circle the best answer.

1. Which of the following is not a definition of prayer?
   - a. lifting our minds and hearts to God
   - b. an invitation from God to spend time with him
   - c. talking and listening to God
   - d. impressing God with our words

2. The prayer in which we use our imagination to connect our lives more closely with God is _____.
   - a. contemplation
   - b. intercession
   - c. Psalms
   - d. meditation

3. Paul taught us to pray _____.
   - a. only in the morning
   - b. with fear of God
   - c. without ceasing
   - d. mainly during the evening hours

4. Which is not a form of prayer found in the Psalms?
   - a. blessing and adoration
   - b. petition
   - c. thanksgiving
   - d. letters

5. Which prayer did Tertullian call a summary of the whole Gospel?
   - a. Nicene Creed
   - b. Our Father
   - c. Glory Prayer
   - d. Apostles' Creed

6. When we pray "Give us this day our daily bread," we _____.
   - a. ask God for the courage to face temptation
   - b. promise to live according to God's will
   - c. ask God to watch over our physical and our spiritual needs
   - d. give glory and praise to God

7. Which of the following people is not a good model of prayer?
   - a. Mary
   - b. Judas
   - c. Abraham
   - d. David

8. In the prayer of invocation, we _____.
   - a. express our sorrow
   - b. call on someone to assist us with our needs
   - c. complain when things go wrong
   - d. praise God for his blessings

9. Which of these is not a true statement about prayer?
   - a. When we pray we show that God is the center of our lives.
   - b. The Eucharist is the greatest prayer of adoration.
   - c. Jesus is the best model of prayer.
   - d. All prayer uses words.

10. In Matthew's Gospel, Jesus taught the Our Father _____.
    - a. in the Temple in Jerusalem
    - b. at the beginning of his ministry
    - c. in the Sermon on the Mount
    - d. at his Crucifixion

233

B. Completing the Paragraph

Fill in the blanks in the paragraph using the words in the word bank.

vocal	contemplation	communion
meditation	prophets	petition
adoration		

The Christian tradition of prayer has its roots in the Old Testament. Abraham, whom we recognize as our father in faith, King David, and the

_____ are some of the Old Testament's models of prayer for Christians. The Old Testament also reveals five basic forms of prayer that Christians use. They are prayers of _____,

_____, intercession, praise, and thanksgiving. Christians express our prayers in three ways. We pray _____ prayers, prayers of _____, and prayers of _____.

By praying regularly each day we grow in friendship and

_____ with God.

C. What I Have Learned

Write three things you learned in this unit.
Share them with the group.

_____

_____

_____

Look at the faith terms in "Words to Know" on page 208.
Circle the terms you know now.

D. From a Scripture Story

The Lord's Prayer teaches us not only how to pray but also how to live as Jesus did. Describe three ways you live the Our Father.

_____

_____

_____

What do the celebrations of the liturgical year help us remember and share in?

235

The Liturgical Year

The Church gathers throughout the year to remember and share in the the saving work of Christ. Each day of the year is made holy by the Church gathering together with Christ, the Head of the Church, to give praise, honor, and glory to the Father through the power of the Holy Spirit. Each week the Church, the new People of God, gathers on Sunday, or the Lord's Day, to celebrate and share in the Paschal Mystery. In addition to Sunday celebrations, the liturgical year of the Church is made up of a cycle of seasons, solemnities, feasts, and memorials. The lessons in this unit focus on the seasons of the liturgical year of the Church. This page lists many of the solemnities, feasts, and memorials that are celebrated throughout the year.

JANUARY
Mary, the Mother of God (January 1)
Elizabeth Ann Seton, Religious (January 4)
John Neumann, Bishop (January 5)
Agnes, Virgin and Martyr (January 21)
Conversion of Saint Paul, Apostle (January 25)
Thomas Aquinas, Priest and Doctor (January 28)

FEBRUARY
Presentation of the Lord (February 2)
Blase, Bishop and Martyr (February 3)
Agatha, Virgin and Martyr (February 5)
Our Lady of Lourdes (February 11)
Chair of Saint Peter, Apostle (February 22)

MARCH
Perpetua and Felicity, Martyrs (March 7)
Patrick, Bishop (March 17)
Joseph, Husband of Mary (March 19)
Annunciation (March 25)

APRIL
Mark, Evangelist (April 25)
Catherine of Siena, Virgin and Doctor (April 29)

MAY
Joseph the Worker (May 1)
Athanasius, Bishop and Doctor (May 2)
Philip and James, Apostles (May 3)
Matthias, Apostle (May 14)
Isidore (May 15)
Visitation (May 31)
Holy Trinity (First Sunday after Pentecost)

Body and Blood of Christ (Sunday after Holy Trinity)
Sacred Heart (Friday following Second Sunday after Pentecost)

JUNE
Charles Lwanga and Companions, Martyrs (June 3)
Barnabas, Apostle (June 11)
Anthony of Padua, Priest and Doctor (June 13)
Birth of John the Baptist (June 24)
Peter and Paul, Apostles (June 29)

JULY
Thomas, Apostle (July 3)
Blessed Kateri Tekakwitha, Virgin (July 14)
Our Lady of Mount Carmel (July 16)
Mary Magdalene (July 22)
James, Apostle (July 25)
Joachim and Ann, Parents of Mary (July 26)
Martha (July 29)
Ignatius of Loyola, Priest (July 31)

AUGUST
Transfiguration (August 6)
Lawrence, Deacon and Martyr (August 10)
Clare, Virgin (August 11)
Assumption (August 15)
Queenship of Mary (August 22)
Rose of Lima, Virgin (August 23)
Bartholomew, Apostle (August 24)
Monica (August 27)
Augustine of Hippo, Bishop and Doctor (August 28)

SEPTEMBER
Birth of Mary (September 8)
Peter Claver, Priest (September 9)
Triumph of the Cross (September 14)
Our Lady of Sorrows (September 15)
Matthew, Apostle and Evangelist (September 21)
Michael, Gabriel, and Raphael, Archangels (September 29)

OCTOBER
Theresa of the Child Jesus, Virgin (October 1)
Francis of Assisi (October 4)
Our Lady of the Rosary (October 7)
Teresa of Jesus, Virgin and Doctor (October 15)
Luke, Evangelist (October 18)
Isaac Jogues and John de Brébeuf, Priests and Martyrs, and Companions (October 19)
Simon and Jude, Apostles (October 28)

NOVEMBER
All Saints (November 1)
All Souls (November 2)
Martin de Porres, Religious (November 3)
Frances Xavier Cabrini, Virgin (November 13)
Elizabeth of Hungary (November 17)
Presentation of Mary (November 21)
Cecilia, Virgin and Martyr (November 22)
Andrew, Apostle (November 30)
Christ the King (Last Sunday in Ordinary Time)

DECEMBER
Immaculate Conception (December 8)
Our Lady of Guadalupe (December 12)
Christmas (December 25)
Stephen, First Martyr (December 26)
John, Apostle and Evangelist (December 27)
Holy Innocents (December 28)

Ordinary Time

Faith Focus

How does the Church worship God throughout the year?

The Word of the Lord

These are the Gospel readings for the Thirty-second Sunday in Ordinary Time. Choose this year's reading. Read and discuss it with your family.

Year A
    Matthew 25:1–13

Year B
    Mark 12:38–44 or
    Mark 12:41–44

Year C
    Luke 20:27–38 or
    Mark 20:27,
        34–38

What You See

The Church uses different colors to celebrate the liturgical seasons. Green is used during Ordinary Time. Green symbolizes life and growth.

The Church's Year of Worship

We celebrate our life and our history by years. The Church also celebrates her life and history on a yearly cycle. We call the Church's yearly cycle of worship the liturgical year. All the seasons and feasts of the Church's liturgical year help us remember the story of God's love for us. Celebrating the Church's year of worship enables us to take part in God's loving plan of salvation.

Advent, Christmas, Lent, Easter, and Ordinary Time are the seasons of the Church's year. We remember and celebrate the announcement and fulfillment of God's plan of salvation in Jesus Christ.

The Triduum is at the center of our year of worship. Beginning on the evening of Holy Thursday and ending on Easter Sunday evening, the Triduum is our three-day celebration of the Paschal Mystery.

The longest part of the Church's year is called Ordinary Time. The word *ordinary* comes from a Latin word meaning "number." During Ordinary Time the Sundays and weeks are named by the use of numbers; for example, the Thirty-second Sunday in Ordinary Time.

The thirty-third or thirty-fourth weeks of Ordinary Time focus on the whole mystery of Christ's life. We listen to the four accounts of the Gospel over a three-year cycle: Matthew in Year A, Mark and John in Year B, and Luke in Year C.

All throughout Ordinary Time we join with the disciples. We walk along the shores of the Sea of Galilee and into Capernaum and the other towns and villages. All the time we listen, we watch, and we learn from our Teacher what it means to be his disciple.

All throughout the seasons of the year we gather on special days called feasts. Some feasts, such as the Transfiguration and the Ascension, celebrate the mysteries of our faith. Other feasts, such as Peter and Paul, Apostles; Our Lady of Guadalupe; and All Saints honor the holy men and women who are part of our faith story.

Living the Great Commandment

On the Thirty–second Sunday in Ordinary Time we listen to Jesus teaching about the Great Commandment (read Mark 12:28–34). In this space create a symbol for each part of the Great Commandment.

Love God with all my heart.

Love my neighbor as myself.

The Family Tree of Jesus

All families have a history and a story to tell. All the people who are part of your family history make up your family tree—your parents, brothers and sisters, grandparents, aunts, uncles, and family members who lived generations ago.

Jesus has a family tree too. We Christians use it to help us celebrate Advent. We call it the Jesse tree. The tree is named for Jesse, a shepherd from Bethlehem. He lived about one thousand years before Jesus. Jesse was the father of David, who grew up to be the greatest king of the people of Israel. David is an ancestor of Jesus.

During Advent we remember the people—like Jesse and David—who are part of Jesus' family tree. We decorate the Jesse tree with symbols of these Old and New Testament figures. The Jesse tree is like our family tree. Each person on the Jesse tree is part of the long story of God's loving plan of salvation that is fulfilled in Jesus.

Remembering the faith stories of the people on the Jesse tree helps us remember God's great love for us—and for all people.

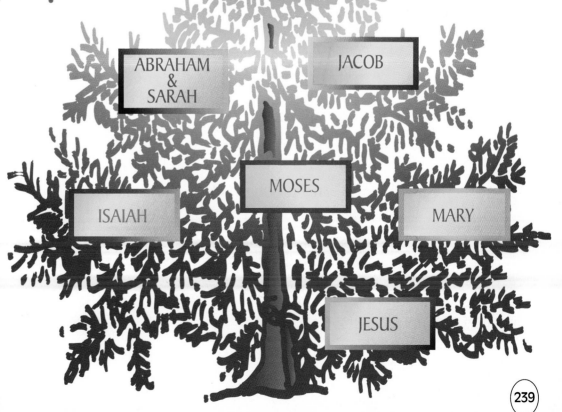

ADAM & EVE

ABRAHAM & SARAH

JACOB

MOSES

ISAIAH

MARY

JESUS

Remembering
the Story of Salvation

Make your own Jesse tree. You can use a small evergreen tree or just some branches. Make a symbol for each of these figures. Add others of your own. Put the symbols on your Jesse tree.

When **Adam** and **Eve** refused to obey,
God promised a savior would come some day.

Noah is a man to note;
while others laughed he built a boat.

Abraham and **Sarah** obeyed God's call.
Their faith is an example for one and for all.

When **Isaac** was born, Sarah was old.
Her laughter rang out, so we are told.

Isaac's son **Jacob** was rich and able;
soon twelve healthy sons sat at his table.

Joseph saved his family from starvation.
In Egypt they grew into a very strong nation.

Moses, leader and man of God,
led Israel through the Red Sea dryshod.

David, the Lord's shepherd and king,
could rule, protect, play, and sing.

Isaiah was one who spoke for his Lord.
The faithful listened to every word.

John the Baptist's announcement was clear.
"Prepare the way! The Lord draws near!"

On **Mary** God's blessings were abundantly poured.
Yes was her response to the angel of the Lord.

Joseph cared for Mary as he promised he would,
Joseph the mild, the patient, the good.

Angels came and shepherds adored,
Jesus is born, our Savior and Lord!

Faith Focus

Faith Focus

What do we prepare for during Advent?

The Word of the Lord

These are the Gospel readings for the Second Sunday of Advent. Choose this year's reading. Read and discuss it with your family.

Year A
  Matthew 3:1–12

Year B
  Mark 1:1–8

Year C
  Luke 3:1–6

Day of the Lord

Advent reminds us of three things:

- The Lord comes in history at Christmas.
- The Lord comes in mystery each day.
- The Lord comes in majesty at the end of time.

The prophets of the Old Testament often used the phrase *day of the Lord* to describe the Lord's coming. Through the prophets, God encouraged the people of Israel to seek out and welcome his Promised One.

Through the prophet Isaiah, God described a day when the Messiah, the Promised One, would come (see Isaiah 11:6–9). Then even enemies would come and live together in peace.

During Advent we make room for the Lord in our lives and hearts. We pray with Mary and Joseph as they prepare to welcome Jesus into their family.

On Christmas Eve, the last day of Advent, we listen to the Scripture, and God speaks to us about that great day, the birthday of Jesus the King and Savior promised to David. We pray:
  Come, Lord Jesus,
  do not delay.

FROM OPENING PRAYER
MASS IN THE MORNING
DECEMBER 24

When we faithfully keep the Advent season, we are ready to welcome Jesus on Christmas Day. Peace rules our hearts and our homes. Peace rules the earth. God's Promised One has come.

On the Day of the Lord . . .

Look up and read Isaiah 11:6–9. Then fill in the spaces with symbols or pictures for the missing words. Then prayerfully reflect on the words of Isaiah.

The   shall be the guest of the   ,

and the   shall lie down with the   ;

The calf and the young   shall browse together,

with a little   to guide them.

The   and the   shall be neighbors;

together their young shall rest;

the   shall eat hay like the   .

The   shall play by the   's den. . . .

There shall be no harm or ruin on all my holy   ;

for the   shall be filled with knowledge of the Lord.

BASED ON ISAIAH 11:6–9

242

How does celebrating Advent strengthen our faith in Jesus' presence with us?

These are the Gospel readings for the Third Sunday of Advent. Choose this year's reading. Read and discuss it with your family.

Year A
    Matthew 11:2–11

Year B
    John 1:6–8, 19–28

Year C
    Luke 3:10–18

The Third Sunday of Advent is the midpoint of the Advent season. In some dioceses the priest may wear rose-colored vestments and the rose-colored candle on the Advent wreath is lit. The color rose signifies our joy at the hope of the coming of our Savior, Jesus Christ.

The Lord's Coming

With joy we welcome new people into our lives. We may prepare for them by cooking special foods and sharing a meal with them. Advent is the time the Church helps us get ready to welcome Jesus. We pray:

Father of our Lord Jesus
    Christ,
ever faithful to your promises
and ever close to your Church:
the earth rejoices in hope of
    the Savior's coming
and looks forward with longing
to his return at the end of time.

FROM ALTERNATIVE OPENING PRAYER,
THIRD SUNDAY OF ADVENT

As we prepare for something wonderful in our lives, we experience many different feelings. We feel excitement and anticipation. We feel happiness and joy. We can hardly wait for the wonderful time that is to come!

During Advent we prepare for our celebration of the birth of Jesus. We remember that the Son of God took on flesh and lived among us. Our faith tells us that this coming of the Son of God among us is a sign that he is with us each moment of every day.

All throughout Advent the Church recalls Israel's waiting for the coming of the Lord. Our hearts are filled with the hope of the prophet Zephaniah:

Shout for joy, O daughter Zion!
    sing joyfully, O Israel!
The LORD, your God, is in
    your midst,
a mighty savior;
He will rejoice over you with
    gladness,
and renew you in his love.

ZEPHANIAH 3:14, 17

We believe that Jesus is our Lord and the promised Messiah. We remember his birth at Christmas. We also look forward to the time when he will come again in glory. During Advent we seek to grow more loving day by day. We pray that we will be ready when the Lord comes to welcome us into the kingdom of heaven.

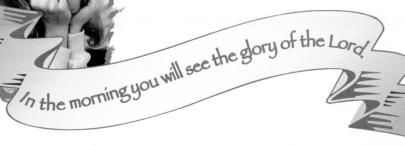

In the morning you will see the glory of the Lord

The Lord Is Near

"Rejoice in the Lord always. I shall say it again: rejoice! Your kindness should be known to all. The Lord is near" (Philippians 4:4–5).

Joy is a gift of a loving person. Joy is yours to keep and yours to spread. Plan three ways your presence and actions will spread joy during Advent this year.

Action	When I Will Do It
_____	_____
_____	_____
_____	_____
_____	_____
_____	_____
_____	_____
_____	_____
_____	_____
_____	_____

Faith Focus

What are the Gospel stories of the Annunciation and the Visitation?

The Word of the Lord

These are the Gospel readings for the Fourth Sunday of Advent. Choose this year's reading. Read and discuss it with your family.

Year A
Matthew 1:18–24

Year B
Luke 1:26–38

Year C
Luke 1:39–45

The Annunciation, stained glass

The Visitation, stained glass

Stories About Jesus' Birth

We like to hear stories about our birth: who visited us just after we were born, why our parents gave us our name. We also like to hear stories about when we were infants and toddlers. Our parents know all these stories, and they share them with us.

The Gospel accounts of Luke and Matthew tell us the stories about Jesus' birth and infancy. Both Luke and Matthew tell us the story of the angel Gabriel's announcement of the birth of Jesus. In Luke we read the story of the angel's announcement to Mary. She said yes to God and agreed to become the Mother of Jesus. We call this announcement to Mary the Annunciation.

In Matthew we read the story of the announcement to Joseph. An angel helped him understand that Mary's child would be the Savior promised by God. Many years before, through the prophet Isaiah, God had announced that "the virgin shall be with child, and bear a son" (Isaiah 7:14). The angel helped Joseph understand that this virgin was Mary. When the angel asked Joseph to take care of Mary, he agreed, and immediately he took her into his home.

During Advent Christians listen to these stories and remember the events. These events help us celebrate Advent.

Luke's account of the Gospel also tells us the story of Zechariah and Elizabeth. For a long time they had prayed for a child. God heard their prayer, and Elizabeth gave birth to a son, whom they named John.

Zechariah praised God for their son and announced John's future work: "And you, child, will be called prophet of the Most High, / for you will go before the Lord to prepare his ways" (Luke 1:76).

After Mary learned about Zechariah and Elizabeth's good news, she went to visit them. We call this story the Visitation. When Mary visited her cousin, Elizabeth said, "Most blessed are you among women" (Luke 1:42).

Praying the Story of Mary

The story of the Annunciation also became a prayer called the Angelus. This prayer is customarily said three times a day: morning, noon, and night. Take the time to pray it now.

Leader: The angel of the Lord declared unto Mary,

All: **and she conceived of the Holy Spirit.**
Hail Mary . . .

Leader: "Behold the handmaid of the Lord.

All: **May it be done unto me according to your word."**
Hail Mary . . .

Leader: And the Word was made flesh

All: **and dwelt among us.**
Hail Mary . . .

Leader: Pray for us, O holy Mother of God,

All: **that we may be made worthy of the promises of Christ.**

Leader: Let us pray.
O Lord, it was through the message of an angel that we learned of the Incarnation of Christ, your Son. Pour your grace into our hearts, and by his Passion and cross bring us to the glory of his Resurrection. Through Christ, our Lord.

All: **Amen.**

Faith Focus

What do we learn from the Gospel story of the angel's announcement to the shepherds of the birth of Jesus?

The Word of the Lord

These are the Gospel readings for Mass on Christmas Day. Choose one reading. Read and discuss it with your family.

John 1:1–18 or
John 1:1–5, 9–14

Shepherds First

Sometimes the people in our lives surprise us. They do something we do not expect. When that happens, we learn a new thing about them. What happened on the night Jesus was born tells us something new about him.

Luke's account of the Gospel includes the announcement of the birth of Jesus to the shepherds. They were the first to receive the good news of Jesus' birth. As the shepherds watched their sheep, an angel appeared to them and said:

> "[T]oday in the city of David a savior has been born for you who is Messiah and Lord." LUKE 2:11

The shepherds hurried to Bethlehem. There they found Jesus and Mary and Joseph as the angel said they would.

Throughout the history of Israel, the writers of the Sacred Scripture used the image of shepherds to speak about God. For the Israelites God was a shepherd who watched over them, his sheep. They often prayed:

> The LORD is my shepherd. PSALM 23:1

However, at the time of Jesus' birth, many people thought that shepherds were of little worth. Their hard, dangerous work kept them in the fields day and night. This meant that they were unable to observe religious practices. Because of this, religious leaders thought shepherds were unfaithful, unimportant people.

But it was to shepherds, Luke tells us, that God announced the birth of the Savior. Jesus is the Messiah and Lord of all.

The Lord Is Our Shepherd

For each letter of the word shepherd, write a word or phrase that tells us about who Jesus is. Then use your words and phrases and write a paragraph telling others about Jesus.

S
H
E
P
H
E
R
D

_____

_____

_____

_____

_____

_____

_____

_____

_____

_____

_____

_____

_____

_____

Faith Focus

How does the Church honor Mary during the Christmas season?

The Word of the Lord

These are the readings for the Solemnity of Mary, the Mother of God. Read and discuss them with your family.

First Reading
    Numbers 6:22–27

Second Reading
    Galatians 4:4–7

Gospel
    Luke 2:16–21

Mary, Mother of God

Each year on Mother's Day we honor our mother. We thank her for taking us to the soccer game. We thank her for cooking our meals and for working to clothe us. We thank her for her love each day of the year. What are some other special times when you honor your mother?

The Church honors Mary, the Mother of God, many times during the year. During the Christmas season we think about Mary in a special way.

While the celebration of the birth of Jesus is at the heart of our Christmas season, we also celebrate the feast of the Holy Family between Christmas and January 1. At our celebration of Mass on that day, we pray that through Mary's prayers and the prayers of her husband, Joseph, our families may live in peace and love.

The Church also sets aside the first day of the new year, January 1, as the Solemnity of Mary, the Mother of God. On this holy day and holiday, we gather to celebrate Mass. We ask God to bless our new year. We ask that Mary's prayer and her motherly love bring us joy forever.

By remembering Mary as the Mother of God and our mother too, we begin the year with blessings. Mary reminds us of what the whole Church desires to do. We all want to say yes to God as she did. We all want to do God's will all our life, just as Mary did.

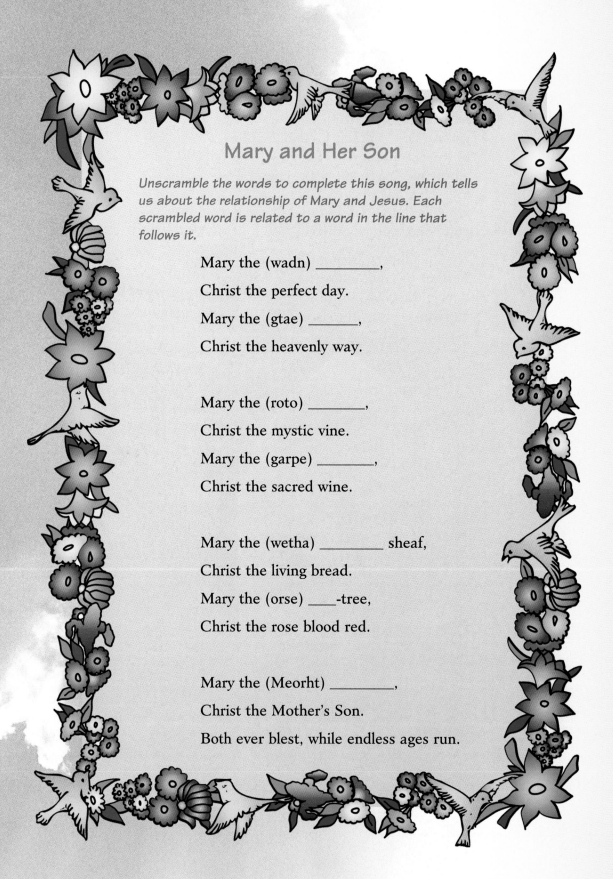

Mary and Her Son

Unscramble the words to complete this song, which tells us about the relationship of Mary and Jesus. Each scrambled word is related to a word in the line that follows it.

Mary the (wadn) _____,

Christ the perfect day.

Mary the (gtae) _____,

Christ the heavenly way.

Mary the (roto) _____,

Christ the mystic vine.

Mary the (garpe) _____,

Christ the sacred wine.

Mary the (wetha) _____ sheaf,

Christ the living bread.

Mary the (orse) ____-tree,

Christ the rose blood red.

Mary the (Meorht) _____,

Christ the Mother's Son.

Both ever blest, while endless ages run.

Faith Focus

What are we called to do during Lent?

The Word of the Lord

Choose this year's Gospel reading for the First Sunday of Lent. Read and discuss it with your family.

Year A
   Matthew 4:1–11

Year B
   Mark 1:12–15

Year C
   Luke 4:1–13

What You See

In our churches we see signs that Lent is a season of discipline. The color of Lent is purple, the color of penitence. No flowers or brightly colored decorations greet us. We sing no joyous Alleluia or Gloria.

Lent

For many of us, the winter landscape seems bare. Leaves fall from trees, flowers die, and grass turns brown. But we trust that after winter, spring will come and bring new life. Each year during Lent we renew the new life of Christ we received in Baptism.

Lent begins on Ash Wednesday. On Ash Wednesday the Church gathers to begin our Lenten journey. As ashes are placed on our head, we hear the words:
   Turn away from sin and be faithful to the Gospel.

During Lent the Church calls us to enter more fully into Jesus' death and Resurrection. We make sacrifices to do this. We may decide to share more of our time and talents with others. We may give up something that we enjoy. We want habits of goodness to live in us. We support one another in our decisions during Lent. Together we look forward to celebrating the joy of Easter.

Choose two small twigs or pieces of wood and tie them with twine to form a simple cross. Place your cross on the prayer table as you gather for prayer. Then pray the prayer together.

Take Up Your Cross

Introduction

LEADER: During Lent we walk with Jesus. We hope to share in his Resurrection at Easter.

The Word of God

READER: *Proclaim Mark 10:35–45.*

LEADER: Jesus looked ahead at the cross he would bear. Are you willing to take up your small cross this Lent?

ALL: **We are.**

Lenten Commitment

LEADER: Let us pause and decide on one thing we know we need to do to be more like Jesus. *(Pause.)*

As I call your name, please come forward.

(Name), will you strive to take up your Lenten cross and follow Jesus?

STUDENT: I will.

Closing Prayer

(Choose a wooden cross from the prayer table.)

LEADER: May the cross of Christ remind us to open our minds and hearts to God.

ALL: **Amen!**

LEADER: May we all walk with Jesus and enter into the joy of Easter.

ALL: **Amen!**

LEADER: May we pray for one another. May we support one another as we take up our cross as a sign of our love of Jesus, who carried his cross because of his love for us.

ALL: **Amen!**

Faith Focus

How did God show his compassion through Jesus?

The Word of the Lord

Choose this year's Gospel reading for the Second Sunday of Lent. Read and discuss it with your family.

Year A
Matthew 17:1–9

Year B
Mark 9:2–10

Year C
Luke 9:28–36

What You Hear

During Lent only a Psalm verse is used before the Gospel reading. The Alleluia that is sung in every season outside of Lent is not said or sung.

The Compassion of God

When something sad or bad happens to someone we love, we feel compassion for that person. The word *compassion* means "to suffer with" another person. Can you remember a time you felt the suffering of another person?

The story of Jesus is the story of a man of compassion. When we see the compassion of Jesus, we see God's compassion for us. At the beginning of his public ministry, Jesus urged his followers to be filled with compassion, just as their heavenly Father was filled with compassion (see Luke 6:36). All through his life, Jesus suffered with the suffering people who came to him for healing and forgiveness.

Toward the end of his life, Jesus looked over the city of Jerusalem. Deeply saddened that so many people turned away from God, he wept and prayed:

"Jerusalem, . . . how many times I yearned to gather your children together, as a hen gathers her young under her wings, but you were unwilling!"

MATTHEW 23:37

During Lent the Church invites us to imitate the compassion of God. He asks us to reach out to those who need our help. Find out what your parish is doing during Lent to help others. As a class, choose a way you will participate in this Lenten outreach. Then pray the prayer together.

The Lord Is Compassionate

LEADER: Bless the Lord, O my soul.

ALL: **Bless the Lord, O my soul.**

BOYS: Bless the Lord, O my soul; bless the Lord, all my being.

GIRLS: Bless the Lord, O my soul; never forget the Lord's greatness.

BOYS: The Lord pardons our offenses and heals our ills.

GIRLS: The Lord redeems us from death and crowns us with goodness and compassion.

BOYS: The Lord fills us with good and renews our strength like the eagle's.

GIRLS: The Lord upholds the poor; the Lord guards the oppressed.

BOYS: Merciful and gracious is the Lord, slow to anger, quick to bless.

GIRLS: The Lord does not treat us with anger; the Lord treats us with mercy and compassion.

BOYS: As high as the heavens are above the earth, so is God abundant in mercy.

GIRLS: Just as parents are compassionate toward their children, so the Lord is compassionate toward those who show reverence to him.

LEADER: The compassion of the Lord lasts forever. May the Lord have compassion on us.

ALL: **Bless the Lord, O my soul. Amen.**

The Third Week of Lent

Faith Focus

What does praying make us more aware of?

The Word of the Lord

Choose this year's Gospel reading for the Third Sunday of Lent. Read and discuss it with your family.

Year A
John 4:5–42, or
John 4:5–15,
19–26, 39,
40–44

Year B
John 2:13–25

Year C
Luke 13:1–9

God Is Near

We like to spend time with our friends, talking and playing and laughing together. But most of us like to spend time alone too. We enjoy a quiet moment to think our own thoughts.

One friend who is with us all the time is God. Faith tells us that God is always near. Prayer helps us become more aware of how close God is to us. Sometimes we pray with others; sometimes we pray alone in the quiet of our heart.

When we pray together, we are sometimes silent together. In fact, our prayer together includes and depends on moments of silence. In silence we are better able to pay close attention to God. The psalmist tells us:

Be still before the LORD;
wait for God.
PSALM 37:7

During Lent we sharpen our awareness of how Jesus taught us to pray. Jesus told us to pray quietly without drawing attention to ourselves. He taught us that prayer should be a normal part of our life. He taught us to pray and to trust that God is near and listens to our prayer.

Lent is a good time to resolve to pray frequently. In prayer you draw near to God, who is always near to you.

Be Still and Wait for God

Pray this prayer together. Then choose one of the petitions and make a bookmark as a reminder to pray always.

LEADER: Let us come together and worship the Lord, our God, who is always near.

ALL: **Be still before the Lord; wait for God.**

LEADER: Let us pray for peace in the world.

ALL: **Be still before the Lord; wait for God.**

LEADER: Let us pray for those who are doing good works during Lent.

ALL: **Be still before the Lord; wait for God.**

LEADER: Let us pray to continue our own prayers and good works during Lent.

ALL: **Be still before the Lord; wait for God.**

LEADER: Lord, hear our prayer that we may be ready to celebrate Easter. We ask this in Jesus' name. Amen.

Faith Focus

Why do we give up things during Lent?

The Word of the Lord

Choose this year's Gospel reading for the Fourth Sunday of Lent. Read and discuss it with your family.

Year A
   John 9:1–41 or
   John 9:1, 6–9,
      13–17,
      34–38

Year B
   John 3:14–21

Year C
   Luke 15:1–3, 11–32

The Eye of a Needle

In Jesus' time, Jerusalem was a city surrounded by a wall. The people there called one of its narrow gates the "Eye of a Needle." So when a rich man asked Jesus what he had to do to get to heaven, Jesus told a parable about a camel passing through the eye of a needle. The camel carried so much baggage on its back that it could not get through the narrow gateway.

In this story Jesus reminds us that things we have can sometimes get in our way on our journey to God. Jesus told the man to give away what he had and follow Jesus. But the man couldn't do it. He went away sad. Remembering this story during Lent helps us remember to share our possessions with others. This is one way we can live as Jesus wants us to live.

Giving and Giving Up

Sometimes we enjoy giving our time to help others. But giving time to others is not always easy. Sometimes we enjoy giving up something that matters to us when someone else needs it. But that is not always easy either.

During Lent the Church invites us to give to others, especially to people who are poor. To give a little more is called almsgiving. Long ago an alms was an amount of money. Almsgiving today includes sharing our time, talents, and goods, as well as our money.

Fasting is another way of doing penance or giving up something for a greater good. When we fast, we voluntarily give up food for a certain amount of time. Following the example of Christ, who fasted often, this practice has long been a part of Catholic tradition. Lent and each Friday of the year, in honor of Jesus' death, are special times of fasting in the Church. On Ash Wednesday and Good Friday, Catholics between the ages of 18 and 59 fast by eating only one full meal a day. Fasting can help us make up for our sins and deepen our relationship with God and others. Some people fast in order to identify more closely with the poor and hungry of the world.

But we can think of fasting in a bigger way. Fasting can include giving up bad habits, such as eating and drinking unhealthy foods, or giving up our greedy desires.

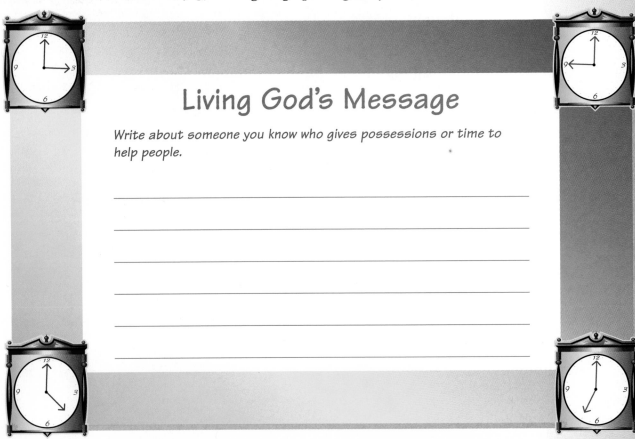

Living God's Message

Write about someone you know who gives possessions or time to help people.

_____

_____

_____

_____

_____

_____

Faith Focus

What does Jesus teach us about repentance?

The Word of the Lord

Choose this year's Gospel reading for the Fifth Sunday of Lent. Read and discuss it with your family.

Year A
   John 11:1–45 or
   John 11:3–7, 17,
      20–27,
      33–45

Year B
   John 12:20–33

Year C
   John 8:1–11

Turn and Live

Think of a time you hurt someone you really care about. How did you feel? What did you want to do? We just want to be forgiven. We wish we had never hurt our friend. We just want things to be fixed. We want to change.

Jesus told us over and over again that God always forgives us. He always wants things to be just right between himself and us.

What we need to do is trust God and repent. We need to turn *from* unloving and hurtful words, actions, and attitudes. We need to turn *to* loving words, actions, and attitudes that bring harmony and life.

In the parable of the Good Shepherd, Jesus told of a shepherd who searched for a single lost sheep. The shepherds of Israel often faced great danger from howling hyenas, baying wolves, sly jackals, and sharp-toothed bears. When a sheep wandered away, the shepherd went out to battle these wild animals and rescue the one who had strayed.

In his parable Jesus said that as the good shepherd in the

Painting of the finding of the lost sheep, painting on wood. Emanuel Vigeland (1875–1948), Norwegian artist.

parable, he would risk his life for his sheep. He is our Good Shepherd, and we are his sheep.

We stray when we sin. Jesus will come after us. He will come in search of us to forgive us and bring us home.

During Lent we celebrate the sacrament of Reconciliation. We recognize and admit our hurtful actions. We confess our sins.

These special celebrations are the welcoming arms of Jesus today. The sacrament of Reconciliation is the Church's way of helping us choose life with God and with one another in harmony and community.

A Litany of Repentance

Lent is a season of repentance. We think about how we are living as followers of Jesus and try to do better. Pray this prayer together with your classmates and with your family.

LEADER: Lord, you announced the good news of God's love for us.

ALL: **Lord, have mercy.**

LEADER: You announced the coming of the kingdom of God.

ALL: **Lord, have mercy.**

LEADER: You preached a message of repentance.

ALL: **Lord, have mercy.**

LEADER: You forgave and healed the sinful man who could not walk.

ALL: **Lord, have mercy.**

LEADER: You invited the tax collectors Levi and Zacchaeus and the good thief into the kingdom.

ALL: **Lord, have mercy.**

LEADER: You forgave the woman who sinned.

ALL: **Lord, have mercy.**

LEADER: You will surely forgive us our sins, especially . . . *(Pause.)* Help us forgive others as abundantly as you forgive us.

ALL: **Lord, have mercy.**

Palm Sunday of the Lord's Passion

Faith Focus

Why do we celebrate Palm Sunday of the Lord's Passion?

The Word of the Lord

Choose this year's Gospel reading for Palm Sunday of the Lord's Passion. Read and discuss it with your family.

Year A
    Matthew 26:14–
        27: 66 or
        27:11–54

Year B
    Mark 14:1–15:47
        or 15:1–39

Year C
    Luke 22:14–23:56
        or 23:1–49

Holy Week

When a well-known person comes to your school or town, you welcome them with a marching band and banners and balloons. When Jesus entered the city of Jerusalem, the people gave him a special welcome.

On that day, the people of Jerusalem welcomed Jesus as a messiah. He did not ride on a mighty horse or in a gilded chariot as a great soldier or a conquering hero. Jesus entered Jerusalem riding a donkey. But as he entered, the people cheered him as they would a great king:

"Hosanna to the Son of David; blessed is he who comes in the name of the Lord; hosanna in the highest."

MATTHEW 21:9

The people proclaimed *Hosanna*, a greeting of joy and praise, which means "Lord, grant salvation."

The people spread cloaks on the road to make the path smooth and less dusty for Jesus. They waved branches taken from palm trees. This welcome of Jesus, as the Messiah riding on a donkey, reminds us that Jesus is the king of everyone, even the lowly. Jesus is a king filled with compassion and care.

The celebration of Palm Sunday begins Holy Week. We begin our celebration with a procession. Everyone walks into church carrying palm branches. This recalls the day Jesus rode into Jerusalem.

Jesus' final entry into Jerusalem, stained-glass triptych, or three-paneled stained-glass window

Blessing of palm branches before the entrance procession into the church, Liturgy of Palm Sunday of the Lord's Passion

Hosanna! A Meditation

Sit quietly.

Close your eyes and breathe slowly.

Remember the story of Jesus' entry into Jerusalem.

Compare the meaning of this story to your own life and share your thoughts with Jesus. Take the time to praise him for the gifts he has brought to your life.

After a few quiet moments, write down any key words or phrases that will help you remember this prayer experience.

_____

_____

_____

_____

What do we remember as the Church celebrates Holy Thursday?

Choose one of the Scripture readings for Holy Thursday. Read and discuss it with your family.

Reading I
Exodus 12:1–8, 11–14

Reading II
1 Corinthians 11:23–26

Gospel
John 13:1–15

Do This in Memory of Me

Do you remember eating a special meal with your family or your friends? What made it special to you? Did you eat special food? Did someone say something that made you feel good about yourself? The Church remembers a special meal that Jesus ate with his disciples.

On the evening of Holy Thursday, we remember the last time Jesus gathered the disciples and shared a meal with them. This meal celebrated the Passover. On this special day the Jewish people celebrate their passage from slavery in Egypt to freedom. They remember the Covenant with God.

All his life Jesus celebrated this greatest of Jewish feasts with his family and friends. Now he shared the foods of the Passover for the last time. But at this Last Supper, Jesus did something special. Jesus changed the bread and wine he shared with his disciples into his own Body and Blood. He took the bread and broke it and said,

"This is my body, which will be given for you." LUKE 22:19

After the meal, he passed the cup of wine for them to drink. He said,

"This cup is the new covenant in my blood, which will be shed for you."   LUKE 22:20

Jesus then commanded his disciples to share this meal with one another. He said,

"[D]o this in memory of me." LUKE 22:19

The Last Supper. Mimida Roveda, contemporary Brazilian painter.

Today, at the celebration of the Eucharist, the Church continues to do what Jesus asked his disciples to do. On Holy Thursday we especially remember his last Passover. We call our celebration on that day the Mass of the Lord's Supper.

The Lord's Supper

Create an announcement inviting your family to join in celebrating the Mass of the Lord's Supper. Display it in your home.

Triduum / Good Friday

Faith Focus

How does the Church remember the death of Jesus?

The Word of the Lord

Choose one of the Scripture readings for Good Friday. Read and discuss it with your family.

Reading I
Isaiah 52:13–53:12

Reading II
Hebrews 4:14–16,
5:7–9

Gospel
John 18:1–19:42

Good Friday

At some time in your life, someone you love will die. This may have already happened to you. You know that when this happens, everyone in your house is sad. People tell stories about the one who has died. The Church does this too, as it remembers the death of Jesus.

On Good Friday our churches have no decorations. The tabernacle is empty; its door is open. There is no altar cloth covering the altar table. The Church gathers to reflect on the Passion and death of Jesus.

Our liturgy on Good Friday is called the celebration of the Lord's Passion. Good Friday is the only day of the year on which Mass is not celebrated. The celebration of the Lord's Passion is made up of three parts:

- The first part is the Liturgy of the Word. The Gospel reading is a proclamation of the Passion and death of Jesus according to John. After the Gospel proclamation, the Church invites us to pray for the needs of the world.

- The second part of the celebration of the Lord's Passion is the Veneration of the Cross. In this part of the liturgy we show reverence and respect for the cross because Jesus died for us on a cross. We might do this by walking in procession, bowing before the cross, and kissing it.

- The third part of the celebration of the Lord's Passion is Holy Communion. The Church invites us to receive the Body and Blood of Christ, which was consecrated at Mass on Holy Thursday.

The celebration of the Lord's Passion ends as it began. The altar cloth is removed from the altar and the tabernacle is empty. In deep silence we leave to begin the long sabbath rest until the celebration of the Easter Vigil.

Veneration of the Cross, Liturgy for Good Friday

Jesus Asks, You Respond

Each day you do many things to show your love for God and others as Jesus did. You make sacrifices. You give your time. You share your gifts. You take up your cross and follow Jesus as he asked you to do.

On one of the beams of this cross, describe something you did for someone. On the other cross beam, describe how it helped the person.

Faith Focus

Why is the Easter season a time of rejoicing?

The Word of the Lord

Choose the Gospel readings for Easter Sunday this year. Read and discuss them with your family.

Year A
  John 20:1–9
    or
  Matthew 28:1–10
    or
  Luke 24:13–35

Year B
  John 20:1–9 or
  Mark 16:1–8 or
  Luke 24:13–35

Year C
  John 20:1–9 or
  Luke 24:1–12 or
  Luke 24:13–35

Alleluia

On our best days, we feel great joy just to be alive. We can do many wonderful things. Easter is a wonderful day in the Church—a day when we rejoice because God has raised Jesus to new life.

Saint Augustine reminds us that we are Easter people and Alleluia is our song. *Alleluia* is a Hebrew word that means "Praise the Lord." At the Easter Vigil the presider solemnly intones the Alleluia, which we have not heard all during Lent. The Church sings "Alleluia!" repeatedly during the Easter season. We continuously thank and praise God for the new life of Easter. We praise God because we have passed from death to life through our Baptism.

Throughout Lent we focused on turning away from sin to become followers of Jesus. During the Easter season we rejoice in our new life in Christ. We sing "Alleluia!" and proclaim, "This is the day the Lord has made, let us rejoice and be glad in it."

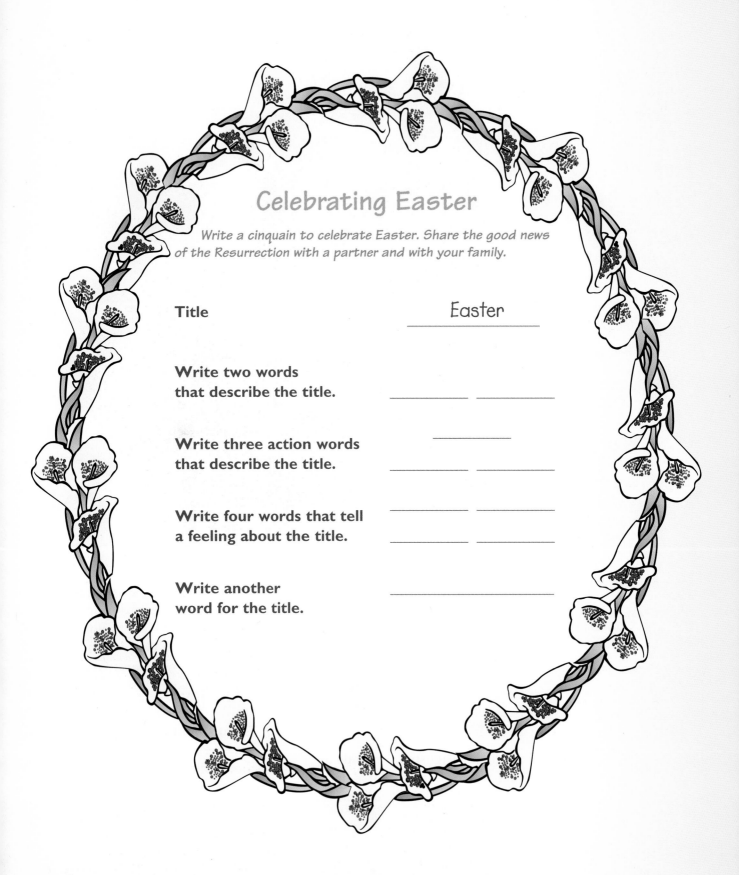

Celebrating Easter

Write a cinquain to celebrate Easter. Share the good news of the Resurrection with a partner and with your family.

Title   Easter
_____

**Write two words
that describe the title.**   _____ _____

**Write three action words
that describe the title.**   _____
_____ _____

**Write four words that tell
a feeling about the title.**   _____ _____
_____ _____

**Write another
word for the title.**   _____

268

Faith Focus

How does the story of Thomas remind us of our gift of faith?

The Word of the Lord

This is the Gospel reading for the Second Sunday of Easter each year. Read and discuss it with your family.

John 20:19–31

Doubting Thomas, detail from stained-glass window

Thomas's Profession of Faith

When someone tells us about an event they have witnessed, we believe them. We believe them because they were there.

When Jesus first appeared to the disciples, Thomas the Apostle was not with them. The disciples told Thomas that Jesus appeared to them, but Thomas refused to believe them. He said he would believe only when he saw the Risen Jesus himself—when he could see Jesus' wounds. This refusal of Thomas to believe the other disciples has become so famous that someone who demands evidence before they believe others is now called a "doubting Thomas."

John's account of the Gospel tells us that a week later the Risen Jesus again appeared to his disciples. This time Thomas was with them. Jesus showed Thomas his wounds and said to him:

"[D]o not be unbelieving, but believe." Thomas answered and said to him, "My Lord and my God!"

JOHN 20:27–28

He then became a strong believer in Jesus, the Risen Lord.

We believe that Jesus was raised from the dead and lives in a new way. This is a gift of faith.

We Believe in Christ

Look up and read 1 John 5:1–6 in the New Testament. Create a symbol of your faith in the Risen Christ. Profess your faith in Jesus. Share and explain your symbol to a partner and to your family.

Called and Sent

At home most of us have chores to do. Our tasks help all our family members and create happiness and harmony within our family. The Gospel tells us that Jesus asks the members of the Church family to serve one another:

"[A]s I have done for you, you should also do."

JOHN 13:15

The Gospel clearly tells us that Jesus told the Apostles that they were to serve others and not want to be served by others. This was a new type of leadership. It was the way Jesus taught them to live through his own life. They were to lead as he led as a good shepherd.

Today bishops are ordained to serve the Church as Christ served others. They are called to serve as Peter and the other Apostles did. All the baptized are also called to live a life in service of others. This service is lived out daily in our homes, in our schools, and in our communities. Each day is filled with opportunities to serve others as Jesus asked us to do.

Faith Focus

How do members of the Church serve one another?

The Word of the Lord

Choose this year's Gospel reading for the Third Sunday of Easter. Read and discuss it with your family.

Year A
Luke 24:13–35

Year B
Luke 24:35–48

Year C
John 21:1–19 or 21:1–14

Live to Serve

Look at the photos on page 271. Think about how you might live Jesus' command to serve others. Write down some of your ideas. Then choose one and do it.

Ideas

_____

_____

_____

_____

_____

My Choice	When I Will Do It
_____	_____
_____	_____
_____	_____
_____	_____
_____	_____
_____	_____
_____	_____

The Fourth Week of Easter

Faith Focus

How has water brought life to God's people?

The Word of the Lord

Choose this year's Gospel reading for the Fourth Sunday of Easter. Read and discuss it with your family.

Year A
  John 10:1–10

Year B
  John 10:11–18

Year C
  John 10:27–30

Water Brings Us Life

At the Easter Vigil the presider blesses water. The prayers of this blessing remind us of waters that brought life to God's people throughout their history. We celebrate that life when we bless ourselves with holy water.

In the beginning God created the vast seas and the rains that nourish the earth and all its creatures. God led the Hebrews to freedom through the waters of the Red Sea. God brought refreshing waters as his people wandered in the dry, stony desert.

The prophet Ezekiel spoke of water when he wrote of a new Covenant between the people and God:

"I will sprinkle clean
    water upon you . . .
I will cleanse you.
I will give you a
    new heart and
    place a new spirit
    within you. . . .
[Y]ou shall be my
    people, and I will
    be your God."
EZEKIEL 36:25–26, 28

The blessing of water at the Easter Vigil also recalls Jesus' baptism in the Jordan River. Water reminds us of our Baptism in the death and Resurrection of Jesus. It reminds us of how we are made new again through the death and Resurrection of Jesus.

Water and New Life

Write a chapter title for a book about ways that water has brought life to God's people. Explain why you chose your title. Share your explanation with a classmate and with your family.

_____

_____

_____

_____

_____

_____

_____

_____

_____

_____

_____

_____

_____

_____

_____

_____

_____

_____

The Fifth Week of Easter

Faith Focus

How can we learn from the early Church to be true followers of Jesus?

The Word of the Lord

Choose this year's Gospel reading for the Fifth Sunday of Easter. Read and discuss it with your family.

Year A
John 14:1–12

Year B
John 15:1–8

Year C
John 13:31–35

Love One Another

When we see someone in need, we can talk about what we have seen. Or we can do something for the person in need. The Church calls us to put our words into action.

During the Sundays of Easter, the first reading of the Liturgy of the Word is always from the Acts of the Apostles. These readings tell us how the early Christians put their faith and words into action.

The early Church remembered that on the night before he died, Jesus gave his disciples a new commandment. He said:

"[L]ove one another. As I have loved you, so you also should love one another. This is how all will know that you are my disciples, if you have love for one another." JOHN 13:34–35

The First Letter of John in the New Testament reminded the early Christians that their love for God must show in their love for one another. If we refuse to love a person we can see, how can we say that we love God, whom we cannot see?

The first followers of Jesus showed this love in many ways. They took care of those who were most in need. They forgave one another.

They welcomed travelers. They gave them food, clothing, and a warm place to live. They prayed for one another. They brought the healing presence of Christ to those who were sick and troubled.

These welcoming and loving followers of Jesus attracted others who wanted to live in this new way. This is still true today. True followers do not simply talk about the good news of Jesus' Resurrection. They show their love for one another.

Bless this House

This blessing is found on the door of Saint Stephen's Church in London.

O God, make the door of this house wide enough
to receive all who need human love and fellowship,
narrow enough to shut out all envy, pride, and strife.

Make its threshold smooth enough to be no stumbling
block to children, nor to straying feet, but rugged and
strong enough to turn back the tempter's power.

God, make the door of this house
the gateway to your eternal kingdom.

Write a blessing to put on the door of your home.

_____

_____

_____

_____

_____

_____

_____

_____

_____

Faith Focus

How were the Apostles to be witnesses to Jesus?

The Word of the Lord

Choose this year's Gospel reading for the Sixth Sunday of Easter. Read and discuss it with your family.

Year A
John 14:15–21

Year B
John 15:9–17

Year C
John 14:23–29

Ascension of Christ, unknown German painter

Promise of the Holy Spirit

Waiting can be hard. But when someone we love promises to give us something, we trust that the waiting will lead to good things. The Apostles waited for the gift Jesus promised to send them.

After his Resurrection, Jesus appeared to many of his followers. He told them that he would send them the Holy Spirit.

One day Jesus led the Apostles to Bethany outside Jerusalem. He reminded them that he had fulfilled all that was written in the Scriptures: He suffered, died, and was raised to new life.

Jesus reminded the Apostles that they had witnessed all that he had done. He told them that they would be his witnesses throughout Judea and Samaria and to the very ends of the earth. They were to tell others about him.

Then Jesus asked them to wait for the coming of the promised Holy Spirit. He then blessed the Apostles and returned to his Father in heaven.

Witnessing Today

Read each modern-day saying. Look up the matching Scripture passage that tells you how Jesus wants you to be a witness to his life today. Then choose one saying and make up an ad featuring some of Jesus' words.

Modern Sayings	Jesus' Advice
Shop 'til you drop.	Matthew 6:19–21
You can have it all!	Luke 9:57–62
Don't get mad. Get even.	Matthew 5:38–41
Might makes right.	Luke 9:46–48

Good News!

Christ is risen to new life! Alleluia! During the seven weeks in the Easter season, we praise God with greater joy than ever before. We celebrate new life with the Risen Jesus.

The Gospel readings for the seven Sundays of Easter tell us of the appearances Jesus made after his Resurrection.

In John's account of the Gospel, we read that Mary Magdalene saw Jesus and proclaimed the good news to the disciples:

"I have seen the Lord."
JOHN 20:18

In Luke's account of the Gospel, we read that two disciples recognized their Risen Lord in the breaking of bread.

Jesus' Resurrection is good news for us too. We share in the new life of Jesus' Resurrection.

Jesus is our Lord and Savior. Each time we gather to celebrate Eucharist, we celebrate our faith. We profess our faith in Jesus, our Risen Lord and God.

Faith Focus

What is proclaimed in the Gospel readings during the Easter season?

The Word of the Lord

Choose this year's Gospel reading for the Seventh Sunday of Easter. Read and discuss it with your family.

Year A
John 17:1–11

Year B
John 17:11–19

Year C
John 17:20–26

Easter

Alleluia! He Is Risen!

Share your Easter joy. Sing your Alleluia!

All: **Alleluia. Alleluia. Alleluia.**

First Reader: Give thanks to the Lord, for he is good,
for his mercy endures forever.
Let the house of Israel say,
"His mercy endures forever."

All: **Alleluia. Alleluia. Alleluia.**

Second Reader: The right hand of the Lord has struck
with power;
the right hand of the Lord is exalted.
I shall not die, but live,
and declare the works of the Lord.

All: **Alleluia. Alleluia. Alleluia.**

Third Reader: The stone which the builders rejected
has become the cornerstone.
By the Lord has this been done;
it is wonderful in our eyes.

All: **Alleluia. Alleluia. Alleluia.**

BASED ON RESPONSORIAL PSALM
SECOND SUNDAY OF EASTER

Faith Focus

How did the gift of the Holy Spirit on Pentecost strengthen the disciples?

The Word of the Lord

Choose this year's Gospel reading for Pentecost. Read and discuss it with your family.

Year A
    John 20:19–23

Year B
    John 20:19–23 or
    John 15:26–27,
        16:12–15

Year C
    John 20:19–23 or
    John 14:15–16,
        23–26

The Holy Spirit

Can you think of a day when you felt as if you could do anything you set your mind to? What had happened to make you feel that way? Did someone say something to you or give you a gift?

The disciples knew a day like that. They received a great gift that made them strong in their belief in the Risen Lord. That day was Pentecost.

Pentecost is a Jewish harvest festival. On this holy day the Jewish people offer the first fruits of the new harvest to God. At the time of Jesus, Jews traveled to Jerusalem for this great feast.

Detail from stained-glass window depicting Pentecost

The disciples gathered in Jerusalem too. As they prayed together in an upper room, they heard the noise of a great wind. Flames gently settled over their heads.

They were filled with the Holy Spirit. They felt new and strong. They went out and boldly proclaimed the Risen Lord. As they spoke, all the people in the crowd heard the message in their own language. People who could not understand one another before suddenly did! People who were separated drew together. The Holy Spirit came upon the disciples as Jesus promised. The Church was born. The work of the Church, filled with the Holy Spirit, had begun.

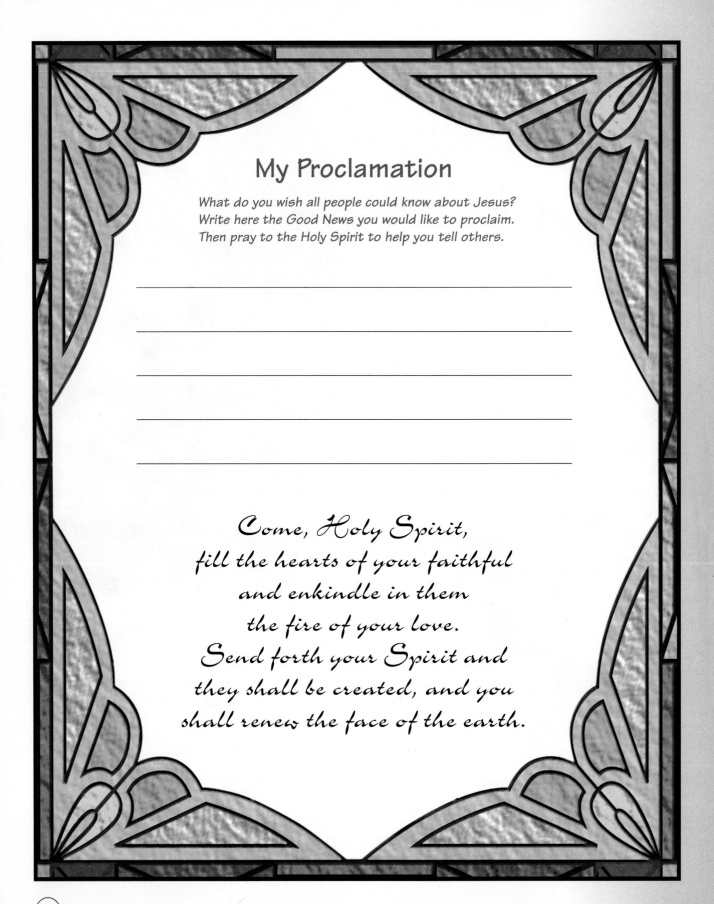

My Proclamation

What do you wish all people could know about Jesus?
Write here the Good News you would like to proclaim.
Then pray to the Holy Spirit to help you tell others.

_____

_____

_____

_____

_____

Come, Holy Spirit,
fill the hearts of your faithful
and enkindle in them
the fire of your love.
Send forth your Spirit and
they shall be created, and you
shall renew the face of the earth.

Catholic Prayers and Practices

Sign of the Cross

In the name of the Father,
and of the Son,
and of the Holy Spirit. Amen.

Glory Prayer

Glory to the Father,
    and to the Son,
    and to the Holy Spirit:
as it was in the beginning, is now,
    and will be for ever. Amen.

Lord's Prayer

Our Father, who art in heaven,
hallowed be thy name;
Thy kingdom come;
Thy will be done on earth
    as it is in heaven.
Give us this day our daily bread;
and forgive us our trespasses
as we forgive those who trespass
    against us;
and lead us not into temptation,
but deliver us from evil.
Amen.

Prayer to the Holy Spirit

Come, Holy Spirit, fill the hearts
    of your faithful.
And kindle in them the
    fire of your love.
Send forth your Spirit and
    they shall be created.
And you will renew the
    face of the earth.

Hail Mary

Hail Mary, full of grace,
the Lord is with you!
Blessed are you among women,
and blessed is the fruit
    of your womb, Jesus.
Holy Mary, Mother of God,
pray for us sinners,
now and at the hour of our death.
Amen.

Act of Contrition

My God,
I am sorry for my sins
    with all my heart.
In choosing to do wrong
and failing to do good,
I have sinned against you
whom I should love above all things.
I firmly intend, with your help,
to do penance,
to sin no more,
and to avoid whatever leads me to sin.
Our Savior Jesus Christ
suffered and died for us.
In his name, my God, have mercy.

Apostles' Creed

I believe in God,
    the Father almighty,
    creator of heaven and earth.

I believe in Jesus Christ,
    his only Son, our Lord.
    He was conceived by the power
        of the Holy Spirit
        and born of the Virgin Mary.
    He suffered under Pontius Pilate,
        was crucified, died, and was buried.
    He descended to the dead.
    On the third day he rose again.
    He ascended into heaven,
        and is seated at the right hand
        of the Father.
    He will come again to judge
        the living and the dead.

I believe in the Holy Spirit,
    the holy catholic Church,
    the communion of saints,
    the forgiveness of sins,
    the resurrection of the body,
    and the life everlasting. Amen.

Nicene Creed

We believe in one God,
    the Father, the Almighty,
    maker of heaven and earth,
    of all that is, seen and unseen.

We believe in one Lord, Jesus Christ,
    the only Son of God,
    eternally begotten of the Father,
    God from God, Light from Light,
    true God from true God,
    begotten, not made, one in Being
        with the Father.

Through him all things were made.
For us men and for our salvation
    he came down from heaven:

by the power of the Holy Spirit
    he was born of the Virgin Mary,
    and became man.

For our sake he was crucified under
    Pontius Pilate;
    he suffered, died, and was buried.
    On the third day he rose again
        in fulfillment of the Scriptures;
    he ascended into heaven
        and is seated at the right hand
        of the Father.
He will come again in glory to judge
    the living and the dead,
    and his kingdom will have no end.

We believe in the Holy Spirit, the Lord,
    the giver of life,
    who proceeds from the Father
        and the Son.
    With the Father and the Son he is
        worshiped and glorified.
    He has spoken through the Prophets.
We believe in one holy catholic and
    apostolic Church.
We acknowledge one baptism for the
    forgiveness of sins.
We look for the resurrection of the dead,
    and the life of the world to come.
Amen.

Morning Prayer

Dear God,
as I begin this day,
keep me in your love and care.
Help me to live as your child today.
Bless me, my family, and my friends
　　in all we do.
Keep us all close to you. Amen.

Evening Prayer

Dear God,
I thank you for today.
Keep me safe throughout the night.
Thank you for all the good I did today.
I am sorry for what I have chosen
　　to do wrong.
Bless my family and friends. Amen.

Grace Before Meals

Bless us, O Lord,
　　and these your gifts
which we are about to receive
　　from your goodness.
Through Christ our Lord.
Amen.

Grace After Meals

We give you thanks for all your gifts,
　　almighty God,
living and reigning now and for ever.
Amen.

A Vocation Prayer

God, I know you will call me
for special work in my life.
Help me follow Jesus each day
and be ready to answer your call.

Act of Faith

O my God, I firmly believe that you are
one God in three divine Persons, Father,
Son, and Holy Spirit; I believe that your
divine Son became man and died for our
sins, and that he will come to judge the
living and the dead. Amen.

Act of Hope

O my God, relying on your infinite
goodness and promises, I hope to obtain
pardon of my sins, the help of your grace,
and life everlasting, through the merits of
Jesus Christ, my Lord and Redeemer.
Amen.

Act of Love

O my God, I love you above all things,
with my whole heart and soul, because
you are all good and worthy of all my love.
I love my neighbor as myself for the love
of you. I forgive all who have injured me
and I ask pardon of all whom I have
injured. Amen.

The Divine Praises

Blessed be God.
Blessed be his holy name.
Blessed be Jesus Christ, true God and
    true man.
Blessed be the name of Jesus.
Blessed be his most sacred heart.
Blessed be his most precious blood.
Blessed be Jesus in the most holy sacrament
    of the altar.
Blessed be the Holy Spirit, the Paraclete.
Blessed be the great mother of God, Mary
    most holy.
Blessed be her holy and immaculate
    conception.
Blessed be her glorious assumption.
Blessed be the name of Mary, virgin and
    mother.
Blessed be Saint Joseph, her most chaste
    spouse.
Blessed be God in his angels and in his saints.

Prayer of Saint Francis

Lord, make me an instrument
    of your peace:
where there is hatred,
    let me sow love;
where there is injury, pardon;
where there is doubt, faith;
where there is despair, hope;
where there is darkness, light;
where there is sadness, joy.

O divine Master, grant that
    I may not so much seek
to be consoled as to console,
to be understood as to understand,
to be loved as to love.
For it is in giving that we receive,
it is in pardoning that
    we are pardoned,
it is in dying that we are born
    to eternal life.
    Amen.

The Angelus

Leader: The angel spoke God's message
to Mary,
Response: and she conceived of the Holy Spirit.
All: Hail Mary . . .

Leader: "I am the lowly servant of the Lord:
Response: let it be done to me according to
your word."
All: Hail Mary . . .

Leader: And the Word became flesh
Response: and lived among us.
All: Hail Mary . . .

Leader: Pray for us, holy Mother of God,
Response: that we may become worthy of the
promises of Christ.

Leader: Let us pray. Lord, fill
our hearts with your grace:
once, through the message
of an angel you revealed
to us the incarnation of
your Son; now, through
his suffering and death
lead us to the glory of his
resurrection. We ask this
through Christ our Lord.
All: Amen.

The Great Commandment

"You shall love the Lord, your God, with all your heart, with all your soul, and with all your mind. . . . You shall love your neighbor as yourself."

MATTHEW 22:37, 39

The New Commandment

[Jesus said:] "I give you a new commandment: love one another. As I have loved you, so you also should love one another. This is how all will know that you are my disciples, if you have love for one another."

JOHN 13:34–35

The Ten Commandments

1. I am the LORD your God: you shall not have strange gods before me.
2. You shall not take the name of the LORD your God in vain.
3. Remember to keep holy the LORD's Day.
4. Honor your father and your mother.
5. You shall not kill.
6. You shall not commit adultery.
7. You shall not steal.
8. You shall not bear false witness against your neighbor.
9. You shall not covet your neighbor's wife.
10. You shall not covet your neighbor's goods.

The Beatitudes

"Blessed are the poor in spirit,
for theirs is the kingdom of heaven.
Blessed are they who mourn,
for they will be comforted.
Blessed are the meek,
for they will inherit the land.
Blessed are they who hunger
and thirst for righteousness,
for they will be satisfied.
Blessed are the merciful,
for they will be shown mercy.
Blessed are the clean of heart,
for they will see God.
Blessed are the peacemakers,
for they will be called children of God.
Blessed are they who are persecuted
for the sake of righteousness,
for theirs is the kingdom of heaven.

Blessed are you when they insult you and persecute you and utter every kind of evil against you [falsely] because of me. Rejoice and be glad, for your reward will be great in heaven."

MATTHEW 5:3–12

Corporal Works of Mercy

Feed people who are hungry.
Give drink to people who are thirsty.
Clothe people who need clothes.
Visit prisoners.
Shelter people who are homeless.
Visit people who are sick.
Bury people who have died.

Spiritual Works of Mercy

Help people who sin.
Teach people who are ignorant.
Give advice to people
   who have doubts.
Comfort people who suffer.
Be patient with other people.
Forgive people who hurt you.
Pray for people who are alive and for
   those who have died.

Gifts of the Holy Spirit

Wisdom
Understanding
Right judgment (Counsel)
Courage (Fortitude)
Knowledge
Reverence (Piety)
Wonder and awe (Fear of the Lord)

Cardinal Virtues

Prudence
Justice
Fortitude
Temperance

Precepts of the Church

1. Participate in Mass on Sundays and holy days of obligation and rest from unnecessary work.

2. Confess sins at least once a year.

3. Receive Holy Communion at least during the Easter season.

4. Observe the prescribed days of fasting and abstinence.

5. Provide for the material needs of the Church, each according to one's abilities.

Basic Principles of the Church's Teaching on Social Justice

The Church's teaching on social justice guides us in living lives of holiness and building a just society. These principles are:

1. All human life is sacred. The basic equality of all people flows from their dignity as human persons and the rights that flow from that dignity.

2. The human person is the principle, the object, and the subject of every social group.

3. The human person has been created by God to belong to and to participate in a family and other social communities.

4. Respect for the rights of people flows from their dignity as persons. Society and all social organizations must promote virtue and protect human life and human rights and guarantee the conditions that promote the exercise of freedom.

5. Political communities and public authority are based on human nature. They belong to an order established by God.

6. All human authority must be used for the common good of society.

7. The common good of society consists of respect for and promotion of the fundamental rights of the human person; the just development of material and spiritual goods of society; and the peace and safety of all people.

8. We need to work to eliminate the sinful inequalities that exist between peoples and for the improvement of the living conditions of people. The needs of the poor and vulnerable have a priority.

9. We are one human and global family. We are to share our spiritual blessings, even more than our material blessings.

Based on the Catechism of the Catholic Church

Rosary

Catholics pray the rosary to honor Mary and remember the important events in the life of Jesus and Mary. There are twenty mysteries of the rosary. Follow the steps from 1 to 5.

5. Pray the Hail, Holy Queen prayer. Make the Sign of the Cross.

3. Think of the first mystery. Pray an Our Father, 10 Hail Marys, and the Glory Prayer.

2. Pray an Our Father, 3 Hail Marys, and the Glory Prayer.

4. Repeat step 3 for each of the next 4 mysteries.

1. Make the Sign of the Cross and pray the Apostles' Creed.

Joyful Mysteries

1. The Annunciation
2. The Visitation
3. The Nativity
4. The Presentation
5. The Finding of Jesus in the Temple

Mysteries of Light

1. The Baptism of Jesus in the Jordan River
2. The Miracle at the Wedding at Cana
3. The Proclamation of the Kingdom of God
4. The Transfiguration of Jesus
5. The Institution of the Eucharist

Sorrowful Mysteries

1. The Agony in the Garden
2. The Scourging at the Pillar
3. The Crowning with Thorns
4. The Carrying of the Cross
5. The Crucifixion

Glorious Mysteries

1. The Resurrection
2. The Ascension
3. The Coming of the Holy Spirit
4. The Assumption of Mary
5. The Coronation of Mary

Hail, Holy Queen

Hail, holy Queen, mother of mercy,
hail, our life, our sweetness,
   and our hope.
To you we cry, the children of Eve;
to you we send up our sighs,
mourning and weeping
   in this land of exile.
Turn, then, most gracious advocate,
your eyes of mercy toward us;
lead us home at last
and show us the blessed fruit
   of your womb, Jesus:
O clement, O loving, O sweet
   Virgin Mary.

Stations of the Cross

1. Jesus is condemned to death.

2. Jesus accepts his cross.

3. Jesus falls the first time.

4. Jesus meets his mother.

5. Simon helps Jesus carry the cross.

6. Veronica wipes the face of Jesus.

7. Jesus falls the second time.

8. Jesus meets the women.

9. Jesus falls the third time.

10. Jesus is stripped of his clothes.

11. Jesus is nailed to the cross.

12. Jesus dies on the cross.

13. Jesus is taken down from the cross.

14. Jesus is buried in the tomb.

Some parishes conclude the Stations by reflecting on the Resurrection of Jesus.

The Seven Sacraments

Jesus gave the Church the seven sacraments. The sacraments are the main liturgical signs of the Church. They make the Paschal Mystery of Jesus, who is always the main celebrant of each sacrament, present to us. They make us sharers in the saving work of Christ and in the life of the Holy Trinity.

Sacraments of Initiation

Baptism

Through Baptism we are joined to Christ and become members of the Body of Christ, the Church. We are reborn as adopted children of God the Father and receive the gift of the Holy Spirit. Original sin and all personal sins are forgiven.

Confirmation

Confirmation completes Baptism. In this sacrament the gift of the Holy Spirit strengthens us to live our Baptism.

Eucharist

Sharing in the Eucharist joins us most fully to Christ and to the Church. We share in the one sacrifice of Christ. The bread and wine become the Body and Blood of Christ through the power of the Holy Spirit and the words of the priest. We receive the Body and Blood of Christ.

Sacraments of Healing

Reconciliation

Through the ministry of the priest we receive forgiveness of sins committed after our Baptism. We need to confess all mortal sins.

Anointing of the Sick

Anointing of the Sick strengthens our faith and trust in God when we are seriously ill, dying, or weak because of old age.

Sacraments at the Service of Communion

Holy Orders

Through Holy Orders a baptized man is consecrated to serve the whole Church as a bishop, priest, or deacon in the name of Christ. Bishops, who are the successors of the Apostles, receive this sacrament most fully. They are consecrated to teach the Gospel, to lead the Church in the worship of God, and to guide the Church to live holy lives. Bishops are helped by priests, their coworkers, and by deacons in their work.

Matrimony

Matrimony unites a baptized man and a baptized woman in a lifelong bond of faithful love to always honor each other and to accept the gift of children from God. In this sacrament the married couple is consecrated to be a sign of Christ's love for the Church.

We Celebrate the Mass

The Introductory Rites

**We remember that we are the community
of the Church. We prepare to listen to the word of God
and to celebrate the Eucharist.**

The Entrance

We stand as the priest, deacon, and other ministers enter the assembly. We sing a gathering song. The priest and deacon kiss the altar. The priest then goes to the chair where he presides over the celebration.

Greeting of the Altar and of the People Gathered

The priest leads us in praying the Sign of the Cross. The priest greets us, and we say,
And also with you.

The Act of Penitence

We admit our wrongdoings.
We bless God for his mercy.

The Gloria

We praise God for all the good he has done for us.

The Collect

The priest leads us in praying the Collect, or the opening prayer.
We respond, **"Amen."**

The Liturgy of the Word

**God speaks to us today.
We listen and respond to God's word.**

The First Reading from the Bible

We sit and listen as the reader reads from the Old Testament or from the Acts of the Apostles. The reader concludes, "The word of the Lord." We respond,
Thanks be to God.

The Responsorial Psalm

The song leader leads us in singing a psalm.

The Second Reading from the Bible

The reader reads from the New Testament, but not from the four Gospels. The reader concludes, "The word of the Lord." We respond,
Thanks be to God.

Acclamation

We stand to honor Christ present with us in the Gospel. The song leader leads us in singing **"Alleluia, Alleluia, Alleluia"** or another chant during Lent.

The Gospel

The deacon or priest proclaims, "A reading from the holy gospel according to (name of gospel writer)." We respond,
Glory to you, O Lord.

He proclaims the Gospel. At the end, he says, "The gospel of the Lord." We respond,
Praise to you, Lord Jesus Christ.

The Homily

We sit. The priest or deacon preaches the homily. He helps the whole community understand the word of God spoken to us in the readings.

The Profession of Faith

We stand and profess our faith.
We pray the Nicene Creed together.

The Prayer of the Faithful

The priest leads us in praying for our Church and its leaders, for our country and its leaders, for ourselves and others, for the sick and those who have died. We can respond to each prayer in several ways. One way we respond is,
Lord, hear our prayer.

The Liturgy of the Eucharist
We join with Jesus and the Holy Spirit to give thanks and praise to God the Father.

The Preparation of the Gifts

We sit as the altar table is prepared and the collection is taken up. We share our blessings with the community of the Church and especially with those in need. The song leader may lead us in singing a song. The gifts of bread and wine are brought to the altar.

The priest lifts up the bread and blesses God for all our gifts. He prays, "Blessed are you, Lord, God of all creation . . ."
We respond,
Blessed be God for ever.

The priest lifts up the cup of wine and prays, "Blessed are you, Lord, God of all creation . . ." We respond,
Blessed be God for ever.

The priest invites us,
Pray, my brothers and sisters, that our sacrifice may be acceptable to God, the almighty Father.

We stand and respond,
May the Lord accept the sacrifice at your hands for the praise and glory of his name, for our good, and the good of all his Church.

The Prayer over the Offerings

The priest leads us in praying the Prayer over the Offerings. We respond, **"Amen."**

Preface

The priest invites us to join in praying the Church's great prayer of praise and thanksgiving to God the Father.

Priest:	The Lord be with you.
Assembly:	**And also with you.**
Priest:	Lift up your hearts.
Assembly:	**We lift them up to the Lord.**
Priest:	Let us give thanks to the Lord our God.
Assembly:	**It is right to give him thanks and praise.**

After the priest sings or prays aloud the preface, we join in acclaiming,
**Holy, holy, holy Lord, God of power and might.
Heaven and earth are full of your glory.
Hosanna in the highest.
Blessed is he who comes in the name of the Lord.
Hosanna in the highest.**

The Eucharistic Prayer

The priest leads the assembly in praying the Eucharistic Prayer. We call upon the Holy Spirit to make our gifts of bread and wine holy and that they become the Body and Blood of Jesus. We recall what happened at the Last Supper. The bread and wine become the Body and Blood of the Lord. Jesus is truly and really present under the appearances of bread and wine.

The priest sings or says aloud, "Let us proclaim the mystery of faith." We respond using this or another acclamation used by the Church,
Christ has died, Christ is risen, Christ will come again.

The priest then prays for the Church. He prays for the living and the dead.

Doxology

The priest concludes the praying of the Eucharistic Prayer. He sings or prays aloud,
Through him, with him, in him, in the unity of the Holy Spirit, all glory and honor is yours, almighty Father, for ever and ever.
We stand and respond, **"Amen."**

The Communion Rite

The Lord's Prayer

We pray the Lord's Prayer together.

The Rite of Peace

The priest invites us to share a sign of peace, saying, "The peace of the Lord be with you always." We respond,
And also with you.
We share a sign of peace.

The Fraction, or the Breaking of the Bread

The priest breaks the host, the consecrated bread. We sing or pray aloud,
**Lamb of God, you take away
the sins of the world:
    have mercy on us.
Lamb of God, you take away
the sins of the world:
    have mercy on us.
Lamb of God, you take away
the sins of the world:
    grant us peace.**

Communion

The priest raises the host and says aloud,
This is the Lamb of God who takes away the sins of the world.
Happy are those who are called to his supper.
We join with him and say,
Lord, I am not worthy to receive you, but only say the word and I shall be healed.

The priest receives Communion. Next, the deacon and the extraordinary ministers of Holy Communion and the members of the assembly receive Communion.

The priest, deacon, or extraordinary minister of Holy Communion holds up the host. We bow and the priest, deacon, or extraordinary minister of Holy Communion says, "The body of Christ." We respond, **"Amen."** We then receive the consecrated host in our hand or on our tongue.

If we are to receive the Blood of Christ, the priest, deacon, or extraordinary minister of Holy Communion holds up the cup containing the consecrated wine. We bow and the priest, deacon, or extraordinary minister of Holy Communion says, "The blood of Christ."
    We respond, **"Amen."** We take the cup in our hands and drink from it.

The Prayer after Communion

We stand as the priest invites us to pray, saying, "Let us pray." He prays the Prayer after Communion. We respond, **"Amen."**

The Concluding Rites

We are sent forth to do good works, praising and blessing the Lord.

Greeting

We stand. The priest greets us as we prepare to leave. He says, "The Lord be with you." We respond, **And also with you.**

Blessing

The priest or deacon may invite us, "Bow your heads and pray for God's blessing." The priest blesses us, saying,
May almighty God bless you, the Father, and the Son, and the Holy Spirit.
We respond, **"Amen."**

Dismissal of the People

The priest or deacon sends us forth, using these or similar words,
The Mass is ended, go in peace.
We respond,
Thanks be to God.

We sing a hymn. The priest and the deacon kiss the altar. The priest, deacon, and other ministers bow to the altar and leave in procession.

We Celebrate Reconciliation

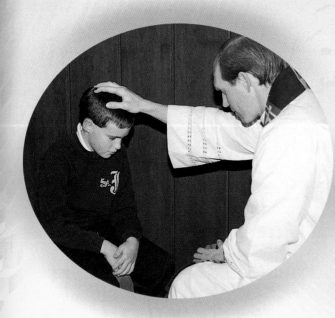

Individual Rite

Greeting

Scripture Reading

Confession of Sins and Acceptance of Penance

Act of Contrition

Absolution

Closing Prayer

Communal Rite

Greeting

Scripture Reading

Homily

Examination of Conscience with a litany of contrition and the Lord's Prayer

Individual Confession and Absolution

Closing Prayer

The Books of the Bible

The Old Testament

Law (Torah) or Pentateuch

Genesis	(Gn)
Exodus	(Ex)
Leviticus	(Lv)
Numbers	(Nm)
Deuteronomy	(Dt)

Historical Books

Joshua	(Jos)
Judges	(Jgs)
Ruth	(Ru)
First Book of Samuel	(1 Sm)
Second Book of Samuel	(2 Sm)
First Book of Kings	(1 Kgs)
Second Book of Kings	(2 Kgs)
First Book of Chronicles	(1 Chr)
Second Book of Chronicles	(2 Chr)
Ezra	(Ezr)
Nehemiah	(Neh)
Tobit	(Tb)
Judith	(Jdt)
Esther	(Est)
First Book of Maccabees	(1 Mc)
Second Book of Maccabees	(2 Mc)

The Poetry and Wisdom Books

Job	(Jb)
Psalms	(Ps)
Proverbs	(Prv)
Ecclesiastes	(Eccl)
Song of Songs	(Sg)
Wisdom	(Wis)
Sirach/Ecclesiasticus	(Sir)

Prophets

Isaiah	(Is)
Jeremiah	(Jer)
Lamentations	(Lam)
Baruch	(Bar)
Ezekiel	(Ez)
Daniel	(Dn)
Hosea	(Hos)
Joel	(Jl)
Amos	(Am)
Obadiah	(Ob)
Jonah	(Jon)
Micah	(Mi)
Naham	(Na)
Habakkuk	(Hb)
Zephaniah	(Zep)
Haggai	(Hg)
Zechariah	(Zec)
Malachi	(Mal)

The New Testament

The Gospels

Matthew	(Mt)
Mark	(Mk)
Luke	(Lk)
John	(Jn)

Early Church

Acts of the Apostles	(Acts)

Letters of Paul and Other Letters

Romans	(Rom)
First Letter to the Corinthians	(1 Cor)
Second Letter to the Corinthians	(2 Cor)
Galatians	(Gal)
Ephesians	(Eph)
Philippians	(Phil)
Colossians	(Col)
First Letter to the Thessalonians	(1 Thes)
Second Letter to the Thessalonians	(2 Thes)
First Letter to Timothy	(1 Tm)
Second Letter to Timothy	(2 Tm)
Titus	(Ti)
Philemon	(Phlm)
Hebrews	(Heb)
James	(Jas)
First Letter of Peter	(1 Pt)
Second Letter of Peter	(2 Pt)
First Letter of John	(1 Jn)
Second Letter of John	(2 Jn)
Third Letter of John	(3 Jn)
Jude	(Jude)

Revelation

Revelation	(Rv)

Glossary

Abba [page 14]
A word meaning "Father," expressing the unconditional trust of a child in a parent's love; the name Jesus used for God the Father, revealing the love and trust that exists between Jesus and God the Father.

Advocate [page 50]
A word meaning "one who is at our side," or "one who speaks for us"; title or name for the Holy Spirit, used by Jesus in John's Gospel.

Annunciation [pages 62, 245]
A word meaning "announcement"; the announcement to the Virgin Mary by the angel Gabriel that God had chosen her to be the mother of Jesus, the Son of God, by the power of the Holy Spirit.

Anointing of the Sick [page 146]
The Sacrament of Healing that strengthens our faith, hope, and love for God when we are seriously ill, weakened by old age, or dying.

Apostles' Creed [page 16]
A summary of the faith of the Church handed down from the time of the Apostles.

Ascension [page 48]
A word meaning "a going up," the return of the Risen Christ in glory to his Father.

assembly [pages 98, 293]
The community of the Church gathered to celebrate the sacraments and the liturgy.

Baptism [page 114]
The Sacrament of Initiation in which we are joined to Jesus Christ, become members of the Church, are reborn as God's adopted children, receive the gift of the Holy Spirit, and original sin and our personal sins are forgiven.

Beatific Vision [page 88]
Seeing God face to face; eternal happiness with God.

Beatitudes [page 72, 169]
A word meaning "ways of happiness or blessedness"; the sayings or teachings of Jesus that are found in the Sermon of the Mount and describe both the qualities and actions of people blessed by God.

bishop [page 63]
A successor of the Apostles; one who has received the fullness of the sacrament of Holy Orders and is a member of the order of bishops, or the episcopal college.

Body of Christ [page 70]
An image for the Church used by Paul the Apostle that teaches that all the members of the Church are one in Christ, the Head of the Church, and that all members have a unique and important role in the work of the Church.

Body of Christ [page 130]
The Eucharist; Christ's true and real presence under the appearance of bread; also a New Testament image for the Church.

Book of Psalms [page 297]
The Old Testament book of the Bible containing 150 prayers in the form of poems and songs.

canon of Scripture [page 25]
The books identified and named by the Church as the inspired word of God that have been collected together in the Bible.

capital sins [page 176]
Seven sins named by the Church that are the sources of other sins; pride, covetousness, envy, anger, gluttony, lust, and sloth.

charisms [page 71]
Graces, or gifts, given by the Holy Spirit to build up the Church on earth for the good of all people and the needs of the world.

Christ [pages 46, 47]
Anointed One, title of Jesus identifying that he is the Anointed One of God, the Messiah who God promised to send to save his people.

Church [page 62]
The Body of Christ, the Temple of the Holy Spirit, the Bride of Christ, the new People of God the Father called together in Jesus Christ by the power of the Holy Spirit.

communion [page 154]
A word meaning "sharing with"; the unity in Christ of all the members of the Church, the Body of Christ.

Communion of Saints [page 70]
All the faithful followers of Jesus, both the living and the dead, those on earth, in purgatory, and in heaven.

confession [pages 259, 296]
The telling of sins to a priest in the sacrament of Reconciliation, an essential part of the sacrament of Reconciliation, another name for the sacrament of Reconciliation.

Confirmation [page 114]
The Sacrament of Initiation that strengthens the grace of Baptism and in which our life in Christ is sealed by the gift of the Holy Spirit.

conscience [page 175]
The gift of God that is part of every person that guides us to know and judge what is right and wrong.

consecrate [page 122]
Set aside and dedicate for a holy purpose.

contrition [page 296]
Sorrow for sins, which includes the desire to make up for the harm our sin has caused; an essential part of the sacrament of Reconciliation.

Covenant [page 22]
The solemn commitment of fidelity that God and the People of God made with one another, which was renewed in Christ, the new and everlasting Covenant.

covet [page 190]
To unjustly desire what rightfully belongs to someone else.

creed [page 14]
A statement of beliefs, a profession of faith; a summary of the principle beliefs of the Church.

Crucifixion [page 48]
The event of Jesus' saving death on the cross.

deacon [pages 154, 155]
One who has received the sacrament of Holy Orders and belongs to the order of deacons, or the diaconate; coworker with the bishops and priests.

Decalogue [page 182]
The Ten Commandments.

distractions to prayer [page 210]
Thoughts and ideas that pull us away from prayer.

divine Revelation [page 38]
God making himself and the divine plan of creation and salvation known over time.

disciple [page 263]
One who learns from and follows the teachings of another person.

E-F-G-H

epistle [page 54]
Lengthy and formal type of letter found in the New Testament.

Eucharist [page 130]
The sacrament of the Body and Blood of Christ; the Sacrament of Initiation in which we receive the Body and Blood of Christ, who is truly and really present under the appearances of bread and wine, and in which we are most fully joined to Christ and to the Church, the Body of Christ.

Evangelists [page 86]
A word meaning "announcers of good news"; Matthew, Mark, Luke, and John; the writers of the four inspired accounts of the Gospel, which are in the New Testament.

evangelization [page 229]
The Church's responsibility to share the Gospel with all people "so that it may enter the hearts of all men and renew the human race."

Exile [pages 231, 232]
The time in the history of God's people when many of them were forced to leave their homeland and live in the country of their conquerors.

Exodus [pages 15, 130]
The saving intervention of God in the history of God's people; the saving of the Hebrews from slavery in Egypt, making of the Covenant with them, and leading them to freedom in the land he promised them.

faith [page 14]
A supernatural gift and power from God; the gift of God's invitation to us that enables us to know and believe in him, and the power God gives us to freely respond to his invitation.

fidelity [page 30]
A word meaning "faithfulness," the virtue of keeping our promises and fulfilling our responsibilities to God and to other people.

forms of prayer [page 218]
The four types of prayer revealed in Sacred Scripture that are the norm for Christian prayer; adoration and blessing, petition, intercession, thanksgiving, and praise.

Gospels [page 86]
The first four books of the New Testament, which pass on the faith of the Church in Jesus Christ and in the saving events of his life, Passion, death, Resurrection, and Ascension.

grace [pages 114–117]
The gift of God's life and love that makes us holy and helps us live a holy life.

holiness [page 166]
The quality, or condition, of a person who is living in communion with and in the right relationship with God, others, and with all of his creation; being in the state of grace.

Holy Orders [pages 154, 155]
The Sacrament at the Service of Communion through which a baptized man is consecrated to serve the whole Church as a bishop, priest, or deacon.

Holy Spirit [page 38]
The third Person of the Holy Trinity, the Advocate sent to us by the Father in the name of his Son, Jesus Christ.

Holy Trinity [page 38]
The mystery of one God in three divine Persons—God the Father, God the Son, God the Holy Spirit.

hope [page 30]
The theological virtue by which we desire and trust that God will fulfill all his promises, especially the promise of eternal happiness.

I-J-K-L

Immaculate Conception [page 78]
Mary's freedom from all sin, both original sin and all personal sin, from the first moment of her existence, or conception, and throughout her entire life.

incarnation [pages 46,47]
A word meaning "take on flesh," or to have a real body.

Incarnation [page 46]
The term the Church uses to name the faith of the Church that the Son of God became fully human in all things except sin, while remaining fully divine.

inspiration of the Bible [page 22]
The Holy Spirit guiding the human writers of Sacred Scripture so that they would faithfully and accurately communicate the word of God, who is the principal author of the Scriptures.

invocations [page 210]
Brief prayers we can learn by heart and pray throughout the day.

Israelites [page 23]
The Old Testament people to whom God revealed himself and with whom he made the Covenant.

justice [page 190]
One of the moral, or cardinal, virtues; the good habit of giving to God and to all people what is rightfully due to them.

kingdom of God [page 86]
The fulfillment of God's plan for all creation in Christ at the end of time when Christ will come again in glory.

liturgical year [page 100]
The Church's yearly cycle of seasons and feasts that celebrate the mysteries of Jesus' birth, life, death, and Resurrection.

liturgy [page 98]
The Church's work of worshiping God.

Lord [page 226]
A title for Jesus that states he is truly God.

Lord's Day [page 109]
The name given to Sunday, the day of the Lord's Resurrection.

M-N-O

Marks of the Church [page 62]
One, holy, catholic, apostolic; the four signs and essential qualities of the Church and her mission founded by Jesus Christ.

Mass [page 130–132]
The main sacramental celebration of the Church at which we gather to listen to God's word and through which we share in the saving death of Christ and give praise and glory to the Father.

Matrimony [page 156]
The Sacrament at the Service of Communion that unites a baptized man and a baptized woman in a lifelong bond, or covenant, of faithful love to serve the Church as a sign of Christ's love for the Church.

Messiah [page 46, 47]
A word meaning "Anointed One"; Jesus, the Anointed One of God, the Messiah, the Savior of the world.

morality [page 174]
A way of judging, or evaluating, whether our choices lead us to God or away from God.

moral decisions [page 174]
The decisions and choices we make to live as children of God and disciples of Jesus Christ.

moral virtues [page 290]
Prudence, justice, fortitude, and temperance; human virtues acquired by human effort and practice; also called the cardinal virtues since other virtues "hinge" on them.

mortal sin [page 176]
A serious failure in our love and respect for God, our neighbor, creation, and ourselves. Three things are necessary for a sin to be mortal, namely, (1) the thing we do or say must be gravely wrong; (2) we must know it is gravely wrong; (3) we must freely chose it.

Nicene Creed [page 16]
A creed, or brief statement of the faith of the Church, written in the fourth century.

oral tradition [page 198]
The passing on of stories and teachings by word of mouth.

original sin [page 38]
The sin of Adam and Even, by which they and all people lost the state of original holiness, and by which death, sin, and suffering entered the world.

P-Q

parable [page 138]
A form of story that compares one thing to another to help listeners understand the main point of the story.

Paschal Mystery [page 48]
The Passion, death, Resurrection, and glorious Ascension of Jesus Christ; the "passing over" of Jesus from death into a new and glorious life.

Passover [page 106]
The Jewish feast that celebrates the sparing of the Hebrew children from death, and God's saving his people from slavery in Egypt and leading them to freedom in the land he promised them.

penance [see Reconciliation]
Prayer or act of kindness that shows we are truly sorry for our sins; an essential part of the sacrament of Penance, or Reconciliation.

Pentateuch [page 22, 23]
Word meaning "five containers," the first five books of the Old Testament: Genesis, Exodus, Leviticus, Numbers, and Deuteronomy; also called the Torah.

Pentecost [page 62]
A word meaning "fiftieth day"; the liturgical feast and holy day when the Church celebrates the coming of the Holy Spirit on the disciples and the birth of the Church.

People of God [page 70]
Biblical image for the Church; the people God has gathered and chosen to be his own; the people through whom God has revealed himself most fully and has invited all nations to live as the one family of God.

prayer life [page 218]
The habit of making prayer part of the rhythm of our day.

precepts [page 182]
Rules or laws that detail responsibilities and impose standards of conduct.

priest [page 155]
One who has received the sacrament of Holy Orders, a member of the order of priests, or presbyterate; coworker with the bishop.

prophet [pages 30–32]
One chosen by God to speak in his name; one who speaks divinely inspired words.

proverb [page 198]
A short, concise saying stating a well-accepted fact or criterion for making a wise decision.

prudence [page 32]
One of the four moral virtues, a virtue that helps us know what is truly good for us and how to choose the right way of achieving that good.

Psalms [page 211]
Prayer-songs found in the Old Testament Book of Psalms, or the Psalter.

public ministry of Jesus [page 47]
The work that God the Father sent Jesus, the Son of God, to do on earth with the help of the Holy Spirit.

Index

Credits

Cover Design: Kristy Howard
Cover Illustration: Amy Freeman

PHOTO CREDITS:

Abbreviated as follows: (bkgd) background;
(t) top; (b) bottom; (l) left; (r) right; (c)
center.

Front matter: Page 7, © Punchstock; 10,
© The Crosiers/Gene Plaisted, OSC; 11 (tl),
© Eric Williams/RCL; 11 (cr), © The
Crosiers/Gene Plaisted, OSC; 11 (bl),
© Stephen McBrady/Photoeditinc.

Chapter 1: Page 13, © Corbis Images; 14,
© Ben Chrisman/AP/Wide World; 17, © Bill
Wittman; 19, © The Crosiers/Gene Plaisted,
OSC; 20, © James Kay/PictureQuest.

Chapter 2: Page 21, © Eric Williams/RCL; 22,
© Annie Griffiths Belt/Corbis; 24, © Nasa; 25
(all), © Bill Wittman; 28, © James L. Shaffer.

Chapter 3: Page 29, © Silvio Fiore/SuperStock;
30, © David Urbina/Photoeditinc; 33 (all),
© Cabrini Mission Corps; 35, © The
Crosiers/Gene Plaisted, OSC; 36, © Stephen
McBrady/Photoeditinc.

Chapter 4: Page 37, © PictureQuest; 38,
© The Crosiers/Gene Plaisted, OSC; 41 (tl),
© Myrleen Ferguson Cate/Photoeditinc; 41 (c),
© The Crosiers/Gene Plaisted, OSC; 41 (br),
© Graeme Outerbridge/SuperStock; 44, ©
PictureQuest.

Chapter 5: Page 45, © National Geographic/
Gettyimages; 46, © Cathy Melloan/
Photoeditinc; 47, © Topham Picturepoint/The
Image Works; 49 (t), © The Crosiers/Gene
Plaisted, OSC; 49 (bl), © Paul Conklin/
Photoeditinc; 49 (br), © AP Photo/Ricardo
Figueroa; 52, © Jeff Greenberg/Photoeditinc.

Chapter 6: Page 53, © SuperStock, Inc.; 54,
© Alan Jacobs Gallery, London/Bridgeman Art
Library; 56, © Conrad Zobel/Corbis; 57 (l),
© Tidings Catholic Newspaper; 57 (r), © Brian
Fahey/Diocese of Charleston; 60, ©
PictureQuest.

Chapter 7: Page 61, © Bill Wittman; 62,
© The Crosiers/Gene Plaisted, OSC; 65 (l),
© Giansanti Gianni/Corbis; 65 (r), © Origlia
Franco/Corbis; 68, © Mark Langford/Index
Stock.

Chapter 8: Page 69, © The Crosiers/Gene
Plaisted, OSC; 70, © Zephyr Pictures/Index
Stock; 72, © Charles Orrico/SuperStock; 73 (l),
© Benedictines for Peace/Erie, PA; 73 (r), ©
The Crosiers/Gene Plaisted, OSC; 76, © Susan
Van Ellen/Photoeditinc.

Chapter 9: Pages 77, 78, © The Crosiers/Gene
Plaisted, OSC; 80, © Bill Wittman; 81 (l),
© Stephanie Maze/Corbis; 81 (c), © Nancy
Sheehan/Photoeditinc; 81 (r), © Myrleen
Ferguson Cate/Photoeditinc; 83, © The
Crosiers/Gene Plaisted, OSC; 84, © Cleo
Photography/Photoeditinc.

Chapter 10: Page 85, © SuperStock, Inc.; 88,
© Nancy Richmond/The Image Works; 89 (t),
© Bill Wittman; 89 (b), © Gabe Palmer/Corbis;
92, © Don Smetzer/Photoeditinc; 95 (all),
© The Crosiers/Gene Plaisted, OSC.

Chapter 11: Pages 97, 98 (all), 99 (all), © The
Crosiers/Gene Plaisted, OSC; 100, © Bill
Wittman; 101 (t), © James L. Shaffer; 101 (c),
© Donald F. Wristen; 101(b), © Sam
Martinez/RCL; 104, © The Crosiers/Gene
Plaisted, OSC.

Chapter 12: Page 105, © A. Ramey/
Photoeditinc; 108, © Farrell Grehan/Corbis;
109 (tc), © James L. Shaffer; 109 (bl), © Bill
Bachman/The Image Works; 109 (br), © Rachel
Epstein/Photoeditinc; 112, © James L. Shaffer.

Chapter 13: Page 113, © Bill Wittman; 114,
© James L. Shaffer; 114 (bkgd), © PhotoDisc;
115, © The Crosiers/Gene Plaisted, OSC; 116,
© Comstock, Inc.; 117 (all), © Bettman
Archives/Corbis; 120, © The Crosiers/Gene
Plaisted, OSC.

Chapter 14: Page 121, © The Crosiers/Gene
Plaisted, OSC; 124 (t, b), © Bill Wittman; 124
(c), © The Crosiers/Gene Plaisted, OSC; 125
(l), © Catholic News Service; 125 (r), © Bob
Roller/Catholic News Service; 128, ©
PictureQuest.

Chapter 15: Page 129, © SuperStock, Inc.;
130 (tl), © Avinoam Danin/Biblical
Archaelogical Society; 130 (tr), © James L.
Shaffer; 130 (b), 132, © The Crosiers/Gene
Plaisted, OSC; 133 (t), © AP/Wide World; 133
(b), © Gamma/Liaison; 136, ©
SuperStock/PictureQuest.

Chapter 16: Page 137, © The Crosiers/Gene
Plaisted, OSC; 138, © Planet Art; 140 (t),
© Spencer Grant/Photoeditinc; 140 (c), © Jeff
Greenberg/Photoeditinc; 140 (b), © Syracuse
Newspapers/The Image Works; 141 (all), ©
Barbara Stephenson/Catholic Campaign for
Human Development; 144, © Brooklyn
Productions/Gettyimages.

Chapter 17: Page 145, © David Joel/Stone;
147 (t), © David Falconer/Words & Pictures;
147 (b), © Myrleen Ferguson Cate/
Photoeditinc; 148 (t), © Dennis McDonald/
Photoeditinc; 148 (b), © Bill Wittman; 148, ©
Al Campanie/Syracuse News/The Image Works;
151, © Naljah Feanny/Corbis Saba; 152, ©
Corbis.

Chapter 18: Page 153, © The Crosiers/Gene
Plaisted, OSC; 154, © Myrleen Ferguson
Cate/Photoeditinc; 155 (all), © Bill Wittman;
156 (t), © Bill Wittman; 156 (c), © Tony
Freeman/Photoeditinc; 156 (b), © Charles
Gupton/Corbis; 157 (tl), © Dennis
Degnan/Corbis; 157 (tr), © Joe Carini/Index
Stock; 157 (bl), © Myrleen Ferguson Cate/
Photoeditinc; 157 (br), © David Young-
Wolff/Photoeditinc; 160, © Pete Saloutos/
Corbis; 163 (tl), © PictureQuest; 163 (cr),
© The Crosiers/Gene Plaisted, OSC; 163 (bl),
© Frank Simonetti/Index Stock.

Chapter 19: Page 165, © Mark Gamba/The
Stock Market; 167 (t, c), © James L. Shaffer;
167 (b), © Michael Newman/Photoeditinc; 169
(all), © Society of St. Andrew; 172, © David
Young-Wolff/Photoeditinc.

Chapter 20: Page 173, © PictureQuest; 174,
© David Young-Wolff/Photoeditinc; 176,
© Image Farm, Inc.; 177, © The Crosiers/Gene
Plaisted, OSC; 180, © Kindra Cineff/Index
Stock.

Chapter 21: Page 181, © Punchstock; 183,
© Jack Kurtz/The Image Works; 184, © Tom
Prettyman/Photoeditinc; 184 (all), © Tony
Freeman/Photoeditinc; 188, © Phoebe
Dunn/PictureQuest.

Chapter 22: Page 189, © Frank Simonetti/
Index Stock; 190, © Network Productions/The
Image Works; 193 (bkgd), © Nasa; 193 (b), ©
Wood River Gallery/PNI; 196, © PictureQuest.

Chapter 23: Page 197, © The Crosiers/Gene
Plaisted, OSC; 200, © Craig Ambrosio/AP/
Wide World; 204, © Myrleen Ferguson
Cate/Index Stock; 207 (tl), © Comstock, Inc.;
207 (cl), Courtesy of Donna Steffen; 207 (bl),
© Bill Wittman.

Chapter 24: Page 209, © Corbis; 210, © Alan
Oddie/Photoeditinc; 212 (t), © Bill Wittman;
212, © Punchstock; 216, © Spencer Grant/
Index Stock.

Chapter 25: Page 217, © Comstock, Inc.; 218,
© Jay Schlegel/Gettyimages; 220 (t), © Mary
Kate Denny/Photoeditinc; 220 (b), © James L.
Shaffer; 221, © Courtesy of Donna Steffen;
224, © Bill Wittman.

Chapter 26: Page 225, © The Crosiers/Gene
Plaisted, OSC; 232, © Tony Freeman/
Photoeditinc.

Liturgical Seasons: Page 235 (tl), © SuperStock,
Inc; 235 (cl, bl), © James L. Shaffer; 237,
© Michael Javorka/Stone; 241, © SuperStock,
Inc.; 243, © Robert W. Ginn/Photoeditinc; 243
(b), © Robert Cushman Hayes; 245 (all), © Bill
Wittman; 247, © Thomas Nebbianges/Image
Collection/National Geography; 249, © James
L. Shaffer; 251 (t, b), © James L. Shaffer; 251
(c), © Corbis/Digital Stock; 253 (t), © James L.
Shaffer; 253 (b), © Michael Newman/
Photoeditinc; 255, © James L. Shaffer; 256,
© Myrleen Ferguson Cate/Photoeditinc; 259,
© The Crosiers/Gene Plaisted, OSC; 260, ©
James L. Shaffer; 261, © The Crosiers/Gene
Plaisted, OSC; 262, © James L. Shaffer; 263,
© SuperStock, Inc.; 265, © Bill Wittman; 266,
© The Crosiers/Gene Plaisted, OSC; 267,
© Stuart McClyment/Stone; 269, © PhotoDisc,
Inc.; 271 (t), © Bob Daemmrich/Stock, Boston;
271 (b), © James L. Shaffer; 273, © Michael
Townsend/All Stock; 275 (t), © David Young-
Wolff/Photoeditinc; 275 (b), © Bill Wittman;
277, © Fine Art Photographic Library; 279 (t),
© James L. Shaffer; 279 (b), © Myrleen
Ferguson Cate/Photoeditinc; 281, © The
Crosiers/Gene Plaisted, OSC; 283, © Robert
Cushman Hayes; 287, © Myrleen Ferguson
Cate/Photoeditinc; 288, © David Young-
Wolff/Photoeditinc; 289 (l), © Society of St.
Andrew; 289 (r), © David Urbina/Photoeditinc;
295, © Tony Freeman/Photoeditinc; 296,
© James L. Shaffer; 297, © Bill Wittman.

ILLUSTRATION CREDITS
Abbreviated as follows: (bkgd) background;
(t) top; (b) bottom; (l) left; (r) right;
(c) center.

Page 8, 9, Amy Freeman; 31, Renee Daily; 39,
Janie Wolverton; 40, Dennis Davidson; 55, Jan
Palmer; 75, 86, © 1966 The Order of St.
Benedict; 87, Jan Palmer; 90, © Dynamic
Graphics, Inc.; 96, 107, Don Morrison; 123,
Renee Daily; 139, Margaret Lindmark; 166,
Amy Freeman; 168, © 1966 The Order of St.
Benedict; 195, Joel Snyder; 200, Amy Freeman;
201, Jan Palmer; 208, 227, Don Morrison; 229,
© Dynamic Graphics, Inc.; 239, Karen
Malzeke-McDonald; 257, Pamela Johnson; 290,
Amy Freeman; 291, drawings by Angela Marina
Barbieri & Joan Lledō Vila.